The *Best* of the
Appalachian Trail
Overnight Hikes

Also by Victoria and Frank Logue
The Best of The Appalachian Trail: Day Hikes
The Appalachian Trail Backpacker
Appalachian Trail Fun Book

Also by Victoria Logue
Backpacking in the 90s: Tips, Techniques and Secrets
Camping in the 90s: Tips, Techniques and Secrets

The *Best* of the
Appalachian Trail
Overnight Hikes

Victoria and Frank Logue

Menasha Ridge Press
Birmingham, Alabama

Appalachian Trail Conference
Harpers Ferry, West Virginia

Please Note:

The hikes in this book describe the route of the Appalachian Trail at the time of publication. But, the trail is occasionally relocated and the route may differ at the time of your hike. Severe damage to the trail caused by storms may impact on your hike as well. If the white blazes differ from the hike described in this book, follow the trail as it is marked.

Neither the authors, nor the publishers, can warrant your safety while on the hikes in this book. Use caution and your best judgement. If you have any changes or suggestions, the authors may be contacted in care of the publishers at either address given below.

Printed in the United States of America
Published by Menasha Ridge Press and The Appalachian Trail Conference
First Edition, Second Printing

Cover photo of a tent on
Wilburn Ridge, Virginia by Frank Logue

Drawings by Dian McCray

Woodcuts by Leslie Cummins

Library of Congress Cataloging-in-Publication Data
Logue, Victoria, 1961-
The best of the Appalachian Trail: overnight hikes/ Victoria and Frank Logue. — 1st ed.
    p. cm.
    ISBN 0-89732-139-1
    1. Hiking—Appalachian Trail-Guidebooks. 2. Backpacking—Appalachian Trail—Guidebooks. 3. Appalachian Trail—Guidebooks.
I. Logue, Frank, 1963- . II. Title.
GV199.42.A68L65 1994
796.5'1'0974—dc20   94-24863
                                CIP

Menasha Ridge Press	Appalachian Trail Conference
3169 Cahaba Heights Road	Post Office Box 807
Birmingham, Alabama 35243	Harpers Ferry, West Virginia 25425
	(304) 535-6331

For Hulda Kramp Kelly,
a great lady, a good friend and
the best grandmother a girl could have.
—Victoria

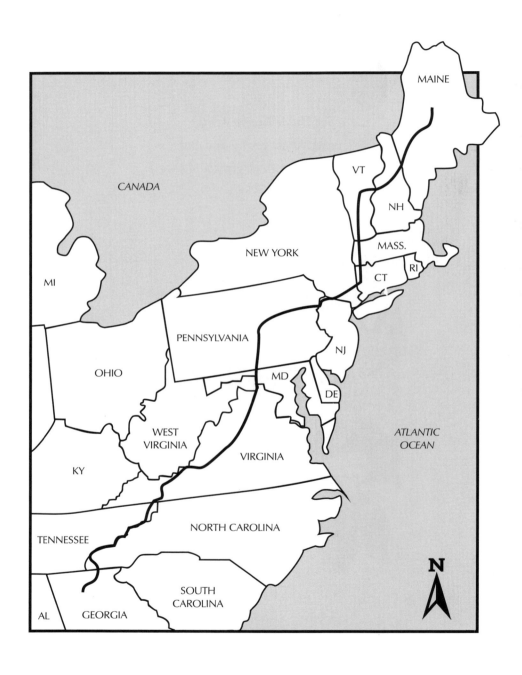

CONTENTS

INTRODUCTION

Dawn is stretching her rosy limbs, slender pink fingers caressing the grassy plain around our tent. The surreality of the night—velvet black sky with crescent moon, feral ponies grazing, the insistent drip of dew—fades as daylight illuminates the sleeping world. Except for the ponies, we are alone.

Wilburn Ridge near Grayson Highlands in Virginia is an exquisitely beautiful area to camp. You must backpack to get there and it is worth every straining muscle to ascend the ridge. Grassy meadows, clumps of firs, rock outcroppings and wild ponies decorate the tableau before you, not unlike a Monet landscape.

Impressionism, surrealism and realism combined, the highlands are always ready for an artist's brush. From the great storms that crash and roar over Mount Rogers to the west to the palette of colors that paint the landscape as the sun rises in the east, you cannot take this place for granted. As you hike the Appalachian Trail (A.T.) across Grayson Highlands and over Wilburn Ridge to Rhododendron Gap, the panorama is awe inspiring. More than two miles from where we set up camp, we could still see the tent's silhouette on the ridge, the wild ponies nosing and tasting the alien structure.

Our daughter, Griffin, frolicked among the ponies, imitating the heel-kicking foals who whickered and neighed as they chased each other about the meadow. She picked daisies, explored rock groupings, and finally settled down snug in her sleeping bag as dusk blanketed the meadows.

This is just one of many experiences possible when hiking overnight along the A.T., experiences we hope this book will help you encounter.

History of the Appalachian Trail

The idea for a trail running the length of the Appalachian Mountains was first considered in the early part of this century. The Appalachian Trail, as we know it, was the vision of Benton MacKaye (rhymes with sky) and others who had been thinking about the concept for more than ten years. In 1921, MacKaye took the initiative and launched the project through an article in *The Journal of the American Institute of Architects*.

In that first article, MacKaye wrote about the purpose of the trail: "There would be a chance to catch a breath, to study the dynamic forces of nature and the possibilities of shifting to them the burdens now carried on the backs of men . . . Industry would come to be seen in its true perspective—as a means in life and not as an end in itself."

MacKaye's original intent was to construct a trail from "the highest peak in the North to the highest peak in the South—from Mount Washington (New Hampshire) to Mt. Mitchell (North Carolina)." He envisioned a fourfold plan including the trail, shelters, community camps, and food and farm camps. The camps never came about. And although MacKaye's larger economic plan for the Appalachian Trail never gained support, his main purpose—an opportunity for American families to commune with nature—is the reason for the trail's continuing existence today.

Within a year after MacKaye's article appeared in the architectural journal, the New York-New Jersey Trail Conference began work on a new trail with the goal of making it part of the Appalachian Trail. In the Hudson River Valley, the new Bear Mountain Bridge would connect the future section in New England with Harriman State Park and eventually with Delaware Water Gap in Pennsylvania.

In 1925, MacKaye and others formed the Appalachian Trail Conference (ATC) to guide the project to completion. By 1936, Myron H. Avery, who would be president of the Appalachian Trail Conference for twenty years, had finished measuring the flagged route of the Appalachian Trail. A year before the trail was completed, he became the to hike the entire footpath, which he had done over many hikes and several years.

On August 14, 1937, the Civilian Conservation Corps (CCC) workers cleared the final link in the 2,025-mile Appalachian Trail. On a high ridge connecting Spaulding and Sugarloaf Mountains in Maine, a six-person CCC crew cut the last two miles of trail. The finished route of the Appalachian Trail was not as originally envisioned by MacKaye; the final product was longer, stretching from Mt. Oglethorpe (the southern terminus of the eastern Blue Ridge) in Georgia to Mt. Katahdin in Maine's Baxter State Park.

The trail did not remain complete for long. The next year, a hurricane demolished miles of trail in the northeast, while the decision to connect Skyline Drive (under construction at the time) with the Blue Ridge Parkway displaced another 120 miles of trail in Virginia. The trail was not made continuous again until 1951, after the world had settled down from World War II.

In 1968, President Lyndon Johnson signed the National Trails System Act and made the Appalachian Trail the first National Scenic Trail. The act charged federal agencies with the task of buying lands to protect the trailway from encroaching development, but ten years passed before the government acted and began protecting the trail lands. By 1993, less than two percent of the A.T. remained unprotected.

Perhaps the most amazing aspect of the world's largest greenway is that the trail was conceived and developed by private citizens. As a testament to the work carried out for decades by volunteers, the federal government left the management of the trail to a private non-profit group—the Appalachian Trail Conference—even after the footpath was brought under federal protection.

Selecting a Hike

The A.T. now offers more than 2,100 miles of hiking possibilities, from scenic rambles along rivers to strenuous scrambles up rocky peaks. The descriptions of hikes in this book often suggest more than great hikes.

The information provided will also tell you good times to hike in the area or when to avoid hiking there. Interesting flora and fauna is mentioned as is notable history. To help you pick out a hike that offers just what you are looking for, several easy-to-find pieces of information are located at the top of each hike description: the hike rating, length and time of the hike, and icons denoting major attractions along the way.

Ratings

The hikes are rated as easy, moderate or strenuous. Easy denotes hikes with little elevation gain or loss that are not more than twenty miles in length. Moderate hikes have no long, steep climbs or descents, though there may be some short, steep grades or long, gradual ascents. Strenuous hikes are steep, sometimes long, and should not be attempted by inexperienced hikers or people in poor physical condition.

Length and Hike Times

A good way to gauge hiking time on the trail is to allow a half hour for each mile to be hiked as well as an additional hour for each thousand feet of elevation gained. This pace allows for a leisurely hike with some time to stop at overlooks and other points of interest. The hikes in this book can certainly be done faster or slower, but this formula will give you an idea of how long you will need to walk.

Many of the hikes in this book are traverses, beginning at one point and ending at a second. All traverses require that you be shuttled or that you have someone drop you off and pick you up.

Icons

Each hike has one or more icons that show the major attractions along the way. The icons (mountain peak, scenic view, pond or lake, waterfall or stream, river, historic area, or bird-watching area) are intended to give you an easy-to-identify symbol that you can use when you flip through the book looking for a hike.

Mountain Peak	Scenic View	Pond or River	Waterfall	Historic Area	Bird-Watching

Equipment for Overnight Hikes

When you decide to begin going on overnight backpacking trips, there are several pieces of equipment that you need beyond what you carry on a day hike. The plethora of equipment out there may seem daunting at first, but basically all you need is food, water and shelter. Many backpacking stores have equipment available for rent so that you can try the gear, and sport, out before you invest in new equipment. For a good book on the subject, try Victoria Logue's *Backpacking in the '90s: Tips, Techniques and Secrets*. Available from most outdoor retailers and many bookstores, it covers the latest equipment as well as time-honored skills for backcountry travel.

Boots

Hiking boots range in price from $50 to $250 and are generally divided into three categories: heavyweight, mediumweight and lightweight. Heavyweight boots, which weigh more than 4 pounds, are generally designed for technically demanding climbs on ice (usually used with crampons) or on snow or alpine rock. You will not need heavyweights for the hikes in this book unless you choose to climb Katahdin in the dead of winter.

Mediumweight boots, which weigh from 2.5 to 4 pounds, are almost entirely made of leather, though many blend in a combination of tough fabric as well. Mediumweights are ideal for the broadest range of hiking situations.

Lightweight boots, which weigh less than 2.5 pounds, are almost always made with a combination of leather and a "breathable" fabric. Lightweights rarely require a "breaking-in" period and are tough enough to handle any of the hikes in this book.

When purchasing a boot, the important factor to keep in mind is proper fit. Even the best boots will make you miserable if they are not fitted properly. This is best done in a store, but you can also purchase boots by mail order if they have a good return policy. Once you buy the boots, make sure to break them in well around town before heading out into the woods. If lightweights fit properly, they won't require breaking in, but even these boots can be purchased too small or too big, too narrow or too wide. Be prepared with moleskin to treat "hot spots" before blisters develop.

Backpacks

Backpacks cost between $50 and $400 and are divided into two categories: internal frame and external frame. The external frame pack is designed to distribute weight equally with a high center of gravity, perfect for established trails. An external pack is cooler to wear because it rides away from your back. The internal frame pack is designed to custom-fit the hiker and has a low center of gravity, which makes it popular for off-trail hiking and mountaineering.

An important feature when purchasing a pack is the hipbelt. Since the hipbelt will carry most of the pack's weight, it should be well-padded. Also make sure that it is well-built and snug-fitting.

Sleeping Bags

Because you will spend one third of your time in a sleeping bag when backpacking, it is important to get a good one. The factors to consider include: comfort rating, filling, weight and shape. The comfort rating provided by the manufacturer gives the lowest temperature at which the bag will still be comfortable. The filling may be goose down or a synthetic, such as Hollofil, PolarGuard HV or Lite Loft. Down gives the most warmth for the weight of the bag, but synthetics provide more warmth when wet. Mummy-shaped bags are the most popular with backpackers because they offer the most warmth and space for the weight. Rectangular bags offer more space but weigh more and provide less warmth than mummy bags. Good sleeping bags range in price from $75 to $400.

Tents
A tent provides protection from bugs and the elements, and is an important purchase. Features to take into consideration include: weight, room, ventilation and "ease-of-setup." For backpacking, you will not want to carry more than 4 pounds of tent per person. When looking at tent size, you will need to decide whether you want to hang your gear up outside the tent or keep it in the tent with you. A two-person tent has room for two people, and if you want to bring your gear inside, you'll need a three-person tent. If you intend to do a lot of summer hiking, a well-ventilated tent is an absolute necessity. Most tents today offer plenty of no-see-um netting for cross ventilation and protection from bugs. Make sure the tent you purchase is well-ventilated. How easily you can set your tent up and take it back down is another important consideration. Practice helps, but if your tent is difficult to set up, you may end up getting soaked in a sudden storm. Good backpacking tents (two or three-person) range in price from $100 to $400.

Stoves and Fuel
It is not only impractical to cook over a fire, but in many areas along the A.T. it is prohibited. Investing in a good backpacking stove, which operates on butane gas cartridges, Coleman fuel, kerosene, or unleaded fuel, will save you many tears, burned fingers, and empty bellies. Good backpacking stoves range in price from $35 to $75.

Clothes
Your choice of clothing, including raingear, will have a big effect on whether or not you enjoy your hikes. Choose clothes that insulate well when wet and don't constrict you as you hike. Raingear, including a jacket, pants, and pack cover, are essential. Whether you choose coated nylon or

Gore-Tex is a matter of preference. Both perform well and each fabric has its share of proponents as well as detractors.

Equipment Checklist
❑ Hiking boots
❑ Backpack
❑ Sleeping bag
❑ Sleeping pad
❑ Tent/tarp and groundcloth
❑ Stove and fuel
❑ Cooking pot and eating utensils
❑ Pocket knife
❑ Water filter or iodine (unless you plan to boil your water)
❑ Food for length of hike
❑ Spices*
❑ One-liter (minimum) water bottle
❑ Drinking cup
❑ Raingear and pack cover
❑ Gaiters*
❑ One pair of shorts
❑ One pair of loose-fitting long pants†
❑ One or two short sleeved shirts
❑ One long sleeved shirt or sweater
❑ Knit cap
❑ Balaclava†
❑ Down or synthetic fill parka†
❑ Two pair of liner socks
❑ Two pair of hiking socks
❑ Bandanas
❑ Long johns†
❑ Two pair of underwear*
❑ Toilet paper and trowel
❑ Biodegradable soap and washcloth
❑ Deodorant*
❑ Toothbrush and toothpaste
❑ Shaving kit*
❑ Nylon cord (at least 10 feet)
❑ Maps and guidebooks
❑ Compass

❑ Flashlight with new batteries
❑ Watch or clock*
❑ Sunglasses*
❑ First aid kit (including moleskin and space blanket)
❑ Swimsuit and towel*
❑ Extra shoes*
❑ Repair equipment for pack, tent, and stove*
❑ Camera and film*
❑ Radio with headphones*
❑ Insect repellent†
❑ Sunscreen and lotion†
❑ Hiking stick*
❑ Crampons and ice axe†

Additional Equipment Needed for Longer Hikes
❑ Repair equipment for clothes
❑ Trash bag
❑ An extra long sleeved shirt or sweater
❑ Long johns
❑ Reading material*
❑ Journal*

* optional equipment
† seasonal equipment

Water

The water sources listed in this book have not been tested and cannot be warranted. If you drink or cook with water from the sources listed in the hike descriptions, you will need to treat the water for giardia and other water-borne contaminants. Backpackers use one or more of these three options: filtering, chemical treatment and boiling. Water filters have become an increasingly popular option. They range in price from $50 to $150 and weigh about 1 pound.

Treating your water with iodine tablets is a second option. Put one tablet in a liter of water and wait a half hour. The unpleasant taste and health concerns about large doses of iodine have lead many hikers to purchase water filters. Some hikers add a couple of drops of chlorine to a liter of water as a form of chemical treatment. According to the Centers for

Disease Control in Atlanta, this is not an effective means for killing water-borne contaminants and should not be used.

The third option is to boil your water. Because Giardia and other contaminants are killed at a temperature less than the boiling point (212° Fahrenheit), bringing water to a boil ensures pure water. The only drawback is waiting for it to cool. (*Note:* you have to treat the water that you use to rinse with when you brush your teeth.)

Minimum Impact

Minimum impact camping is a philosophy once summed up by the National Park Service as, "Take nothing but pictures, leave nothing but footprints." The following sub-headings discuss measures you can take to help eliminate traces of your presence along the trail. This is not a list of rules but rather a way of living that is becoming increasingly important to adopt. If these techniques are not used by everyone (and currently they're not), the A.T. will lose its natural beauty. Nature is resilient, but its ability to fight back is limited. A little bit of help goes a long way toward improving the world we're escaping to. If everyone pitches in, we'll be able to enjoy our backcountry experiences even more.

Carry Out All of Your Trash

Pack it in, pack it out, and you're already one giant step toward improving the environment. Keep a sack handy to store your trash. Trash includes everything, even organic material. Orange peels, apple cores and egg shells may strike you as natural trash, easily biodegradable. Why not toss it into the brush? Because it takes five months for an orange peel to rot and become one with the earth.

There is nothing worse than heading back into the woods to relieve yourself and discovering a trail of paper proving you weren't the first to have this idea at this spot. Soggy, used toilet paper is probably one of the uglier reminders of human presence.

Following trails littered with cigarette butts is disheartening. If you want to smoke, that's your prerogative, but don't think of the outdoors as one big ashtray. Not only is the litter of cigarette butts ugly, but it only takes one stray spark to start a forest fire that will turn the woods into a huge ashtray.

Carry Out Trash Left by Others

The trails abound with trash. For some reason, people who wouldn't dare throw trash on the ground at home do so freely in the outdoors. Unfortunately, the enviro-conscious do not outnumber the users and abusers of America's trails. We have to make up for their ignorance and sloth by picking up after them.

You can make the outdoors an even better place by stopping occasionally to pick up other people's trash. You don't have to be ridiculous and carry out nasty toilet paper or rotting organic material , but you can take a minute to cover it with leaves, moss, dirt, and twigs. Pick up trash, you'll find you feel a lot better about yourself.

Switchbacks

Stay on designated trail; switchbacks are there for a reason. They slow down the trail erosion on steep climbs. It may seem easier to scramble up the hillside to the next section of trail, but if too many people did that, rain would start using the newly exposed earth as a watercourse—washing away both trail and mountain. You may curse the person who blazed it and those who attempt to keep it passable for you, but remember that just about any trail you hike was built and maintained by volunteers.

Solid Waste Management

In other words, how to dispose of your excrement. Disposing of your feces when backpacking is absolutely necessary. Always, always, always (I can't say it too many times) dig a hole. More importantly, make sure you're at least 150 feet from the nearest water source. If you're hiking alongside a stream, climb up. There's more to being green than just packing out your trash. Disposing properly of your solid waste will keep the wilderness much more appealing.

Trail Maintenance

Give back to the trail and the hiking community by becoming involved in trail maintenance. Maintaining a section of existing trail or helping out with blazing new trails is a good way to pay back the outdoors for the good times you have received from it. Trails are beginning to criss-cross the entire country, and there is sure to be a new or old trail somewhere near you. Contact your local trail clubs to see what you can do to help out. Most backpacking shops can tell you about clubs in your area.

The entire Appalachian Trail is maintained by volunteers. To find out more about the clubs that maintain the Appalachian Trail, contact the Appalachian Trail Conference (see appendix).

Finding Solitude

Many hikers retreat to the Appalachian Trail seeking a wilderness experience, only to find themselves on a crowded section of trail sharing their "wilderness experience" with more hikers than they bargained for. Here are a few tips for finding a little solitude on America's most popular long distance trail.

Start your hike each day early in the morning. We once took this advice to the extreme and enjoyed the best hike of our lives. We started climbing Katahdin at 2:30 A.M. and arrived at Baxter Peak by 5:30 A.M., in time for the sunrise. The view was spectacular and we didn't share the summit with another hiker. That was on a Labor Day weekend, when later in the day hikers marched in a long, single-file line from Baxter Peak to Pamola Peak. By making an extra effort to get up early (and hike the tricky section of trail in the dark), we had the peak to ourselves on perhaps the busiest day of the year.

Another way to find your own piece of the Appalachian Trail is to hike during the off-season. Roan Highlands on the Tennessee/North Carolina state line is very crowded during peak bloom of the rhododendron garden. In June, visitors flock to see the awesome spectacle—thousands of big catawba rhododendrons in bloom at once—but during the winter we have camped alone on the summit. We didn't see the rhododendron in bloom, but the snow-covered mountain was a magnificent sight.

A third way to find solitude on the country's most popular long distance trail is to discover your own special places. After enjoying the hikes in this book, branch out and discover more of the trail on your own. To help you in your search, the Appalachian Trail Conference publishes a set of eleven guidebooks. They cover the entire 2,100-mile footpath, mile by mile.

Safety

Trouble is rare on the Appalachian Trail, but theft is not uncommon. Cars parked at trailheads are usually targeted for break-ins because thieves know that the owner will be away for awhile. Do not leave visible anything worth stealing, or better yet, leave all valuables at home. Also, do not leave any notes on your car stating where you are going and how long you intend to be gone. You might as well advertise for your car to be broken into.

It is doubtful you will run into any troublesome humans on the A.T., but if you do run into someone that gives you a bad feeling, keep moving.

Weather is something else you need to be concerned about when hiking. While it is neither impossible nor necessarily uncomfortable to hike in rain, snow, or intense heat, there are certain precautions you should take. Clothing suitable to the situation is important—raingear for rain, layered clothing for snow and cold weather, and lightweight, porous clothing for hot days. With the appropriate clothing, you can go a long way toward avoiding both hypothermia and hyperthermia.

Some of the hikes mentioned in this book are along sections of trail that are above treeline or in other exposed areas. In some cases, an alternate bad-weather route is available, but in many places, this is not an option. If inclement weather is predicted, it might be wise to take a rain check. For above-treeline hikes, carry raingear just in case because storms can form suddenly at high elevations.

Lightning kills more people each year than most other natural disaster, including earthquakes, hurricanes and tornadoes. If you get caught on the trail during a lightning storm, there are a few things you can do to reduce your chances of being struck. Avoid bodies of water and low places where water can collect. Avoid high places, ridges, open places, tall objects, metal objects, rock outcroppings, wet caves and ditches. If possible, find a stand of trees and sit with your knees pulled up to your chest, head bowed and arms hugging knees.

Getting lost is rarely a problem on the A.T., but anyone can become distracted and miss a blaze that indicates a turn off. The Appalachian Trail is marked with white blazes at least every quarter mile, and usually more often. Most maintainers try to blaze so you can see the next blaze as soon as you have passed the previous one. So, if you have walked for more than five minutes without seeing a blaze, it would be wise to backtrack until you see a blaze and then continue on your way.

First Aid

The risk of serious injury on an overnight hike is not high, but being unprepared would be tempting fate. You can still get stung by a bee, twist an ankle, develop blisters, become hypothermic, or have a heatstroke. The following information will give you some ideas about how to deal with these situations if they arise.

Hypothermia

Shivering, numbness, drowsiness and marked muscular weakness are the first signs of hypothermia. These symptoms are followed by mental confusion, impairment of judgement, slurred speech, failing eyesight and unconsciousness. The most serious warning sign of hypothermia occurs when the shivering stops. If the victim stops shivering, he is close to death.

Fortunately, hypothermia is easy to treat. If you or a friend is feeling hypothermic, get warm. In the case of a short overnight hike, this may mean nothing more than hurrying back to your car, stripping yourself of wet clothes, and turning the heater on. For an overnight hike you should, however, have the equipment to warm yourself—dry clothes, a sleeping bag, and a stove to heat water. If you are hiking with friends, they may be able to help you get warm. As long as you are hiking, your body will continue to try and warm itself. Keeping still could mean death, unless you are taking action to warm back up.

Hyperthermia
This ailment develops in three steps: heat cramps, heat exhaustion and heatstroke. The best treatment for hyperthermia is prevention. If you are hiking in particularly hot weather, make sure you maintain a continual and consistent intake of fluids. Dehydration is what usually leads to heat-related ailments. Also, if hiking is making you too hot, take a break, find some shade, drink some water, and give your body a few minutes to cool off.

If you progress to heat cramps (legs or abdomen begin to cramp), you are on your way to heat exhaustion and heatstroke. Take a break and sip water slowly. It is best to add a bit of salt to the water if possible. Rather than continue hiking, you should call it a day, and if possible, return to your car.

Heat exhaustion can follow heat cramps. Although the body temperature remains fairly normal, the skin is pale, cool and clammy; you may also feel faint, weak, nauseated and dizzy. Sit in the shade and sip water. Lower your head between your knees to relieve the dizziness. You can also lie down, loosen your clothes (or take them off if you're not shy), and elevate your feet about one foot. Bathe in cool water if there is any available. Vomiting signals a serious condition and medical help should be sought.

When suffering from heatstroke, the skin becomes hot, red, and dry; the pulse, rapid and strong. Unconsciousness is common. The victim should be undressed and bathed in cool water until the skin temperature is lowered, but do not over-chill the victim, which can be as dangerous as overheating. Medical attention should be sought as soon as possible.

Blisters
Blisters develop slowly and can make you miserable. As soon as you feel a hot spot, cover it with moleskin. If not treated properly, blisters can become infected. If you do get a blister, leave it unbroken; if it is already broken, treat it like an open wound, cleansing it and bandaging it. Do not continue to hike if you are in too much pain.

Bee Stings
Although most insects (other than black flies, deer flies, and ticks) will try to avoid you, bees (yellow jackets in particular) are attracted to food, beverages, perfume, scented soaps and lotions, deodorant, and bright-colored (and dark) clothing. Yellow jackets nest anywhere that provides cover—logs, trees, even underground. And they don't mind stinging more than once!

If you're sensitive to stings, carry an oral antihistamine to reduce swelling. A topical antihistamine, such as Benadryl, will help reduce itching. If you are allergic and a potential victim of anaphylactic shock, carry an Anakit whenever you hike. The Anakit, which must be prescribed by a doctor, contains a couple of injections of epinephrine as well as antihistamine tablets. If you use the kit, seek medical attention as soon as possible.

Pests
Deer, bears, boars, moose, raccoons, snakes, skunks and porcupines can all be found along the A.T., but these animals rarely cause problems for hikers, although overnight hikers have to worry about some of these critters stealing their food.

Bee stings discussed in the first aid section because the problem is immediate and potentially fatal, but there are other insects on the trail that can be a problem—no-see-ums, black flies, deer flies, horse flies, mosquitos, and ticks. The first five insects all produce itchy, painful bites that can be treated with a topical or oral antihistamine (or both, depending on how badly you react to their bites). Wearing lots of clothing, including a hat, will put the bugs at a disadvantage, but you may be uncomfortable. A bug repellent that is a thirty-five percent DEET works best.

Along the A.T., the tick is the biggest problem because some are infected with Lyme disease. You will need to take a little extra precaution. The tiny (about the size of a pinhead) deer tick is the carrier of Lyme disease. Whenever you hike in tick country (tall grass and underbrush), make sure you check yourself afterwards for ticks. It takes a while for a tick to become imbedded, so a thorough check at the end of the day will help you catch the tick before it catches you.

Wear a hat, long sleeved shirt, and pants with cuffs tucked into socks to discourage ticks.Too uncomfortable? Use a repellent with permethrin and stick to the center of the trail to avoid brushing against branches and shrubs. Ticks, like mosquitos, are attracted to heat and have been known to hang around for months waiting for a hot body to pass by. Try wearing light colored clothing so you'll be able to see the ticks more clearly.

If a tick attaches itself to your body, the best way to remove it is by grasping the skin directly below where the tick is attached and removing the tick along with a small piece of skin. Then carefully wash the bite with soap and water. Following its removal, keep an eye out for the symptoms of Lyme disease: fever, headache, and pain and stiffness in joints and muscles. If left untreated, Lyme disease can produce lifelong impairment of muscular and nervous systems, chronic arthritis, brain injury, and in ten percent of victims, crippling arthritis. If you suspect Lyme, see your doctor. Tick season is from April to October with a peak between May and July.

To avoid potential problems with bears, mice and raccoons, hang your food and garbage whenever you make camp. Make sure the bundle is heavy so that a raccoon can not haul the rope back up to the branch. If you leave your pack outside or in a shelter, you might want to leave the pockets open so that mice won't chew their way in. Mice aren't looking only for food. They also love clothing. It makes good nesting material.

Porcupines never attack unless provoked and are found along the A.T. only north of Massachusetts. The only problem with these animals is they gnaw boots. They are looking for salt, and sweat (especially on leather) is a good source. When you're hiking up north, hang your boots or stick them in the end of your sleeping bag at night.

Hantavirus
This deadly disease made the news in 1994 with an outbreak in the Four Corners area of the southwest. About that time, the Trail community learned that an A.T. thru-hiker had contracted hantavirus about 18 months earlier while hiking through southwest Virginia. The hiker had been hospitalized for a month in 1992 with the disease, but returned to the A.T. in 1994 to complete his thru-hike. Meanwhile, many hikers were left with grave concerns about this new infectious disease.

Hantavirus is rare and difficult to contract. You must have contact with the feces or urine of deer mice, or breathe air infected with the disease through evaporated droppings. Federal and state authorities have trapped and tested mice in shelters in southwest Virginia without finding evidence of the disease. To be safe, avoid all contact with mice and their droppings. Air out a closed, mice-infested structure an hour before occupying it.

Dogs

If you hike with a dog, you may have additional problems. Dogs can be sprayed by skunks, barbed by porcupines, and bitten by snakes. Plus, if you choose to hike with a dog, be prepared for your friend to scare up trouble. Dogs like to find dead things and roll in them, competing with the skunk for the most obnoxious odor.

Dogs can also cause other problems. A.T. hikers have been bitten by other hikers' dogs. If your dog does not like other people, leave him at home or keep him restrained while hiking. If you come upon a threatening dog, a hiking stick makes a good weapon. (*Note:* Dogs need as much water as you do on hot days.)

MAINE

MAINE

The Appalachian Trail in Maine is more rugged and remote than in any of the other thirteen trail states. The northern terminus of the A.T. is at Baxter Peak on top of Katahdin in Maine's Baxter State Park. From that peak, you can look to the southwest and see the Maine lake country that the A.T. crosses in this part of the state.

The trail in Maine traverses several prominent mountains including the twin peaks of the Bigelow Range, the Crockers, Saddleback, Old Blue, the Baldpates, and the Mahoosuc Range. In the Mahoosucs, the A.T. has what is often described as the "toughest mile." This section through Mahoosuc Notch is a testament to a trail builder's imagination and a hiker's stamina; here the A.T. goes over and under an incredible boulder-filled notch. The A.T. continues over Goose Eye and Mount Carlo on its way to the state line of New Hampshire.

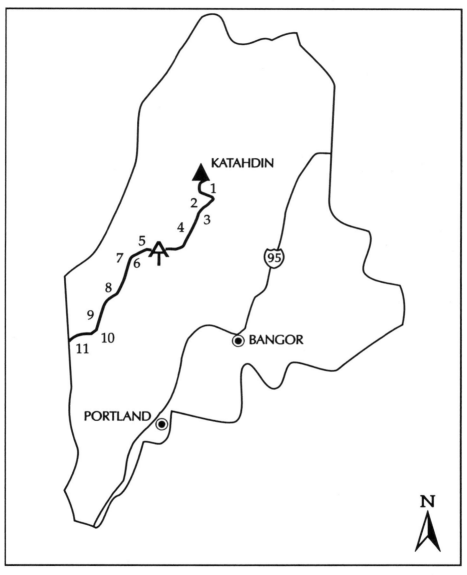

1. Rainbow Lake
2. Nahmakanta Lake to Abol Bridge
3. White Cap Range Loop
4. Barren-Chairback Range
5. Moxie Bald
6. Carry Ponds

7. Bigelow Range Loop
8. Saddleback Range
9. Baldpates
10. Bemis Range Loop
11. Mahoosuc Range

RAINBOW LAKE

MODERATE
25.4 miles roundtrip

This hike an little ambitious length for an overnight hike, but will reward you richly for your effort. And, if you would like to go to Rainbow Ledges but don't have the time to fit in the entire roundtrip, an optional hike is included. Along the hike, you'll find views of Katahdin and the surrounding lake country as you climb over Rainbow Ledges. The destination is a campsite near the dam at the western end of the Rainbow Lake, where the wild piercing cry of the loon can often be heard. From the campsite, there is an awe inspiring view of Mount Katahdin over the lake. This hike is at the northern end of the One Hundred Mile Wilderness,which stretches from Abol Bridge to Monson, Maine. This is the wildest section on the A.T.'s entire 2,100-mile route.

The Hike
The hike begins at Abol (short for Aboljackamegassic, Abenaki for "bare of trees") Bridge on the West Branch of the Penobscot River. The views of Katahdin from the bridge are the first of many fine views along this hike. Hiking south along the A.T., work your way over bog bridges, through a swampy area, and at mile 3.4 , arrive at Hurd Brook Lean-to, where water is available.

If you don't have time to hike the entire 25.4-mile roundtrip, you could hike into Hurd Brook one evening or early one morning. Using the lean-to as a base camp, hike up to Rainbow Ledges (or even to Rainbow Lake).

From Hurd Brook Lean-to, the trail soon begins to climb up Rainbow Ledges, gaining about 750 feet in elevation over the next 2 miles. Just over 2 miles from the lean-to, you will reach the highpoint of the Ledges—enjoy more excellent views of Mount Katahdin. Hike another 1.6 miles to Rainbow Lake. The trail wanders along the shore of the lake for the next 5 miles.

Locate a short side trail 2.3 miles after reaching Rainbow Lake. This spur leads to the pristine Rainbow Lake Spring. The spring is the best source of water for the campsite, which is another 1.8 miles south on the A.T. The campsite is located a short distance off the A.T., down an old road near the dam.

After spending the night at the campsite, return north via the A.T. to Abol Bridge.

Trailhead Directions
From Millinocket, Maine, travel 16 miles on Baxter Park Road to the turn for Baxter State Park. Instead of turning to the right to go to the Park, follow the main road and drive 4 miles to Abol Bridge. You can arrange to park your car in the campground at the bridge by talking to the camp's owner.

NAHMAKANTA LAKE TO ABOL BRIDGE

MODERATE
25 mile traverse

A short float-plane flight from Millinocket, Maine, brings you to the trailhead for this wilderness hike. The trip covers the top quarter of the One Hundred Mile Wilderness, which stretches from Abol Bridge south to Monson, Maine, and is the wildest section on the A.T.'s entire 2,100-mile route. Nahmakanta Lake offers good swimming at several points near the A.T. The lake's wild surroundings make the cold swim all the more enjoyable. The only two climbs along the route—Nesuntabunt and Rainbow Ledges—have some steep sections, but are relatively easy and reward you with good views of Mount Katahdin and the surrounding lake country.

The Hike
This overnight trip begins with a plane ride from Millinocket Lake. The hike begins at the south end of Nahmakanta Lake. The A.T. stays near the shore of the lake for 2.1 miles. After leaving the lake, you will cross Wadleigh Stream (.25 mile), and reach Wadleigh Stream Lean-to in another .1 mile. Water for the lean-to is available from the stream.

From the lean-to, hike 1.8 miles to the summit of Nesuntabunt Mountain. There are no views from the summit, but a short side trail leads to a rock ledge with fine views of Nahmakanta Lake and Mount Katahdin. Descend 1.1 miles to the base of the mountain and continue .75 mile to Crescent Pond, which the trail skirts for .4 mile. After leaving Crescent Pond, you will reach a logging bridge over Pollywog Stream in 1.4 miles, and Rainbow Stream in another .4 mile.

For the next 2 miles, the trail follows Rainbow Stream, which offers several swimming holes. Just before crossing the stream, you will reach Rainbow Stream Lean-to. Water for the lean-to is available from the stream. The lean-to, one of two suggested campsites for this hike, is at mile 10.4. The other campsite, near Rainbow Lake Dam and located just off the A.T. on an old tote road, is at mile 12.3. Camping at the lean-to breaks the trip up into a 10.4-mile day and a 14.6-mile day. Pushing on to the campsite at the dam breaks the hike up more evenly into a 12.3-mile day followed by a 12.7-mile day.

From the old road near Rainbow Lake Dam, hike 1.8 miles to Rainbow Lake Spring, a ten-foot wide spring on a short side trail. After passing the spring, the A.T. continues to follow the shore of Rainbow Lake for another 3.3 miles and then begins to climb Rainbow Ledges. The highest point of the Ledges is reached 1.6 miles after you leave the lake. Several points along Rainbow Ledges afford excellent views of Mount Katahdin.

From the high point along the Ledges, hike 2.6 miles to Hurd Brook Lean-to. Water is available from the brook. From Hurd Brook, hike 3.4 miles of often boggy trail to Abol Bridge on the West Branch of the Penobscot River. Return transportation should be arranged with the Air Service when you set up your flight.

Trailhead Directions
To make arrangements for the flight, contact Katahdin Air Service in Millinocket Lake, Maine, at (207) 723-8378. They offer reasonably priced flights to a number of points along the trail in Maine, including Nahma-kanta Lake.

Where and how to meet up with your flight can be arranged when you call the Katahdin Air Service.

WHITE CAP RANGE LOOP

STRENUOUS
18 miles roundtrip

Steep climbs and descents are often a part of this tough, but beautiful, loop hike in the One Hundred Mile Wilderness. Stretching from Abol Bridge south to Monson, Maine, it is the wildest section on the A.T.'s entire 2,100-mile route. You will cross Gulf Hagas Mountain, West Peak, Hay Mountain, and the summit of White Cap (on a side trip). From White Cap Mountain's rocky summit, you can see Mount Katahdin's planed-off top in the distance. In this section, the A.T. is crossed only by logging roads.

If time permits a side trip, you can visit Gulf Hagas. The Gulf is a wonderful wilderness area along a canyon, where the rushing waters of Gulf Hagas Brook cut through the rock. A 1.2-mile roundtrip will take you to Hammond Street Pitch. Here the Gulf is at its deepest.

The Hike

From the parking area on Steep Hill Road, walk toward Hay Brook, cross over the brook, and continue to the A.T., about a mile down the road. Follow the A.T. north and enter the Hermitage, a grove of one-hundred-foot trees purchased by the Maine Chapter of the Nature Conservancy to protect them from logging or development. These trees were once used as masts for sailing ships.

From the sign in the center of the Hermitage, hike 1 mile to the junction with the Gulf Hagas and Screw Auger Falls Trails, two worthwhile side trips. If you don't have much time, at least hike over and back to see the canyon. The Gulf Hagas Trail is a 5.2-mile loop trail. The Screw Auger Falls Trail leads about .25 mile to a magnificent waterfall.

From the junction of these two trails, follow the A.T. north for 4.7 miles to reach Carl Newhall Lean-to, just after crossing Gulf Hagas Brook. North of this lean-to, the A.T. becomes more strenuous, climbing and descending over peaks in the White Cap Range. From the lean-to, hike .5 mile to the top of Gulf Hagas Mountain (elevation 2,683 feet), then descend .75 mile, often steeply, to a sag (at mile 8.2) where water is available from a small spring. Campsites are scarce but available in this sag.

Ascend West Peak, reaching the summit (elevation 3,181 feet) in .6 mile, and then reaching the summit of Hay Mountain (elevation 3,244 feet) in another 1.3 miles. From the tree-covered peak of Hay Mountain, hike .5 mile to the junction of the A.T. with the White Brook Trail, which takes you back to your car to complete the loop. The 2.2-mile roundtrip to the rocky summit of White Cap is included in the mileage for this hike. The views from White Cap (elevation 3,644 feet) are magnificent.

Return to the trail junction between Hay Mountain and White Cap, and follow the White Brook Trail for 4 miles. Turn right on the Diamond Logging Road and take the next left onto Steep Hill Road. You will reach your car shortly after passing the gravel pit. The road walk is approximately 1.5 miles. The mileages for the road walk down from White Cap and back to the car are approximates due to periodic changes in the trail's route.

Trailhead Directions
Access to this part of the One Hundred Mile Wilderness is through the Katahdin Iron Works Gate. From Brownville Junction, Maine, go north on Maine 11 for 5.5 miles to Katahdin Iron Works Road. Turn right and reach the Katahdin Iron Works Gate in 7 miles. After passing through the gate, turn right on Diamond Logging Road. After crossing High Bridge, turn left and take your next left onto Steep Hill Road. The parking area is on the right after you pass the gravel pit.

BARREN-CHAIRBACK RANGE

STRENUOUS
15.4 mile traverse

This rough and rocky mountain range has a lot to offer. You'll be traversing the five peaks of the Barren-Chairback Range in the heart of the One Hundred Mile Wilderness, which stretches from Abol Bridge near Baxter State Park south to Monson, Maine. It is the wildest section on the A.T.'s entire 2,100-mile route. In this section, the A.T. is crossed only by logging roads. Short side trails lead to three mountain-top ponds—Cloud, West Chairback and East Chairback.

Elevation changes considerably between the peaks and gaps along the range, a net gain in elevation of nearly 4,000 feet no matter which direction you hike. The Barren-Chairback Range is for experienced hikers looking for a wilderness trek.

Because this hike is a traverse, it will require a drop-off/pick-up, shuttle, or two vehicles.

The Hike
From the trailhead on the St. Regis Logging Road, hike south on the A.T. and immediately begin climbing Chairback Mountain. The trail climbs steeply for the first mile and then moderately for .75 mile before you reach a .25-mile side trail that leads to East Chairback Pond. From the junction with the pond side trail, hike 1.9 miles, crossing several ridges and then ascending sharply to the summit of Chairback Mountain (elevation 2,219 feet).

From the rocky, open summit of Chairback Mountain, enjoy noteworthy views of White Cap and the surrounding lakes and ponds. Hike .5 mile down Chairback Mountain to Chairback Gap Lean-to located in the gap between Chairback and Columbus Mountains. Water is available from a spring. From the lean-to, climb .5 mile to the top of Columbus Mountain (elevation 2,342 feet). The trail crosses a rocky viewpoint near the summit and then descends for 1.2 miles to a gap where an old tote road leads .25 mile to West Chairback Pond.

From the gap, a .75-mile climb brings you to Monument Cliff at the top of Third Mountain (elevation 2,069 feet), and 1.2 miles will bring you over to the top of Fourth Mountain (elevation 2,379 feet). After leaving this tree-covered peak, hike 3.3 miles to the side trail for Cloud Pond Lean-to. The .25-mile side trail leads to where the shelter sits on a small rise overlooking the lovely wilderness pond for which it is named. This is our favorite of the three shelters in the range. There is a spring along the side trail on the way to the shelter.

Continuing on the A.T., hike 1 mile to the summit of Barren Mountain (elevation 2,660 feet), the fifth, and last, peak you'll encounter on the Barren-Chairback Range. Enjoy the fine 360° view of the surrounding area. From Barren Mountain, descend 1.7 miles to Barren Ledges where you'll find fine views of Lake Onawa and Boarstone Mountain. In another 1.2 miles, you will reach the .1-mile side trail that leads to Long Pond Stream Lean-to. Water is available from the stream.

From the lean-to, hike for .25 mile to Long Pond Stream, follow its banks for the next .75 mile, and then ford the stream (about knee deep). Take care because the rocks can be quite slick and the streambed is uneven in places. After crossing the stream, you will reach the end of the hike, Bodfish Farm Road.

Trailhead Directions
Access to the northern end of the hike is through the Katahdin Iron Works Gate. From Brownville Junction, Maine, go north on Maine 11 for 5.5 miles to Katahdin Iron Works Road. Turn right and reach the Katahdin Iron Works Gate in 7 miles. After passing through the gate, turn right on the Diamond Logging Road. Take your first left onto the St. Regis Logging Road and travel 7 miles to the trailhead.

The southern end of this hike is on Bodfish Farm Road. Take Elliotsville Road north out of Monson, Maine, and travel 12 miles to the Long Pond Stream Tote Road, which the trail crosses in just over 4 miles.

MOXIE BALD

MODERATE
12.8 miles roundtrip

This picturesque hike gets a moderate rating because of the more than fifteen-hundred-foot elevation gain when climbing Moxie Bald Mountain. Most of the elevation is gained in 2 miles (on the initial and the return trip). The 360° view from Moxie Bald Mountain (elevation 2,630 feet) makes the climb worthwhile. There are also two large ponds on the hike—at the onset of the hike and at the recommended campsite. Moxie (Indian for "dark water") Pond and Bald Mountain Pond offer great opportunities for swimming. There are several stream fordings on this hike, including a traverse of Baker Stream. Be careful crossing this particularly wide stream. If the water is too high to cross at the ford, there is a double-cable crossing available .1 mile downstream. The cable crossing is trickier than the ford, so use the cable only in extreme weather conditions.

The Hike
To begin this hike, follow Moxie Pond Road. The A.T. follows this gravel road (built over an old Central Maine railroad bed abandoned in the 1930s). The section of pond the road follows is called Joe's Hole. At mile .1, where Baker Stream empties into Moxie Pond, you will pass the wire cables used to cross the stream when it is too high to ford.

Carefully ford Baker Stream at mile .25. The A.T. begins a slow and gradual ascent of Moxie Bald Mountain to the east. In the next mile, you will pass beneath a power transmission right-of-way before reaching Joe's Hole Brook Lean-to, which sits next to a small brook. About 1.5 miles later, you will cross through an old lumber camp clearing and ford the small Bald Mountain Brook.

The A.T. begins to ascend steeply up the face of Moxie Bald Mountain. In 1.5 miles, you will reach the junction of the blue-blazed trail that bypasses the summit. This .5-mile trail can be used to avoid the summit in foul weather. Take the A.T. for another .4 mile to the summit of Moxie Bald Mountain, and enjoy the 360° view. Look west to view the Bigelow Mountain Range and northeast to view the Barren-Chairback Range. On especially clear days, you can see Mount Katahdin. There are also the remains of an old Maine Forest Service firetower on the summit of this mountain.

Descend north from the summit toward the sag in the ridge, and follow the ridge toward the north peak of Moxie Bald. In just over .25 mile, you will reach the junction with the northern end of the trail that bypasses the summit. Water is available from a spring .1 mile down this blue-blazed trail. Before descending steeply toward Bald Mountain Pond, you will reach the junction of the side trail that leads .75 mile to the north peak of Moxie Bald. This trail crosses many open ledges with great views. The north peak also features outstanding blueberrying in season.

About a mile after beginning a steep descent, you will cross a small brook and reach the short side trail to Moxie Bald Lean-to, which sits on the shore of Bald Mountain Pond. Camp at the shelter or along the shores of this pond. To return, hike south on the A.T.

Trailhead Directions
From Bingham, Maine, follow Maine 16 east for about 1.5 miles. Turn left onto a gravel logging road, and go north up the Austin Stream Valley to the south end of Moxie Pond. It is about 14 miles from Bingham to the A.T.

CARRY PONDS

MODERATE
13.9 mile traverse

Carry Ponds would be rated easy except for the tough ascent and descent of Roundtop Mountain. With more than 1,000 feet gained in elevation and then lost within 2 miles, this climb makes for an invigorating end to this pleasant lake country hike. On this section, the A.T. passes three ponds— East Carry, Middle Carry and West Carry—before going up and over Roundtop Mountain and reaching Long Falls Dam Road.

This hike is suffused in history. The area and trails were used both by Indians and the Benedict Arnold expedition. In 1775, George Washington charged Arnold with leading a detachment of 1,100 men through the wilderness of Maine to Quebec where a surprise attack would be staged against the British. Arnold followed the Kennebec River north to the Carry Pond area (called The Great Carrying Place by the Indians who used the trails and the ponds in the area to avoid rapids in the Dead River). Using the Abenaki Indians' portage route, Arnold and his men followed the Dead River to the St. Lawrence River Basin and finally entered Canada near Lake Megantic.

Battered by Maine's weather and landscape—it was late autumn and they were forced to slog in the bitter cold through swamps, bogs, and rivers—Arnold's expedition reached Quebec with only 700 men. The six weeks it had taken them to get through Maine had taken its toll and the campaign against Quebec was unsuccessful.

The A.T. now uses 2 miles of the Arnold Trail between West and Middle Carry Ponds. The Arnold Trail continues on to Flagstaff Lake, which can be reached by Long Falls Dam Road. The Dead River is now a part of this reservoir, which filled the Dead River Valley in 1949 when Long Falls Dam was built. Two towns—Flagstaff and Dead River, both farming communities—now lie underwater. Occasionally, when the waters of the dam are drawn down, parts of the towns can still be seen, including foundations, roadbeds and old bridge abutments.

The Hike
From the gravel logging road, follow the A.T. south. After about .25 mile, you will pass the side trail to Harrison's Camps, which is only .1 mile away to the south. Lodging and meals can be obtained here. A side trail also leads north to Pierce Pond.

Continue on the A.T. for another .1 mile to a waterfall that drops forty feet into Pierce Pond Stream and then cross an old wooden dam at the outlet of Pierce Pond. Be careful of the logs when wet. They can be slippery! After crossing the dam, you will reach the junction of another side trail leading to Harrison's Camps, which is now .25 mile away. There is another brook .1 mile down this side trail.

At mile .5, you will pass the Pierce Pond Lean-to, which is located on an arm of the pond, and at mile .75, you will cross a cold mountain stream and begin a gradual ascent of Bates Ridge. For the next 3.2 miles, ascend, pass over and descend Bates Ridge, a total elevation gain of 250 feet. At the bottom of this ridge, mile 4.1, you will cross the North Branch of Carrying Place Stream.

One mile past the North Branch, you will cross a gravel logging road that leads 18 miles to Bingham by way of Wyman Lake on the Kennebec River. To the right, the road leads 7 miles to Long Falls Dam Road.

Continue on the A.T., reach the northern shore of East Carry Pond in 1.5 miles, and follow the north and east shore for the next .6 mile. At the northeastern corner of the pond, you will cross over rocks along the shore, and about .4 mile later, you will reach a small sand beach. This pond has leeches so watch out! When you reach the western shore of East Carry Pond .1 mile past the beach, the A.T. leaves the pond and heads westward toward Middle and West Carry Ponds.

Before reaching another gravel logging road, you will cross a boggy area on bog bridges. The trail follows the road to the right for a short distance, crosses over Sandy Stream (the main inlet to Middle Carry Pond), and continues along the gravel road. At the fork, go left and turn sharply right off the road. For the next couple of miles, the A.T. follows the Arnold Trail, which crosses a wide bog and a meandering stream on bog bridges. (The Arnold Expedition didn't have these bridges and were greatly slowed down by the mucky earth.)

Less than a mile after turning onto the Arnold Trail, you will reach the high point between Middle and West Carry Ponds, and after another mile, you will reach the shore of West Carry Pond near Arnold Point, where there is a small gravel beach. Follow the pond to the east and south for the next 1.3 miles, and about .5 mile after you leave the east shore of West Carry Pond, reach West Carry Pond Lean-to. It is not far from a side trail leading to a small and sandy beach on the shore of the pond nor from a rocky berm that must be crossed. Use the bypass trail when the water is too high.

After the lean-to, the trail skirts the southeast corner of the pond, turns west, and leaves the pond entirely. Begin your ascent of Roundtop Mountain, crossing the broad summit (elevation 2,200 feet) in less than .5 mile. Descend gradually off the mountain and cross yet another gravel logging road in .5 mile. Cross Jerome Brook (previously the site of Jerome Brook Lean-to) in another .25 mile and reach the paved Long Falls Dam Road. The town of North New Portland is 20 miles south (left). Though there are several good campsites along this hike, you may want to make a long day of it and camp overnight at the lean-to. That way, you can enjoy a leisurely morning walk over Roundtop Mountain to Long Falls Dam Road.

Trailhead Directions
In Bingham, pick up the gravel logging road that intersects the A.T. just .5 mile north of Pierce Pond (Ask for the road that leads to Wyman Lake). Travel 11 miles to the head of Wyman Lake (the west side) and another 6

miles to the road's crossing with Pierce Pond Stream. The A.T. is just north of the stream crossing. About 11 miles north of Bingham, the road branches off to the left, bearing west and intersecting the A.T. about 1.5 miles north of East Carry Pond. Remain on the right branch of the road if you want to start your hike at Pierce Pond.

For the ending point, take Long Falls Dam Road out of North New Portland. You will intersect the A.T. about 20 miles north of town.

BIGELOW RANGE LOOP

STRENUOUS
11.7 mile loop

This short, but challenging, overnight hike traverses a section of the Bigelow Range and is one of the best wilderness hikes in a state known for its wilderness trails. The A.T. ascends Bigelow Mountain to a wonderful mountain tarn—Horns Pond—at more than 3,000 feet in elevation. From Horns Pond, the A.T. ascends South Horn and the West Peak of Bigelow, where there is an awe-inspiring view of Flagstaff Lake and numerous surrounding mountains including Sugarloaf and the Crocker Mountains to the southwest.

The return trip on the Firewarden's Trail and along Stratton Brook Pond Road makes a nice two-day trip. A side trip to the summit of Avery Peak is an optional .75-mile hike that will richly reward you for your efforts. Like the West Peak, Avery Peak boasts a commanding 360° view of the surrounding mountains and lakes.

This hike is located almost entirely in the Bigelow State Preserve. The Preserve is a 33,000-acre wilderness area the people of Maine set aside by a 3,000-vote margin in a general election in the 1970s. Prior to the legislation, developers had hoped to develop the Bigelow Range as a ski area. Led

by the Friends of Bigelow, the Maine Appalachian Trail Club and numerous other conservation groups helped force the referendum that saved the Range from future development.

The Hike
From the trailhead on Stratton Brook Pond Road, hike north on the A.T. In .1 mile, cross Stratton Brook and hike up a slight grade for the next .9 mile. The climb up Bigelow starts gradually and gets steeper. This tough climb reaches the highpoint on the ridge above Horns Pond at mile 3 and gains more than 2,000 feet in elevation. After topping the ridge, hike 1.1 miles along the ridge to a short side trail that leads to a memorable view of Horns Pond with North and South Horn in the background.

Reach the junction with the Horns Pond Trail .1 mile after the first side trail, and in another .25 mile, arrive at the twin Horns Pond Shelters. There are several tent sites nearby, and water is available from a spring in the camping area. The solar privy was built to minimize hikers' impact on the pond's ecosystem.

From the lean-tos at Horns Pond, climb .6 mile to the open summit of South Horn (elevation 3,831). Descend to a ridge that continues for 1.7 miles and then ascend for .4 mile to the West Peak of Bigelow (elevation 4,150). The 360° view from the rocky summit is tremendous. The Appalachian Mountain Chain marches off to the southwest. Close by, view Crocker and Sugarloaf; on a clear day, Mount Washington in New Hampshire. Down below, view Flagstaff Lake, which was built in the 1940s. Remember, the plants on the summit are fragile. Stick to the trail.

Climb steeply for .25 mile to Bigelow Col and the junction with the Firewarden's Trail. From the Col, there is an optional .75-mile hike to the Avery Peak of Bigelow, a rewarding side trip. For the return portion of this loop, hike down the Firewarden's Trail from the Col and off the mountain. The first .75 mile is very steep; afterwards the trail descends more moderately. Reach the junction with the Horns Pond Trail 2.9 miles after leaving the Col. Hike another 1.4 miles to Stratton Brook Pond Road. Follow the road for about a mile back to the trailhead.

Trailhead Directions
Stratton Brook Pond Road is about 4 miles south of Stratton, Maine, on Maine 27. Turn left on Stratton Brook Pond Road and drive 1 mile to the trailhead.

SADDLEBACK RANGE

STRENUOUS
22.3 mile traverse

Western Maine offers some excellent hiking opportunities, but the Saddleback Mountain Range heads the list, boasting a 3-mile, above-treeline section with outstanding views. Before you climb Saddleback Mountain, The Horn and Saddleback Junior, you will pass Piazza Rock, an overhanging rock that juts out from a cliff, and the shores of Ethel and Eddy Ponds. From Saddleback Junior's treeless peak, there are views in all directions of the surrounding western Maine wilderness. You will ford the cold, clear waters of Orbeton Stream before you climb Lone Mountain, Spaulding Mountain and Maine's second highest peak—Sugarloaf Mountain—located on a .6-mile side trail. The trail then descends sharply to the sometimes tricky ford of the South Branch of the Carrabassett River.

The ridge between Spaulding and Sugarloaf Mountains was the last section of the Appalachian Trail to be cleared. When a CCC Crew blazed this section of trail in 1937, it completed the more than 2,000-mile Appalachian Trail from Maine to Georgia.

This is a strenuous hike and should not be taken lightly. The above-treeline sections leave the unprepared hiker exposed to the elements; weather changes quickly in these mountains. The Saddleback Range offers no protection from lightning or severe rain or snow. Follow the Boy Scout creed and "Be Prepared." Avoid this hike in inclement weather.

The Hike
From the trailhead on Maine 4, follow the A.T. north and cross Sandy River on a footbridge in .1 mile. From Sandy River, hike 1.3 miles to Piazza Rock Lean-to. Water is available from the nearby stream. A short side trail leads to Piazza Rock.

After leaving the lean-to, the A.T. leads .9 mile to Ethel Pond and another .5 mile to Eddy Pond, which sits at the base of the climb up Saddleback. The trail ascends steeply up the west side of the mountain, gaining well over 1,000 feet in elevation during the first mile. Reach the junction with Saddleback Trail in 1.8 miles and the open summit of Saddleback (elevation 4,116 feet) with outstanding views of the western

Maine mountains in .6 mile. Water is available from a spring located on a short side trail .1 mile before reaching the summit.

Descend 1 mile to the gap between Saddleback and the Horn and then ascend the Horn steeply, reaching the summit (elevation 4,023 feet) in .6 mile. Just .25 mile from the summit of the Horn, the trail drops below treeline again, continuing to descend sharply off the Horn and reaching the short, steep climb up Saddleback Junior. The distance between the Horn and the treeless summit of Saddleback Junior (elevation 3,640 feet) is 2 miles. After enjoying Saddleback Junior's fine 360°, descend and reach Poplar Ridge Lean-to in 1.3 miles. Water is available from the nearby stream.

From the lean-to, hike .25 mile to the high point on Poplar Ridge, and descend steeply for .5 mile, losing 1,000 feet in elevation. Reach the ford of Orbeton Stream, 1.3 miles from the top of the ridge. The trail climbs steeply and then moderately out of Orbeton Stream Valley and reaches the summit of Lone Mountain (elevation 3,280 feet) in 3.1 miles. Arrive at the junction with the side trail to Mount Abraham (elevation 4,043 feet) in 1.1 miles. If you allow three days for this hike, you may want to add a trip to Abraham, 3.4 miles roundtrip. There are outstanding views from both the mountain and the ridge.

Continue following the A.T. and reach Spaulding Mountain Lean-to in 1 mile. Water is available from a spring near the shelter. From the lean-to, hike .75 mile to the side trail that leads to Spaulding Mountain. It is just .1 mile along the side trail to Spaulding's tree-covered summit (elevation 3,988 feet). Continue following the A.T. and reach the side trail to Sugarloaf Mountain (elevation 4,237 feet) in 2 miles. It is .6 mile along the side trail to the building on the top of Sugarloaf.

Continue following the A.T. for 1.1 miles to the top of an open ravine. It is more than 500 feet to the forest below. Descend, sometimes steeply, for .75 mile to the South Branch of the Carrabasset River. This ford can be difficult, particularly after heavy rain. The hike ends after another .1 mile at Caribou Valley Road.

Though this can be done as an overnight hike, it is easier if done in three days. By setting up cars at both ends late one afternoon, you can hike the 1.4 miles to Piazza Rock Lean-to and then walk the remainder of this hike the following two days.

Trailhead Directions
The trailhead on Maine 4 is 9 miles south of Rangeley, Maine. The trailhead on Caribou Valley Road is a logging road that turns off Maine 27 at the top of a hill, 1 mile north of Sugarloaf USA's access road and about 7 miles south of Stratton, Maine. Follow the logging road 4.5 miles to the trail crossing.

BEMIS RANGE LOOP

STRENUOUS
13.9 mile loop

This relatively difficult hike features the four open peaks of the Bemis Range and the ledges that connect them. You hike the A.T. for 7.3 miles and connect with the Bemis Valley Trail (also called the Bemis Stream Trail) for the last 5.6 miles. At the beginning of the hike, there is a .6-mile roadwalk from the parking area at the trailhead of the Bemis Valley Trail to the Appalachian Trail. In season, blueberries are abundant along the ledges; and on clear days, there are excellent views of the Rangeley lakes to the north as well as most of the major peaks of Northwest Maine.

The Hike
After parking at the Bemis Valley Trailhead on Maine 17, hike .6 mile up the road to its junction with the A.T. The A.T. crosses Maine 17 at a turnout, which offers views of Lake Mooselookmeguntic and the Bemis Range. The A.T. begins to descend immediately into the Bemis Valley.

Bemis Stream runs along the valley's floor and can be difficult to ford when the water is high. Just over .25 mile after fording the stream, you will cross a gravel road built over a former line of the Rumford and Rangeley Lakes Railroad, abandoned in the 1930s. Begin to ascend the Bemis Range.

In about .1 mile, pass a small spring and continue the ascent to the first of many open ledges and knobs. A large cairn marks the eastern peak of the

Bemis Range (elevation 2,604 feet). Just under a mile later, the second peak is reached (elevation 2,923 feet).

Continue along the A.T. and you will reach the Bemis Mountain Lean-to in another 1.5 miles. The lean-to is located in a sag, and water is available from a nearby spring. Consider spending the night here, leaving yourself an 8.3-mile hike for the following day. If you go on, stock up on water because this spring is the only sure water source in the Bemis Range.

From the shelter, hike less than .5 mile to the summit of the third peak in the Bemis Range (elevation 3,110 feet). The main summit of Bemis is made up of two peaks—the east and the west. In just over a mile, you will top the east peak (elevation 3,532 feet) and .1 mile later, the west peak (elevation 3,592 feet). The A.T. then descends from the west peak into 'the saddle between Bemis and Elephant Mountain.

In 1 mile, you will reach the junction of the A.T. with the Bemis Valley Trail. Take this trail and descend south and east down the valley for about 6 miles to Maine 17.

Trailhead Directions
The A.T. is 26 miles north of Rumford on Maine 17.

THE BALDPATES

STRENUOUS
10.2 mile traverse

The Baldpates and the spectacular waterfalls of Dunn Notch are the outstanding features of this trip. The net elevation gain of 3,300 feet over rough terrain creates a tough but short hike for experienced backpackers. Like many peaks in this wilderness state, the Baldpates offer incredible views of the mountains and lakes of western Maine. The 1,000-foot cliffs at Grafton Notch on Maine 26 are outstanding.

The Hike
This hike begins at East B Hill Road, which also connects to the northwest with Maine 26 near Upton Village. From East B Hill Road, the A.T. crosses a brook and heads south and west toward Dunn Notch.

Reach Dunn Notch in less than a mile and cross the West Branch of the

Ellis River, a mountain stream. Downstream from the trail crossing is a sixty-foot double waterfall that spills into a deep gorge. A tote road on the south bank of the river provides access to the bottom of the falls. You can also follow the river upstream to the upper falls, which spill into a small gorge.

From the falls, the A.T. ascends steeply out of the notch's south rim, reaching the top of the rim in .25 mile. The trail begins to ascend more gradually for the next 2 miles before swinging around the east arm of Surplus Mountain. At mile 4.6, reach your destination for the day—Frye Notch Lean-to and the adjacent Frye Brook.

Less than a mile beyond the lean-to, you will arrive at the junction of an unmarked side trail, which leads 2.8 miles down the Frye Brook valley to East B Hill Road (about 2.5 miles east of the A.T.). From here, the shoulder of East Baldpate Mountain, hike just over .25 mile to treeline and another .1 mile to the peak of Little Baldpate. Continue your ascent up the Baldpates and arrive on the open summit of East Baldpate (elevation 3,812 feet), marked by a large cairn.

The trail heads into the sag between the East and West Peaks of Baldpate (there is a small canyon at the bottom of the sag) and arrives on the partially open summit of West Baldpate (elevation 3,680 feet) after nearly a mile.

Descending from the West Peak toward Grafton Notch, you will pass over a small stream in just under a mile, located at the base of the main climb up the peak. In another 1.4 miles, you will reach the junction with the Table Rock Trail, which leads just over .5 mile to Table Rock, which overlooks the sheer cliffs that fall away into Grafton Notch. The Table Rock Trail meets up with the A.T. at the bottom of the notch near Maine 26 in another .9 mile.

Follow the A.T. for .5 mile and reach the side trail that leads to Grafton Notch Lean-to. In another .25 mile, you will reach the second junction with the Table Rock Trail, and in .1 mile, you will reach Maine 26. There is a small parking area for hikers' cars on the opposite side of the highway.

Trailhead Directions
The A.T. is 8 miles northwest of Andover at East B Hill Road. East B Hill Road also connects to the northwest with Maine 26 near Upton Village. The A.T. and Grafton Notch are 12 miles north of US 2 on Maine 26 (18 miles from Bethel).

MAHOOSUC RANGE

STRENUOUS
15 mile, 13.7 mile, or 9.4 mile traverse

The Mahoosuc Range is the most rugged section of A.T. in the state of Maine. A lot of elevation is gained and lost. The mountains in this chain are all over 3,500 feet in elevation. Because you will be hiking along the crest of the ridge, water will be scarce. Be sure to carry plenty.

The treadway is often wet and rough, and the trails cross many boggy areas, high on the ridge and in the sags. Because these areas can get so muddy, many bog bridges have been installed to protect the delicate ecosystem. Please remain on these bridges.

The most outstanding feature of the Mahoosuc Range (and these hikes) is Mahoosuc Notch. This deep cleft between Mahoosuc Arm and Fulling Mill Mountain is filled with enormous boulders that have fallen from the sheer cliffs on either side of the notch. Even in July, you can find ice in some of the caves formed by the boulders. The moss and boulders are slick and wet. Be careful. This is not the place to have an accident! Once you're down among the boulders, there is no way around them except over, under and to either side. Although less than 1 mile in length, Mahoosuc Notch can take several hours to maneuver through. Be sure to account for the extra time.

All three of these hikes begin and end on Success Pond Road and use side trails to get to and from the A.T. However, there are several miles between where the hikes begin (Speck Pond Trail) and where they end (Carlo Col, Goose Eye, and Mahoosuc Notch Trails), so you will need a shuttle, drop-off/pick-up, or two vehicles.

The Hikes
Speck Pond Trail to Carlo Col Trail (15 miles): Hike 3.3 miles up the Speck Pond Trail to reach Speck Pond, a mountain tarn between Old Speck and Mahoosuc Arm, and the A.T. The Speck Pond Trail and A.T. join at the Speck Pond Campsite. From here, follow the A.T. sharply left and skirt the eastern side of Speck Pond. The A.T. follows the Appalachian Mountain Club's (AMC) Mahoosuc Trail along the crest of the ridge.

After crossing the outlet of Speck Pond, you will begin your ascent up Mahoosuc Arm (elevation 3,777 feet). Less than 1 mile after passing the junction with the Speck Pond Trail, the A.T. tops the open summit of Mahoosuc Arm. From here, descend gradually, then more steeply, over ledges into Mahoosuc Notch, which is 1 mile further.

Before entering the notch, you will cross a brook, turn right, and head upstream along the Bull Branch of the Sunday River. The route through the notch is both difficult and dangerous and care should be taken. Follow the white blazes through the notch for 1 mile, and at its western end, reach the junction of the Mahoosuc Notch Trail. The A.T. turns sharply left and begins its ascent of Fulling Mill Mountain. The Mahoosuc Notch Trail descends out of the range to Success Pond Road 2.8 miles away. (This is where the Speck Pond Trail to Mahoosuc Notch Trail hike ends; a total of 9.4 miles.)

Continue on the A.T. and reach the crest of the South Peak of Fulling Mill Mountain (elevation 3,420 feet) in 1 mile. From here, turn right and descend, passing the Full Goose Shelter just past the bottom of the sag. There is a short side trail at the shelter that leads to water, a scarce commodity along this hike. Beyond the shelter, the A.T. ascends steeply for .25 mile and then levels off a bit. One mile past the shelter, you will reach the summit of the North Peak of Goose Eye Mountain (elevation 3,680 feet).

Turning left toward a long line of cairns, descend and ascend out of the sag ahead and reach the summit of the East Peak of Goose Eye Mountain (elevation 3,794 feet) just over 1 mile later. Turn right and descend into the col. About .25 mile later, you will reach the junction with the Goose Eye Trail. The Goose Eye Trail tops the summit of the West Peak of Goose Eye (elevation 3,860 feet) in .1 mile. Descend west off the range for 3.1 miles to Success Pond Road. (This is where the Speck Pond Trail to Goose Eye Trail hike ends; a total of 13.7 miles.)

The A.T. turns left, bypassing the west peak, and descending steeply into a sag. From the bottom of the sag, the A.T. ascends for .5 mile to the summit of Mount Carlo (elevation 3,565 feet). Then, the A.T. bears right, descends toward the col ahead, and meets the junction with the Carlo Col Trail less than .5 mile later. Follow this trail for .25 mile to the Carlo Col Shelter. Hike another 2.3 miles on the Carlo Col Trail, descending off the range to the northwest, to Success Pond Road. (This is where the Success Pond Trail to Carlo Col Trail hike ends; a total of 15 miles.)

Using the above description as a guide, follow the Mahoosuc Notch Trail out of the Mahoosuc Range to Success Pond Road at the point in the text that notes the end of the third hike.

Trailhead Directions

Success Pond Road, which provides access to the trails used for all three hikes—Speck Pond, Mahoosuc Notch, Goose Eye and Carlo Col—can be reached from Berlin, New Hampshire. Cross the Androscoggin River at the 12th Street Bridge on Upper Main Street. Turn right on Hutchins Street and drive .4 mile to Morris Lumber Company. Then, turn left at the stop sign, cross the railroad tracks, and turn right at Liberty Market. Continue for .4 mile and take the second dirt road in the mill yard of the James River Company. Cross the yard and continue along Success Pond Road. A radio tower is visible on the left and you will soon cross a powerline cut-through. It is about 9 miles down Success Pond Road to the trailhead (on right) for both the Carlo Col and Goose Eye Trails; 12 miles to the trailhead (on right) for the Mahoosuc Notch Trail; and 14 miles to the trailhead (on right) for the Speck Pond Trail. If you pass Success Pond (on left), you have gone too far.

NEW HAMPSHIRE

New Hampshire

From the Mahoosuc Range on the Maine border, the A.T. in New Hampshire heads west over the rugged Carter-Moriah Range and the Wildcat Range to Pinkham Notch. From the Notch, the trail heads up into the Northern Presidential Range with miles of above-treeline trail. This is a very rugged and remote section of trail. In the White Mountain National Forest, which attracts thousands of visitors each year, many hikers underestimate the ruggedness of the terrain. The weather can quickly turn severe in these high elevations; even if the weather in the valleys is expected to be nice, be prepared for the worst when hiking in the Whites. Mount Washington can get snow year round.

As the A.T. crosses the White Mountains, it goes up and over some of the area's best-known peaks, including Mt. Madison, Mt. Washington, Mt. Lafayette, Franconia Ridge, Kinsman Mountain, and Mt. Moosilauke. From the Whites, the trail traverses Mt. Cube and Smarts Mountain on the way to Hanover, New Hampshire. The trail goes right through town and passes Dartmouth College, home of the Dartmouth Outing Club that maintains the trail in this area.

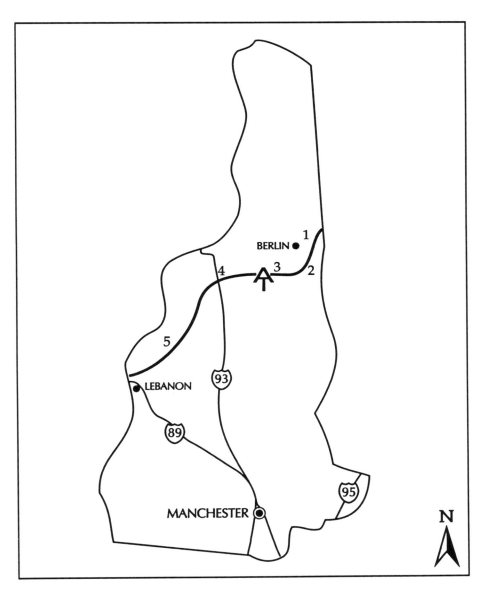

1. Gentian Pond
2. Mount Moriah
3. The Northern Presidential Range
4. Franconia Ridge/Lonesome Lake
5. Western New Hampshire

GENTIAN POND

MODERATE
22.2 miles roundtrip

The highlights of this overnight hike are four mountain tarns. You will hike by Page Pond, Dream Lake and Moss Pond before reaching Gentian Pond, where you can spend the night at the shelter or camp on the hill overlooking the pond.

This hike will also take you over the east summit of Mount Hayes (elevation 2,555 feet) where you'll find fine views of the northern Presidentials and the Carter-Moriah Range. The peak is reached on a .25-mile side trail. It is a rollercoaster hike, but there are no major changes in elevation following the 3-mile climb to the east summit of Mount Hayes, during which you'll gain 1,500 feet.

The Hike
From the trailhead on Hogan Road, follow the A.T. north into the woods and begin ascending Mount Hayes. At mile 2.7, reach the east summit of Mount Hayes, and at mile 3.1, reach the Mahoosuc Trail. The peak of Mount Hayes (elevation 2,555 feet) is .25 mile along this trail. Continue following the A.T., descend to the col between Mount Hayes and Cascade Mountain, and immediately begin a moderate ascent up Cascade Mountain.

At mile 5, reach the top of Cascade Mountain (elevation 2,631 feet). The trail takes a hard left turn, continues along the top of the mountain, and begins the occasionally steep, 1.1 mile descent to Trident Col.

Hike 1 mile to Page Pond, then 1.1 miles to Dream Lake, and another 1.7 miles to Moss Pond, the smallest of the four tarns along the hike. From Moss Pond, descend moderately to Gentian Pond. Water is available just upstream of the trail where the A.T. crosses a creek on a footbridge prior to arriving at Gentian Pond. You will reach the Gentian Pond Shelter and Campsite at mile 11.1. A solar privy near the shelter is designed to lessen hikers' impact on the area. Return by way of the A.T. to the trailhead.

Trailhead Directions
From Gorham, New Hampshire, drive 3.6 miles east on US 2, and turn left

onto North Road. Note the white blazes along North Road as the A.T. follows the road on this section of trail. Turrn left onto Hogan Road in .5 mile and travel another .25 mile down this gravel road. Parking is available where the trail turns into the woods.

MOUNT MORIAH

STRENUOUS
11.2 miles roundtrip
or 10.1 mile traverse via Carter-Moriah Trail

From 800 feet above sea level in the Androscoggin River Valley, the Appalachian Trail climbs to the top of Mount Moriah, gaining more than 3,000 feet in elevation. This is a beautiful but tough hike. The rugged Carter-Moriah Range features an uninterrupted footpath for its 20-mile length. This hike follows the Rattle River up the mountainside, passes through a pretty, marshy sag on bog bridges, and reaches the summit of Mount Moriah.

At the summit of Mount Moriah, the Carter-Moriah Trail descends northward to the town of Gorham. If you do not wish to retrace your steps, you can take this shorter trail back down the mountain for a 10.1-mile hike. Because this latter hike is a traverse, it requires a drop-off/pick-up, shuttle or two vehicles.

The Hike
The hike begins in the parking lot at the junction of US 2 and the Appalachian Trail. Ascend gradually through the woods, passing a lumber campsite at mile .75. In just over .5 mile, reach the Rattle River Shelter, and in another .5 mile, take the right fork of the trail, crossing over a brook and ascending steeply.

Following the river, you will continue your ascent and cross the Rattle River at mile 3.1. This might be your last source of water, so you may want to pick some up, particularly if you intend to camp atop Mount Moriah. The climb becomes steep and reaches a junction at mile 4.1 where the A.T. turns right and joins the Kenduskeag Trail. (The Kenduskeag Trail heads left to the Shelburne Trail.)

The A.T./Kenduskeag Trails continue to climb over the wooded summit of Middle Moriah Mountain. In .75 mile, you will pass through a pretty, marshy sag on bog bridges and continue your ascent up the mountain. Hike another .75 mile to the junction of the Carter-Moriah Trail and the end of the Kenduskeag Trail.

The A.T. turns left and descends to the south along the Carter-Moriah Trail. The Carter-Moriah also turns right and heads northward, shortly reaching the summit of Mount Moriah (elevation 4,049 feet). Take the Carter-Moriah Trail (right) to the summit of Mount Moriah, the midpoint of the hike. From here, you can either take the Carter-Moriah Trail for 4.5 miles to US 2 in the town of Gorham, New Hampshire, or you can follow the A.T. north back down the mountain and along the Rattle River to the parking lot at US 2.

Trailhead Directions
The A.T. can be reached at US 2 by driving 3.8 miles east of Gorham, New Hampshire. The Carter-Moriah Trail is also on US 2 (in the town of Gorham, New Hampshire).

THE NORTHERN PRESIDENTIAL RANGE

STRENUOUS
17 mile loop

The A.T. traverses all but 4.1 miles of this magnificent loop around the Northern Presidential Range of the White Mountains. The loop uses the Tuckerman Ravine Trail to descend from the summit of Mount Washington, the highlight of this hike, to Pinkham Notch. The Presidentials are the highest mountain group traversed by the A.T. north of Clingmans Dome (located in the Great Smoky Mountains National Park, North Carolina/Tennessee).

The trail runs above treeline for more than 8 miles of this hike. Treeline in the Presidential Range is at 4,200 feet, and above this elevation the only vegetation is krummholz (stunted spruce) and alpine plants, both extremely vulnerable to foot traffic. Please remain on the trails. Because of the potential for inclement weather in the Whites—rapidly arising storms with hurricane-force winds and freezing conditions—it is best to keep to the trails anyway.

Mount Washington is said to have the worst weather in the world, producing record gusts of wind atop its 6,288-foot peak. In 1934, the weather observatory, established in 1870, recorded a wind velocity of 231 miles per hour that has yet to be matched. Standing well above treeline, Mount Washington, along with the rest of the Presidentials, forms an arctic island with permafrost and arctic flora. Come prepared to throw on raingear and wool sweaters at a moment's notice.

The first path to the summit was cut in 1819. The first summit house was built in 1852. The second summit house, the Tip Top, was built in 1853 and is still standing. It is open daily during season as a museum. The summit also features the Sherman Adams Building, which houses the weather observatory and its museum, as well as a snack bar, souvenir shop, post office, restrooms, and telephones. The Mount Washington Auto (Toll) Road climbs 8 miles from New Hamshpshire 16 to the summit, and the world's first mountain-climbing railway, the Mount Washington Cog Railway, has been carrying tourists to the summit of Washington since 1869. The 3.5-mile railroad climbs at a 37.4 percent grade, the steepest in the world.

If you intend to stay at one of the huts (as opposed to a tentsite or shelter), you must make reservations through the Appalachian Mountain Club (AMC). Call (603) 466-2727 or write to Reservations Secretary, AMC, Pinkham Notch Camp, Gorham, New Hampshire 03581. Fees are inexpensive for tentsites and shelters (usually just a few dollars), but hut fees can cost as much as $54, which includes lodging, breakfast, and dinner.

The Hike

You will start out on the Tuckerman Ravine Trail at Pinkham Notch, following this trail for a short distance before turning right onto the Old Jackson Road Trail. At mile 1.4, make a sharp left away from the roadbed near a brook and begin to climb steeply.

You will soon reach the junction of Raymond Path (leading left across the mountain to Tuckerman Ravine Trail). Not long after the A.T. crosses a brook, you will reach the junction of the Nelson Crag Trail (leading left past Nelson Crag to the Mount Washington Auto Road).

At mile 1.7, you will cross the Mount Washington Auto Road at its 2-mile post and take the Madison Gulf Trail into the Great Gulf Wilderness. In another .1 mile, a side trail leads a short distance to Lowe's Bald Spot and great views of the Northern Presidentials and the Carter-Moriah Range.

In another .5 mile, you will cross twin brooks and continue your ascent. At mile 3.7, the A.T./Madison Gulf Trail joins the Great Gulf Trail for a short distance. You will soon cross the West Branch of the Peabody River over a suspension bridge, ascend a ridge, and then cross a footbridge over Parapet Brook.

The A.T./Madison Gulf Trail then turns left while the Great Gulf Trail heads right (downstream). Shortly thereafter, make a sharp left (still along Madison Gulf Trail) for .25 mile to the junction of the Osgood Cutoff. The A.T. then follows the Osgood Cutoff to its intersection with the Osgood Trail while the Madison Gulf Trail continues ahead toward Madison Springs Hut.

It is less than .5 mile to the Osgood Trail. Osgood Tentsite is at mile 4.3. Water is available from a spring on the right. It is the last sure water until Madison Springs Hut, 3 miles away. Turn left onto the Osgood Trail and ascend steeply.

At mile 5.5, you will reach treeline on the crest of Osgood Ridge. For the next 8 miles or so, you will be above treeline. In .5 mile, cross the first peak on Osgood Ridge, and in another .25 mile, reach Osgood Junction. Here, the Daniel Webster Trail and Parapet Trail intersect the A.T.

The A.T. continues up the ridge on Osgood Trail and passes over a second peak. You will pass the intersection of the A.T. with the Howker Ridge Trail before reaching the summit of Mount Madison (elevation 5,363 feet) at mile 6.7. Watson Path descends right and the A.T. continues, descending the southwest ridge of Mount Madison.

In another .4 mile, you will reach Madison Springs Hut. From the hut, the A.T. follows Gulfside Trail, soon crosses Snyder Brook, and ascends southwest. In .25 mile, you will reach the junction of the A.T. with the Air Line Trail to the right; a short distance further, the Air Line Trail leaves the A.T. to the left, climbing .75 mile to the summit of Mount Adams (elevation 5,798 feet). The A.T. continues to ascend gradually to the southwest.

At mile 8, reach Thunderstorm Junction. It is marked by a massive rock cairn more than ten feet high. Lowe's Path heads left .25 mile to the summit of Mount Adams and descends to the right to Gray Knob Cabin. Spur Trail descends to Crag Camp Cabin, and the Great Gully Trail heads north to King Ravine. The A.T. continues along Gulfside Trail, passing a grassy area between Mount Adams and Mount Sam Adams.

In .25 mile, reach the intersection of the A.T. with Israel Ridge Path, which also leads to the summit of Mount Adams. In another .25 mile, you will pass intermittent Peabody Spring in a swampy, grassy area. There is a more reliable water source just past this spring at the base of a boulder to your right.

At mile 8.6, reach another trail junction where Israel Ridge Path descends .9 mile to The Perch Shelter. The A.T. continues ahead, following the narrow ridge between Castle Ravine on the right and Jefferson Ravine on the left.

In .75 mile, you will reach Edmands Col, where Randolph Path heads right .25 mile to Spaulding Spring, and Edmands Col Cutoff heads left, passing Gulfside Spring a short distance later. The A.T. continues along the eastern side of Mount Jefferson, reaching Jefferson Loop in .1 mile. The loop heads right for .25 mile to the summit of Mount Jefferson (elevation 5,715 feet).

Continuing along the eastern flank of the mountain, the A.T. soon reaches its intersection with Six Husbands Trail (left to Jefferson Ravine and Great Gulf Wilderness; right to the summit of Jefferson). In another .25 mile, the A.T. passes a smooth, grassy plateau known as Monticello Lawn. Jefferson Loop enters from the right.

The Cornice Trail descends to the right in another .25 mile, the Sphinx Trail to the left .4 mile later. Reach Clay-Jefferson Col at mile 10.8., where the Mount Clay Loop heads left to the summit of Mount Clay (elevation 5,532 feet). Avoiding the summits, the graded A.T./Gulfside Trail continues along the western side of the ridge.

In just over .5 mile, when you pass the junction of Jewell Trail, the A.T. descends slightly. At mile 11.7, the Mount Clay Loop enters from the left and the trail begins to ascend gradually. In .1 mile, the Westside Trail leads to right to Lakes of the Clouds Hut. The A.T. ascends between the edge of the Gulf and the Mount Washington Cog Railway.

At mile 12.3, when the Great Gulf Trail descends into the Great Gulf, the A.T. turns right, crosses the railway, and continues across the side of Mount Washington. In just over .5 mile, you will reach the summit of Mount Washington (elevation 6,288 feet).

From here, you take the Tuckerman Ravine Trail for 1.7 miles to Hermit Lake Shelter and Tentsite, and another 2.4 miles to Pinkham Notch at New Hampshire 16 where you began your hike.

Trailhead Directions
Pinkham Notch and trailhead for the A.T. can be reached by following New

Hampshire 16 for 8 miles north of Jackson, New Hampshire, or for 12 miles north of Gorham, New Hampshire.

FRANCONIA RIDGE/LONESOME LAKE

STRENUOUS
13 mile loop

This hike begins in Franconia Notch at the junction of US 3 and the A.T. You will hike northward over Franconia Ridge, descend to Franconia Notch via the Old Bridle Path, pick up the Lonesome Lake Trail and follow it to Lonesome Lake Hut where you will reconnect with the A.T. and hike north to Franconia Notch.

This is a beautiful loop hike, taking in both the splendor of Franconia Ridge and the beauty of the Lonesome Lake area. The hike along Franconia Ridge is above treeline and passes over the summits of Mount Lafayette and Mount Lincoln. Treeline occurs at 4,200 hundred feet; you will hike several miles across the ridge among the krummholz (stunted spruce) and alpine vegetation. Keep to the trail to avoid damaging these very fragile plants. Franconia Ridge is exposed to sudden and severe storms. Be prepared by bringing along raingear and a warm sweater or coat.

Lonesome Lake is a high mountain tarn on the shoulder of Cannon Mountain. The A.T. follows Cascade Brook, passing its waterfalls and cascades, downstream to Franconia Notch. The Lonesome Lake Trail ascends to Lonesome Lake Hut from Lafayette Campground through the woods along the shoulder of Cannon Mountain.

Franconia Notch—the beginning, middle and end of the hike—features several interesting geological features that can be viewed after your hike. They can all be reached off US 3. The Basin, located 1 mile north of the A.T. crossing on US 3, is a glacial pothole more than 20 feet in diameter; it was carved in granite at the base of a waterfall more than 25,000 years ago. Also nearby on US 3 is the Old Man of the Mountains, a 40-foot stone profile of a man formed by five ledges of Cannon Mountain. It stands more than 1,200 feet above Profile Lake and can be viewed from Profile Clearing. The Flume, also in Franconia Notch, is about a mile south of the trail crossing off US 3. This natural chasm is 800 feet long with granite walls sixty to seventy feet high, and twelve to twenty feet wide.

If you intend to stay at one of the huts (as opposed to a tentsite or shelter), you must make reservations through the Appalachian Mountain Club (AMC). Call (603) 466-2727 or write to Reservations Secretary, AMC, Pinkham Notch Camp, Gorham, New Hampshire 03581. Fees are inexpensive for tentsites and shelters (usually just a few dollars), but hut fees can cost as much as $54, which includes lodging, breakfast and dinner. Lodging is also available at Lafayette Campground, operated and maintained by the New Hampshire Division of Parks. It is 2.5 miles north of the trail crossing and has ninety-eight tentsites, showers, water, a telephone and some provisions. A fee is charged.

The Hike
The hike begins at the intersection of the paved bike path and Liberty Spring Trail near US 3 in Franconia Notch State Park. To get here, park a mile south at the Whitehouse Trail and Flume Complex, and take the bike path back to Liberty Spring Trail.

Entering the woods on Liberty Spring Trail (also the Appalachian Trail), you will soon cross two small brooks and then follow an old logging road. At mile .4, you will reach the junction of the the Flume Slide Trail. The A.T. ascends straight ahead, crossing a brook in another .25 mile. In the next .25 mile, you will cross two more brooks and begin to ascend very steeply.

At mile 2.4, you will pass Liberty Spring Campsite. Water is available from the spring just off the trail to the right. Continue to ascend steeply, and reach Franconia Ridge in another .25 mile. The A.T. turns north onto Franconia Ridge Trail, ascending gradually then steeply over rough ledges. The Franconia Ridge Trail leads south .25 mile to the summit of Mount Liberty. The Osseo Trail begins here and descends south to Kancamagus Highway.

At mile 4.6, you will top Little Haystack Mountain (elevation 4,760 feet). Falling Waters Trail descends to Lafayette Campground on US 3, but you will reach the same campground later by way of the Old Bridle Path.

Continue ahead on the A.T., which is now above treeline. At mile 5.3 mile, you will reach the summit of Mount Lincoln (elevation 5,089 feet), and at mile 5.7, a minor peak. Ascend steeply up the rocky cone of Mount Lafayette (elevation 5,249 feet), and reach the summit at mile 6.3.

At the summit of Mount Lafayette, you will see the remains of the summit house foundation. Take the Greenleaf Trail to the left, descend a short distance to a spring, and hike 1.1 miles to Greenleaf Hut. At Greenleaf

Hut, pick up the Old Bridle Path and hike 2.5 miles down the mountain to Lafayette Campground at US 3.

The Lonesome Lake Trail leaves Lafayette Campground at US 3 and travels just over 1 mile to Around-Lonesome-Lake Trail. This .25-mile trail leads around the northern shore of Lonesome Lake to Lonesome Lake Hut and the Appalachian Trail.

In .1 mile, you will reach the end of Fishin' Jimmy Trail, where the A.T. turns right onto Cascade Brook Trail. The A.T. follows this trail along Cascade Brook, the outlet brook of Lonesome Pond, for the next couple of miles.

In 1 mile, the Kinsman Pond Trail enters from the right. Continue downstream along the A.T. for .5 mile and cross the wooden bridge over Cascade Brook. Shortly thereafter, reach the Basin-Cascade Trail, which heads left to The Basin on US 3.

Soon after crossing the rocks over Whitehouse Brook, a mile or so later, you will reach US 3. Go under both lanes and locate the paved bike path. Take the bike path right to the Whitehouse Trail and Flume Complex, a mile away.

Trailhead Directions
The Appalachian Trail crossing at U.S. 3 is 5.8 miles north of North Woodstock. You must park south of the A.T. at the Whitehouse Trail and Flume Center (also called the New Hampshire State Park Flume Complex) and hike 1 mile north to the trail crossing via a paved bike path.

WESTERN NEW HAMPSHIRE

STRENUOUS
19.4 mile traverse

During this overnight hike, you might be lucky enough to spot a Peregrine Falcon. A reintroduction program at Holts Ledge has been successful, and there are at least seven nesting pairs in the state, with one nesting site here. There are signs posted around the Ledge to keep hikers away from the nesting area. Human intrusion could jeopardize the endangered species further, so please don't be tempted to venture beyond the signs.

On this traverse, there are a few steep climbs and descents along the way, but the mountains offer spectacular views of the surrounding countryside. You can hike from either direction, but we suggest starting at New Hampshire 25A and traveling south. It gets the toughest climbs out of the way early and leaves the easier sections for the second day. If you prefer to tackle the tougher climbs and descents on the second day, you will want to hike north from Goose Pond Road. Smarts Mountain Shelter and Tentsite makes a nice location to camp, and it divides the hike up into two hikes of roughly equal length.

The Hike
From the trailhead at New Hampshire 25A, hike south on the A.T. and begin ascending Mount Cube at mile .25. At mile 1.8, cross Brackett Brook on a bridge and continue climbing. In another 1.5 miles, reach the col between the summits of North and South Cube. A short side trail leads to the summit of North Cube, which of the two peaks, affords the better view of the White Mountains. Continue on the A.T. and reach the summit of South Cube (elevation 2,911 feet) in .1 mile. From the open summit, you can look ahead to your next climb, Smarts Mountain.

Follow the A.T. down from Mount Cube for 1.5 miles then cross a small stream just before the .25-mile side trail to Hexacube Shelter. Water for the shelter is available from the creek at the junction of the side trail with the A.T. Continue following the A.T. south, crossing two brooks and a couple of old logging roads in the next 1.5 miles. The second brook, at mile 6.1, is at the base of the climb up Smarts Mountain. The trail climbs steadily for 3.8 miles to the summit of Smarts (elevation 3,240 feet).

The old Firewarden's Cabin is maintained as a hiker shelter, and there is a tent platform on the summit as well. Water is available from a spring .1 mile away on a blue-blazed side trail. The view from the firetower is outstanding, but the view from the privy is one of the best on the mountain.

From the summit of Smarts Mountain, descend on the A.T. and reach the junction with the Smarts Mountain Ranger Trail in .5 mile. Continue following the A.T. and cross the rocky Lamberts Ridge, where there are fine views from several points on the ridge, and reach the parking lot on the Lyme-Dorchester Road 3.8 miles south of Smarts Mountain.

Continue following the A.T. along a short road walk and re-enter the woods in .4 mile. In 1.5 miles, the trail turns left onto the Lyme-Dorchester Road, and in .25 mile, the trail leaves the road and begins a moderate climb up to Holts Ledge. From the road, hike .9 mile to the .25-mile side trail for Trapper John Shelter. Water is available from a creek near the shelter. Reach the highpoint of the trail on the Ledge .5 mile past the shelter side trail. A .1-mile side trail leads to the top of the Dartmouth College Skiway and the viewpoint at Holts Ledge. Follow the A.T. down from the Ledge for 2 miles and reach Goose Pond Road.

Trailhead Directions
The A.T. crosses New Hampshire 25A 4.3 miles west of Wentworth, New Hampshire. Limited parking is available. The southern end of this hike is on Goose Pond Road, 3.3 miles east of New Hampshire 10. Goose Pond Road turns left off New Hampshire 10 about 3 miles south of Lyme.

VERMONT

VERMONT

From the Connecticut River at the Vermont/New Hampshire border, the Appalachian Trail passes from east to west for over 40 miles. Crossing through lowland hardwood forests and climbing over steep hills dotted with pastures and fields, the A.T. joins the Long Trail at Sherburne Pass where it heads 101 miles south to the Vermont/Massachusetts border.

The northern section of the trail in Vermont passes through an area once populated by many farms. The area from the Connecticut River to Sherburne Pass features cleared hills, pastures, ravines, steep hills and patches of timber. Stone walls, cellar holes and other remnants of the farms that once dominated this area can still be seen. The area is now reverting back to forest.

At Sherburne Pass, the Long Trail heads north about 160 miles to Canada and south with the A.T. to the Vermont/Massachusetts border. The A.T. climbs up the slopes of Killington and Pico Peaks in the Coolidge Range, reaching its highest point in Vermont just below Killington Peak (elevation 4,235 feet). Once the trail passes through the Coolidge Range, it descends again to rolling hills and farmlands then crosses Clarendon Gorge on a suspension bridge before climbing back up into the Green Mountains.

From here, the A.T. follows the ridge of the Green Mountains, passing several mountain ponds (Little Rock Pond, Griffith Lake and Stratton Pond). The trail also crosses several peaks, including Peru Peak, Spruce Peak, and Stratton Mountain. The latter is said to be the birthplace of the Appalachian Trail. It is here that Benton MacKaye first envisioned a trail along the Appalachian Mountains.

From Stratton, the trail continues to Glastenbury Mountain before descending to Vermont 9 near Bennington, Vermont. The trail then climbs to follow a rolling ridge for 14 miles until it meets the Vermont/Massachusetts border. It is another 4 miles to Massachusetts 2 in North Adams, the nearest road crossing to the border.

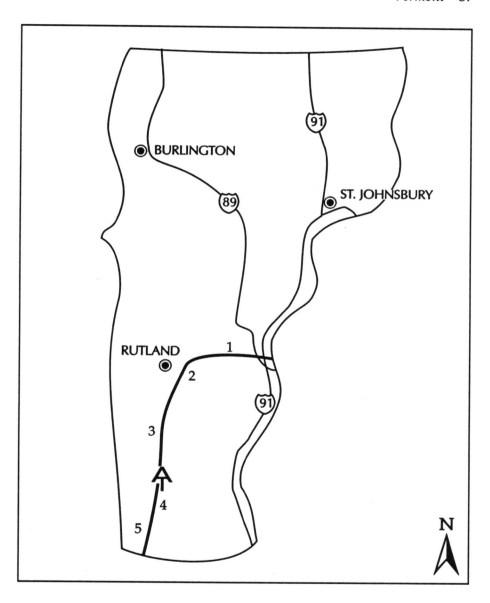

1. Eastern Vermont
2. Killington Peak
3. Griffith Lake Loop
4. Stratton Mountain/Lye Brook
   Wilderness Loop
5. Glastenbury Loop

EASTERN VERMONT

MODERATE
21.3 mile traverse

On this hike, you will be traversing an intermountain range section as the A.T. makes its way from the White Mountains of New Hampshire to the Green Mountains of Vermont. The elevations along this hike are not that extreme, between 1,500 and 2,500 feet above sea level, but there are plenty of ups and downs along the way.

You will enjoy fine views at Lakota Lake Lookout, pass the beautiful Kent Pond, and cross a portion of Gifford Woods State Park. The State Park is along a major migratory bird flyway, and bird watchers flock to the park in the spring and fall to see the varied birds that use the park as a rest area during their migration. The park also boasts a virgin grove of forest made up largely of sugar maples.

There is an optional .6-mile side trip at the end of this hike. The Deer Leap Trail climbs to the top of Deer Leap Cliffs and affords outstanding views of Sherburne Pass and its surrounding peaks.

The Hike
From the trailhead on Bernard Gulf Road, follow the A.T. south. At mile 1.2, enjoy good views from an open ridgetop, and at mile 2.2 and mile 3, cross old roadbeds. At mile 3.9, reach the .25-mile side trail to Wintturi Shelter. Water is available from a small spring near the shelter.

The trail then ascends more steeply as you continue to climb Sawyer Hill. At mile 5.4, the A.T. turns right onto an old road. In another .25 mile, the trail turns off the road—watch for the turn.

At mile 6.4, reach the junction with the Lookout Spur Trail. Continue following the A.T. for 1.8 miles to reach the Lakota Lake Lookout. There are good views of the lake as well as the surrounding countryside while the White Mountains appear in the distance.

For the next several miles, you will be following a ridge with occasional knobs to climb. The end of the ridge is descended by way of switchbacks, and at mile 13, you will reach the short side trail to Stony Brook Shelter immediately before the first of two stream crossings.

Cross Stony Brook Road in .1 mile and begin climbing steadily. Reach the top of a ridge and cross a shoulder of Quimby mountain on the way to the highest point of the hike, an unnamed mountain (elevation 2,640 feet) 2.1 miles past Stony Brook Road. Descend steeply on switchbacks to a ridge and cross under powerlines in .6 mile, where there are good views from the powerline right-of-way. Climb to another unnamed point and descend gradually. From the powerlines, hike another 1.1 miles to a viewpoint from an old logging road.

At mile 17.7, cross gravel River Road and follow Thundering Brook Road across the Ottauquechee River. The A.T. turns off the road, climbs gradually over a hill, and rejoins the road again in .4 mile. The Mountain Meadows Lodge is to your left just after you pass the dam for Kent Pond. As you follow the shoreline, you will pass a swimming area and cross a few small creeks.

At mile 19.3, the A.T. joins Vermont 100 for a short distance before turning off the highway into Gifford Woods State Park. Shelters and tentsites are available for rent from the park. The A.T. winds its way through the park, passing the caretaker's house, showers, the camping area, and more. Beyond the park, the A.T. ascends, sometimes steeply, and reaches Maine Junction at mile 20.7. The A.T. and the L.T. go south and share the same trailway to the Massachusetts border. The L.T. also heads north to the Canadian border. Continue following the A.T. and descend to Sherburne Pass in .6 mile.

There is an optional .6-mile side trip at the end of this hike. Hike .5 mile past Maine Junction and turn right on the Deer Leap Trail. The trail climbs sharply up to the top of Deer Leap Cliffs in .3 mile. From the top of the cliffs, enjoy outstanding views of Sherburne Pass and its surrounding peaks.

Trailhead Directions
The trail crosses Vermont 12 at Barnard Gulf Road, 4.4 miles north of Woodstock, Vermont. There is a parking area at the road crossing. Sherburne Pass is located 10.3 miles east of Rutland, Vermont, on US 4.

KILLINGTON PEAK

STRENUOUS
16.9 mile traverse

This hike traverses the Coolidge Range of the Green Mountains and reaches the highest elevations along the Appalachian Trail in Vermont. Short side trails lead to Pico Peak (elevation 3,957 feet) and Killington Peak (elevation 4,235 feet). It is from the summit of Killington that the state was christened "verd mont" or "green mountains" in 1763. From the top of Killington, you can see the Green Mountain Range of Vermont; from Glastenbury Mountain to the south to Mount Mansfield to the north. There area also views of the White Mountains of New Hampshire, the Taconics and Adirondacks of New York, and on especially clear days—Massachusetts, Maine, and even Canada.

The evergreen forests and dense hardwoods along this section provide for an especially spectacular traverse in the fall. In the lower half of this section, you will find yourself descending into the foothills, winding through pastures, fields, open woods, and second-growth conifers.

The Hike
From US 4 (elevation 2,150 feet), enter the woods on the south side of the road. You will cross a section of the old highway and pass east of the ruins of the former Long Trail Lodge. In .75 mile, pass the junction with the .1-mile side trail to the upper station of the Little Pico Ski Lift and the top of the Pico Alpine Slide.

Ascend through hardwoods on the northeastern slope of Pico Peak for .5 mile and pass a stream that disappears into a sinkhole on your right. At mile 2.1, you will pass a spring that is a short distance to the right of the trail and shortly before Pico Junction. Follow a ski trail uphill for a short distance and then turn left into the woods.

At mile 2.5, you will pass Pico Camp. This enclosed cabin shelters twelve. Water is available from a spring a short distance north on the A.T. Behind the cabin, the blue-blazed Pico Link Trail leads .4 mile to the summit of Pico Peak (elevation 3,957 feet). The trail continues south with minor elevation changes.

In just over a mile, you will pass a gully; and a short distance later, a spring. Climbing gradually to the south, you will pass to the right of West Glade Ski Trail and begin to climb steeply.

At mile 5.4, turn right and a short distance later pass Cooper Lodge (elevation 3,900 feet). There is a spring 100 feet south of the cabin. (*Note:* A relocation of the present trail between Cooper Lodge and Governor Clement Shelter is being considered. The new trail will be cut west of the current trail. Watch the blazes carefully.) In front of the lodge, the Bucklin Trail descends west to Wheelerville Road. Behind the lodge, the A.T. climbs a short distance to the .25-mile side trail that leads to the summit of Killington Peak (elevation 4,235 feet), the second highest mountain in Vermont. There is a very expensive snack bar on the summit as well as a chair lift (open Memorial Day through Labor Day).

From the side trail, the A.T. continues south along the western slope of Killington, passing through spruce-fir forest and crossing the Juggernaut Ski Trail. One mile from Cooper Lodge, the Shrewsbury Peak Trail heads left. Shortly thereafter, cross the Juggernaut Ski Trail again and then reach Consultation Point (elevation 3,760 feet) at mile 6.7. From here, you will descend steeply on rough trail. In another .5 mile, you will descend steadily through hardwoods, passing several overgrown logging roads and turning right onto a wide logging road at mile 9.2.

At mile 9.5, turn right off the road, and soon reach the Governor Clement Shelter (elevation 1,860 feet) located in an overgrown field on the right. Water is available at a large stream east of the logging road. Continue across the clearing and into the woods, and turn right onto a woods road in .1 mile.

A short distance later, the trail turns left off the road, crosses Robinson Brook, ascends, and then turns left along the western bank of the brook. The trail continues with minor elevation changes. At mile 9.9, you will cross a stone wall and ascend into a clearing. About .25 mile later, cross another stone wall to the left of a deer camp and descend. Reach an old road at mile 10.3, turn sharply left, cross Sargent Brook, turn right, and follow the brook downstream.

In .6 mile, you will cross Upper Cold River Road and continue to descend along Sargent Brook. In another .75 mile, cross Gould Brook and descend along its left bank until you reach a wide trail. Nearly a mile later, turn right on Cold River Road (Lower Road), cross a concrete bridge, turn left into the woods, and follow the western bank of Northam Brook uphill. In .25 mile, leave the brook and soon cross a field. In another .1 mile, leave the field and turn left onto Keiffer Road.

After .1 mile, you will turn right off the road and ascend along a stone wall. You will reach the crest of the ridge in just over a mile and pass the unreliable Hermit Spring .25 mile later.

At mile 14.6, you will enter a pasture, and about .25 mile later, cross the unpaved Lottery Road. Be sure to close the farm gates as you ascend another pasture, climbing to a grove of sugar maples. At mile 15.2, you will reach the airport beacon atop Beacon Hill (elevation 1,760 feet). Then, the trail drops steeply and crosses a brook in .5 mile.

Reaching the old town road (Crown Point Military Road—built during the French and Indian Wars), turn left and descend for .1 mile to Clarendon Shelter. The trail continues south, crosses a town road, climbs gradually to a rock promontory, and descends through a steep gorge.

At mile 16.7, pass under a powerline, then through the woods, cross a stile, and hike through an open field to another stile to Vermont 103. Clarendon Gorge is on the other side of Vermont 103 and is spanned by the Mill River Suspension Bridge. There is good swimming here as long as you refrain from diving off the rocks.

Trailhead Directions
The trailhead at Sherburne Pass is located 10.3 miles east of Rutland, Vermont, on US 4. The A.T. crossing at Vermont 103 is 2.2 miles east of US 7, 7.7 miles east of Rutland, and 3 miles west of Cuttingsville.

GRIFFITH LAKE LOOP

MODERATE
14.1 mile loop

Griffith Lake, a beautiful mountain pond with good swimming, is the goal of this overnight hike. You will cross Baker Peak on your way to Griffith Lake. The return is by way of the Old Job Trail, which follows Lake Brook down the mountain to rejoin the A.T. This loop makes for a great fall foliage hike. It is hard to beat the grandeur of leaf season in Vermont, but the crowds can be a bit much. If possible, hike this section during the week to avoid these crowds.

A number of options exist for camping along this hike—three shelters and one campsite. The campsite at Griffith Lake has a caretaker during peak season—mid May to mid October—who collects a fee. The other shelters are free of charge. The only water available at Griffith Lake is .5 mile beyond the campsite. Bring enough with you or plan to make the side trip to Peru Peak Shelter.

The Hike

From the trailhead on USFS 10, hike south on the A.T. for 1.3 miles to Big Branch Shelter. The caretakers here have been waging a loosing battle against porcupines that like to eat the wood from the shelter that is flavored with hikers' sweat. Wherever you camp on this hike, be sure to keep your boots packed away at night because porcupines are attracted by the sweat-stained leather.

Reach a suspension bridge over Big Branch .1 mile beyond the shelter, and the junction with the Old Job Trail at mile 1.5. Continue following the A.T. and climb steadily for 1.5 miles to Lost Pond Shelter. Water is available from the small creek nearby. From Lost Pond Shelter, the trail continues to climb steadily and reaches the summit of Baker Peak (elevation 2,580) at mile 5. Enjoy outstanding views of the Green Mountains and the Dorset Valley.

In .1 mile, reach the junction with the Baker Peak Trail; and in 1.7 miles, the junction with the Lake Trail. Continue on the A.T. for .1 mile to the northern end of Griffith Lake. The Old Job Trail comes up from the left. In .25 mile, reach Griffith Lake campsite on the banks of this high mountain pond (elevation 2,580). Water is available at Peru Peak Shelter, which is .5-mile south on the A.T.

To return, leave the Griffith Lake campsite, hiking north on the A.T. In .25 mile, reach the junction with the blue-blazed Old Job Trail. Descend gradually along the Old Job Trail, following an old logging road to Lake Brook. The trail will descend, sometimes steeply, along the brook and reach an old logging road 3 miles from the A.T. junction. In another 1.3 miles, you will reach a large clearing where the Old Job Shelter is the only remaining development. The town of Griffith was once located here. Water is available from the brook.

From Old Job Shelter, continue following the Old Job Trail and reach its northern junction with the A.T. in 1 mile. Follow the A.T. north and cross the suspension bridge over Big Branch in .1 mile. Hike another .1 mile to Big Branch Shelter. From the shelter, hike 1.3 miles to the trailhead on USFS 10.

Trailhead Directions
The A.T. and the L.T., which share the same treadway on this section, cross USFS 10 (Danby-Landgrove Road) 3.5 miles east of US 7 at Danby, Vermont. There is a parking lot at the trailhead.

STRATTON MOUNTAIN/LYE BROOK WILDERNESS LOOP

MODERATE
21 mile loop

This is actually a figure-eight hike that will take you through some of the best the Green Mountains have to offer. The hike uses the A.T. and L.T., the Lye Brook Trail, the Branch Pond Trail, and the Stratton Pond Trail to wind you through the Vermont wilderness. Stratton Mountain is topped with a firetower offering a commanding view of the Green Mountains and surrounding Vermont countryside. You will also hike to Stratton and Bourn Ponds and pass through the Lye Brook Wilderness.

There are five shelters along this hike, supplying numerous options for breaking up this outstanding hike. Although rated moderate, the hike up and back down Stratton is definitely strenuous. Don't despair; the rest of the hike is much easier.

The Hike
From the trailhead on the Arlington-Wardsboro Road (locally known as Kelly Stand Road), hike north on the A.T., which shares the same trailway with the L.T. on this section. You will gradually begin ascending, and in 1.3 miles, you will cross a dirt road. The ascent becomes more strenuous as you climb Stratton Mountain. At mile 2.8, pass a small spring on the uphill side of the trail.

At mile 3.4, reach the wooded summit of Stratton Mountain (elevation 3,936 feet). A ranger-naturalist with the Green Mountain Club is on duty mid-May through mid-October at the small cabin near the firetower. The cabin is the ranger's residence and is not open to hikers. However, it is worth the effort to climb to the top of the firetower and take in the tremendous view. Stratton and Bourn Ponds can be seen to the west far below. Mount Equinox, the highest peak in the Taconic Range, is also to the west.

Follow the A.T. off the summit and descend steeply for the first mile, then more gradually. Reach an old road 1.9 miles past the summit of Stratton. At mile 6, reach Stratton Pond Junction (elevation 2,550 feet), where water is available from a small spring. A good swimming area is also nearby.

From the Stratton Pond Junction, follow the blue-blazed Lye Brook Trail. Reach Bigelow Shelter in .1 mile and the Vondell Shelter .1 mile beyond. Stratton Pond is the busiest camping spot on the L.T. A caretaker is on duty in peak season and fees are charged for camping or staying in the shelters.

From Vondell Shelter, hike .4 mile to a log bridge over the Stratton Pond Outlet. At the bridge, you will reach the junction with the western end of the North Shore Trail, which leads .75 mile around the north shore of Stratton Pond back to the Stratton Pond Junction. Continue following the Lye Brook Trail and cross the upper reaches of the Winhall River in .6 mile. As you cross the river, which at this point is a small stream, you enter the 14,300-acre Lye Brook Wilderness.

From the Winhall River, hike 1.2 miles to South Bourn Pond Shelter on the southwest bank of the mountain pond. Water is available from a spring located on a short side trail. From the South Bourn Pond Shelter, follow the Branch Pond Trail north for .5 mile and pass a short side trail leading to the North Bourn Tenting Area, which offers a privy and a couple of tent platforms. Near the platforms, there is a good view of Stratton Mountain rising above the pond.

From the camping area, hike .75 mile to where the trail crosses Bourn Brook. The trail follows the brook 2.3 miles to the William B. Douglas Shelter. Water is available from a spring along the trail before you reach the shelter. From the Douglas Shelter, hike .5 mile to the junction with the A.T. Turn back hard to your right and follow the A.T. south for 2.4 miles to a bridge over the Winhall River. Cross the bridge, and climb along the side of an unnamed ridge for 2.2 miles to Stratton Pond Junction.

From Stratton Pond Junction, follow the blue-blazed Stratton Pond Trail south. This was the route of the A.T. until a 1989 relocation over Stratton Mountain. With little elevation change, the Stratton Pond Trail leads 3.9 miles to Arlington-West Wardsboro Road. When you reach the road, turn left and walk the .75 mile back to the parking area at the trailhead.

Trailhead Directions
The A.T. crosses Arlington-West Wardsboro Road (locally known as Kelley Stand Road) 13.2 miles east of US 7 at Arlington, Vermont.

GLASTENBURY LOOP

STRENUOUS
21.5 mile loop

Following a rolling ridge along the southern Green Mountains, the Glastenbury Loop uses the A.T. and L.T., the West Ridge Trail, and the Bald Mountain Trail. The highlight of this loop is the summit of Glastenbury Mountain (elevation 3,748 feet), which is completely covered with tall spruce. However, there is an old firetower that offers great views of the surrounding mountains.

The Hike
From the parking area on the Bennington-Brattleboro Highway (Vermont 9), the A.T. heads east into the woods. In .1 mile, you will cross City Stream on the William A. McArthur Memorial Bridge. Follow the north bank of City Stream downstream and turn uphill for a tough ascent to Split Rock.

In another .1 mile, you will cross an old woods road and climb to a lookout. At mile .6, you will pass through the fissure of Split Rock. Then, in another .25 mile, you will cross another woods road, climb gradually and cross yet another woods road.

At mile 1.5, you will reach the side trail to the Melville Nauheim Shelter. From here, the A.T. ascends north and crosses Black Brook. After .5 mile, you will reach a powerline at its highest point on the southern side of Maple Hill (elevation 2,620 feet). There are great views of Bennington and Mount Anthony to the west, and Mount Snow, Haystack Mountain and the northern end of the Hoosac Range to the east.

Cross under the powerline and reach the high point just east of the summit of Maple Hill in about .25 mile. Descend and cross over twin brooks in .5 mile, and cross the bridge over Hell Hollow Brook nearly .5 mile after that. This is the last reliable water source until Glastenbury Shelter.

In another .25 mile, you will cross an old woods road and pass through a balsam and spruce swamp on bog bridges. Then, begin climbing steadily northeast for nearly a mile and reach the summit of Porcupine Ridge (elevation 2,815 feet). Follow the ridge northeast to a lookout and continue along the ridge, first descending a bit, then climbing again.

At mile 5.4, you will reach the summit of Little Pond Mountain (elevation 3,100 feet). Descending briefly, you will continue along a narrow ridge. In .25 mile, you will pass Little Pond Lookout (elevation 3,060 feet). Continue northeast along the ridge, climbing steadily toward an unnamed peak, passing just west of its summit at mile 6.3.

Descending steeply northwest along the western side of the ridge, the grade eventually becomes moderate as the trail climbs back onto the ridge. At mile 7.4, you will reach Glastenbury Lookout and the view of Glastenbury Mountain and the connecting ridge to Bald Mountain.

Descend north for .5 mile, cross an old woods road in a shallow sag, and begin a gradual ascent. In .4 mile, you will cross another woods road and continue to climb steadily. In just over .25 mile, you will pass a large rectangular boulder atop the summit of another nameless peak (elevation 3,150 feet).

At mile 8.8, you will follow a woods road down the ridge a short way before turning off the road and ascending once again. At mile 9.5, you will cross an old skid road and climb very steeply before leveling off.

Reach Goddard Shelter at 9.8 miles. Water is available from a spring a short distance east on the A.T. If you choose to spend the night here, it is a .25-mile climb to the summit of Glastenbury Mountain (elevation 3,748 feet). The sunset, viewed from the firetower, can be spectacular.

From the shelter, take the blue-blazed West Ridge Trail, which leaves the A.T. and heads 7.8 miles southwest along the ridge, with little elevation change, to the Bald Mountain Trail.

After passing near a beaver pond, the trail climbs and crosses a logging road at mile 12.3. The trail then continues to climb the ridge and swings around the west side of a minor summit before continuing in a southerly direction. Passing several limited views, the trail continues on or near the top of the ridge for 5.2 miles, reaching the summit of Bald Mountain (elevation 2,857 feet) at mile 17.5.

Descend from the summit for .1 mile to the junction with the Bald Mountain Trail. Head left on the Bald Mountain Trail, descends via switchbacks for .25 mile to the side trail that leads .25 mile to a spring at Bear Wallow.

At mile 19.5, the Bald Mountain Trail reaches a public road. Hike .75 mile south along the road to the junction with the Bennington-Brattleboro Highway. Turn left (east) and walk 1.2 miles to the parking area at the A.T. crossing.

Trailhead Directions
The Appalachian Trail crossing on the Bennington-Brattleboro Highway (Vermont 9) is 5.1 miles east of Bennington and 2.8 miles west of Woodford.

MASSACHUSETTS

MASSACHUSETTS

The A.T. enters Massachusetts 4 miles north of where it crosses Massachusetts 2 in North Adams, and descends along the rocky ridge of East Mountain. From North Adams, the trail continues up Prospect Mountain Ridge over Mount Williams and Mount Fitch to the summit of Mount Greylock, the highest point in Massachusetts (elevation 3,491 feet).

From Mount Greylock, the A.T. descends to Cheshire, continues over to Dalton, and climbs the Berkshire Highlands. The trail traverses High Top and passes Finerty Pond before entering October Mountain State Forest. After crossing US 20 at Greenwater Pond, the A.T. continues to Goose Pond and descends into the Tyringham Valley. From Tyringham, the Appalachian Trail continues into the Beartown State Forest, skirting Benedict Pond.

From here, the trail heads southwest into East Mountain State Forest, crosses over Warner and June Mountains, and descends to the Housatonic River. The last miles of the A.T. in Massachusetts cross the valley to the Taconic Range, climbing Mount Everett and Mount Race, and passing beautiful Bear Rock Falls before descending to the Connecticut border in Sages Ravine. The many scenic ponds, such as Upper Goose, Benedict, and Finerty, are perhaps the dominant feature of the A.T.'s 89 miles in Massachusetts.

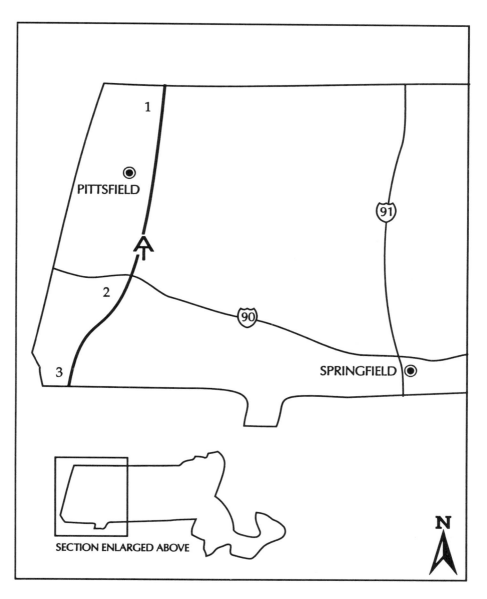

1. Mount Greylock Loop
2. Upper Goose Pond to Benedict Pond
3. Jug End/Mount Everett/Sages Ravine

MOUNT GREYLOCK LOOP

MODERATE
11.1 mile loop

This short overnight loop uses the Hopper Trail, the Money Brook Trail, and the A.T. to form a hike around the Mount Greylock State Reservation, which is situated on 11,000 acres. The highlight of the hike is the summit of Mount Greylock (the highest point in Massachusetts), where the first observation tower in the nation to charge admission is located. The summit of Greylock boasts the Massachusetts War Memorial, a stone tower on the site of the former observation tower.

The summit also houses Bascom Lodge, owned by the state and operated by the Appalachian Mountain Club (AMC). The lodge offers bunkroom sleeping quarters and a shower for under $30. Meals are also available here.

You will also pass Wilbur Clearing, named for Jeremiah Wilbur who used to pasture his animals on the 1,600 acres around this old corral—a small grassy area in the middle of a red spruce grove.

The Hike
The hike begins at Hopper Road where both the Hopper Trail and the Money Brook Trail begin. From the farm gate on the road leading between two pastures (step over the electric wire immediately after the gate), follow the road for .25 mile until you reach the second farm gate with stone walls on both sides.

In another .1 mile, you will reach the junction with the Money Brook Trail, which leads downhill to a brook. The Hopper Trail heads right into an overgrown pasture. After taking the right fork onto the Hopper Trail, hike through the pasture, enter the woods, and reach a barbed wire fence in .5 mile. In another .5 mile, the trail leaves private property (along with some logging activity) and enters Greylock State Reservation. Begin a steady climb through an open hardwood forest.

At mile 1.4, a side trail heads left, downhill, to the Money Brook Trail. In another .1 mile, you will reach several springs that come out of the side of the hill and cross the trail. This is the only available water on the Hopper Trail.

In another .75 mile, after a steady, and at times quite steep ascent, the trail levels off in a red spruce grove and enters Site 16 of the Sperry Campground at Sperry Road. The Hopper Trail follows Sperry Road for .1 mile before heading left back into the woods opposite the campground's contact station. The trail here is both steep and wet.

In .1 mile, you will see the remains of an old CCC log dam and spring house below a cliff, and a small waterfall to the right. In another .1 mile, the Hopper Trail turns left sharply as the Deer Hill Trail (the old Greylock Stage Coach Road) enters from the right. For the next .5 mile, you will follow this road up Mount Greylock. Reach the junction with the Overlook Trail to the left and hike another .1 mile to the junction with Rockwell Road.

Walk .25 mile through the woods to reach Rockwell Road at its junction with the A.T. and the Cheshire Harbor Trail. Take the A.T., cross Rockwell Road, and skirt the south side of an old water-supply pond for .25 mile before reaching the junction of Notch Road, Summit Road, and Rockwell Road. For the next .25 mile, you will hike through woods of stunted spruce and fir before emerging into a clearing next to a television tower.

In another .1 mile, you will reach the summit of Mount Greylock (elevation 3,491 feet). And, .5 mile later, after turning north toward the end of the parking lot, the A.T. descends and crosses Summit Road, eventually leveling off on the ridgeline where two ski trails head east.

At mile 5.4, on the west side of the trail, you will pass the first of two campsites that are within .1 mile of each other. The A.T. continues ahead over an unusual outcropping of milky quartz near the round, tree-covered top of Mount Fitch.

In .75 mile, a side trail leads .25 mile to Notch Road. The trail continues to ascend steadily for another .25 mile, passing the blue blazes and granite marker that indicate the western boundary of the North Adams Watershed. At mile 6.4, the trail arrives at a register atop Mount Williams. There is a campsite on the north side of the ledges and views of Mount Haystack in Vermont.

Cross Notch Road nearly a mile later (near the day-use parking area), and hike .1 mile to the junction of the Money Brook Trail, also the side trail to the Wilbur Clearing Lean-to.

Heading through the red spruce grove on the Money Brook Trail, you will soon pass a spring, and in .25 mile, the Wilbur Clearing Lean-to will appear on the right. In the next .25 mile, a short-cut trail to Notch Road comes in from the left as you pass through a beech and northern hardwood forest.

After a steep sidehill descent, you will come to a huge old hemlock at a hairpin turn in the trail, where there is a side trail to the left to Money Brook Falls. Descending through a hemlock grove, you will cross Money Brook for the first time at mile 8.4.

Continue to descend gradually along a shelf parallel to the brook, and reach the junction of the Mount Prospect Trail in another .75 mile. The Mount Prospect Trail ascends steeply from the brook to the right.

In .1 mile, you will cross Money Brook again and then one of its tributaries. Continue downstream along Money Brook for nearly .5 mile to the side trail short cut to the Hopper Trail on your left. Take a sharp left across a tributary of Money Brook, and find a large pool at the junction of the two main tributaries that form Hopper Brook.

The trail follows an old logging road for just over .5 mile, and crosses Hopper Brook. In another .1 mile, you will reach a fence next to a brookside pasture. Follow the farm road uphill and reach the junction with the Hopper Trail in about .25 mile. In .1 mile, you will once again pass the gate, which has stone walls, and then reach the electric wire near the first farm gate.

Trailhead Directions
Hopper Road can be reached off Massachusetts 43 in Williamstown. The trailhead is at the end of Hopper Road. Parking is allowed only along the side of the road near the last telephone pole at Haley Farm.

UPPER GOOSE POND TO BENEDICT POND

MODERATE
20.7 mile traverse

From the scenic Upper Goose Pond at the northern end of this section to the glacial Benedict Pond near the southern end, you will pass through the beautiful Massachusetts woods and near the picturesque town of Tyringham. This section also crosses Webster Road, the site of a two-school community that thrived in the early 1800s. It was home to Widow Sweets, a self-taught bonesetter and local legend.

South of Tyringham, you pass the site of the former Tyringham Shaker Community (1792-1875). All that remains are cellar holes and wide stone walls. This section leads through farm and hay fields before it reaches the Beartown State Forest. The trail also passes through a steep valley before climbing to The Ledges with views of Mount Everett and the Catskills.

The Hike

Following the A.T. south from US 20, you will cross a stream on a high bridge at a historic mill site beside the outlet of Greenwater Pond. In another .1 mile, you will cross the Massachusetts Turnpike (Interstate 90) on twin bridges, enter the woods, and climb steeply up a rough trail.

Within the next .6 mile, you will cross two intermittent brooks and reach the top of the ridge at mile 1, where there is a trail junction and register box. Because this is a protected natural area, you might find a caretaker on duty.

In just over .5 mile, the A.T. takes a sharp left turn at its junction with the side trail to the Upper Goose Pond Cabin, .5 mile away. A caretaker is on duty at the cabin, and there is a fee for both tentsites or bunkroom space, $2 and $3 respectively.

Continue along the A.T. for .25 mile and pass an old chimney and a plaque marking the site of the former Mohhekennuck fishing and hunting club. Hike for .5 mile along the shore of Upper Goose Pond, named for the Canada Geese that nest upon its shores, and cross the inlet of the pond. In .25 mile, you will pass a spring to the right and soon thereafter leave this protected natural area as the trail heads away from the pond and begins to climb steeply. At mile 3.1, the trail levels off and descends across large rocks. In another .75 mile, you will see where the former trail continued to the right across private property toward Lower Goose Pond.

The new trail continues straight ahead, descending through a deciduous forest. At mile 4.1, reach the outlet to a beaver marsh on a long bridge constructed of telephone poles. The trail continues through ferns and ground pine with the marsh to the left. In .1 mile, you will parallel a stone wall and then cross a small brook.

There is a house visible to the left as the trail passes through a mostly level pine forest. Cross the dirt Goose Pond Road (Tyringham Road) in another .1 mile. For the next .75 mile, the trail gently ascends and descends through a hemlock grove before reaching a side trail that leads to a view of a pond.

At mile 6.7, after crossing a swiftly flowing inlet, you will reach Webster Road. For the next .25 mile, you will pass over cobbles before reaching a plateau and overgrown fields. Hike 1.7 miles to Main Road, which leads right 1 mile to the town of Tyringham.

After crossing Main Road, you will pass over Hop Brook on a bridge. For the next .5 mile, use bog bridges to follow fencing and hedgerows around wet fields. You will also pass over a buried gasline swath and reach criss-crossing brooks in a hemlock grove at mile 9.4.

Hike another .25 mile, cross a stile, then cross Jerusalem Road. Enter the Tyringham Cobble Reservation. Here, open fields are managed to help out the wildlife; no camping or fires are permitted. Climb up Cobble Hill and reach the summit at mile 10, where there is a good view of the Tyringham Valley. Following the trail through the field, you soon enter a pine forest.

In another .5 mile, you will begin to switchback down through a hemlock grove, reach a barbed wire fence, and leave the Trustees of Reservation lands. Hike just over .25 mile and enter another hay field. Follow the edge of the field for .1 mile.

Crossing a hedgerow and another small brook, you will enter another hay field. Follow the edge of this field, too, and enter the woods in .1 mile. After passing over a cleared gas-pipeline crossing and another hayfield with good views of the valley to the north, you will enter the woods to the left over a small dirt berm and cross two small streams.

In another .1 mile, you will cross three small brooks. Find the waterfall and old homestead foundation 100 yards upstream of the third brook. Hike .1 mile past the third brook and begin to switchback uphill for .25 mile to Fernside Road, where there is a spring a short distance east on the road. Cross the road and follow the A.T. up the steep bank, and soon reach a logging road that switchbacks up the ridge.

In .5 mile, you will reach the top of a white pine knoll and begin to descend. Turn sharply at a boulder gulch along cliffs covered with fern. You might notice that the temperature is cooler here. At mile 12.6, you will reach a view of the Tyringham Valley, and at mile 13.3, three stone walls to the right that mark the boundary of the Beartown State Forest.

In another .5 mile, the A.T. turns sharply west into a hemlock grove in order to avoid a swamp. After crossing a west-flowing brook between the swamps, the A.T. reaches another corner of the Beartown State Forest and turns south again.

At mile 14.5, below a series of beaver dams, the trail crosses a brook; and at mile 14.9, the trail crosses Beartown Mountain Road at a culvert for a brook that supplies the beaver ponds. In .25 mile, after skirting a planted Norway spruce grove, the A.T. crosses a motorcycle trail and ascends.

After .5 mile, the A.T. turns right onto the old trail at the top of a ridge. At mile 15.6, reach the .25-mile side trail (left) to the Mount Wilcox North Shelter. It sleeps eight to ten, but the water source is uncertain during the dry season.

Continue along the A.T. for .1 mile and turn left onto another new section of the A.T. After .5 mile, the trail skirts the east side of Beaver Pond and crosses its outlet, and in another .5 mile, reaches the top of a plateau with a view to the south.

At mile 17.4, locate the Mount Wilcox South Shelter a short distance to the left of the trail. Water is available from a spring on a side trail. Another spring is a short distance south on the A.T. The trail then crosses a woods road and two small brooks before climbing steeply.

At mile 18.1, the A.T. skirts the edge of The Ledges. Enjoy views of East and Warner Mountains, Mount Everett, and the Catskills. After .25 mile, the trail crosses the outlet of a swamp and beaver dam, then turns left and descends steeply down the slope of a ravine.

After turning left onto an abandoned road .25 mile later, cross a bridge, turn right off the road, and skirt the eastern shore of Benedict Pond. A short distance later, you will cross a state forest road that leads right to a picnic area, telephone, and outhouse.

Hike just under .5 mile, ascend slightly, turn right and follow a woods road for .5 mile. After passing an old charcoal pit, reach the top of a cliff with views of East Mountain State Forest. In .1 mile, descend steeply down rock steps to Blue Hill Road.

In another .25 mile, cross about 100 yards of swamp over bog bridges and rock steps, then turn southeast away from the corner of a pasture. After a gentle ascent and descent of an overgrown pasture (another .5 mile), the trail crosses an intermittent stream in a steep gully. Reach the junction with the former A.T. route. The new A.T. turns left and partially follows the old route.

Leave the gullies (old trail route and road) for higher ground a few feet to the west in .1 mile. After .25 mile, the trail circles back toward the Monterey-Great Barrington line and the old trail, and after passing through a field, the trail reaches Massachusetts 23.

Trailhead Directions
The trail crossing at US 20 is 5 miles east of Exit 2 on the Massachusetts Turnpike (I-90). The trail crossing at Massachusetts 23 is 4 miles east of Great Barrington.

JUG END/MOUNT EVERETT/ SAGES RAVINE

STRENUOUS
16.5 mile traverse

Some of the best hiking the A.T. has to offer in Massachusetts and Connecticut is packed into this one overnight hike. You will pass several magnificent viewpoints, but the high point of this hike is perhaps at its lowest point, Sages Ravine.

There are several particularly good tentsites that break up the trip nicely into two sections. One camp lies near the banks of Sages Ravine Brook, which tumbles through the lush growth of the ravine in a seemingly unending series of beautiful small waterfalls and pools of clear, cold water. Another, Bear Rock Falls camping area, has more than fifty acres surrounding this area, an area donated to the Appalachian Trail Conference in memory of three hikers—Susan Hanson, who died in a 1990 plane crash, and Geoffrey Hood and Molly LaRue, who were murdered during a southbound thru-hike of the A.T. in 1990. A granite marker has been placed at the bottom of Bear Rock Falls, a cascade of more than 300 feet, in memory of the three hikers.

The Hike

From Jug End Road, hike south on the A.T. and begin a moderate ascent. In .25 mile, the trail ascends more sharply, and steadily climbs up Jug End. The summit is reached at mile 1.1, where you are treated to a spectacular view, the first of many along this hike.

Hike another 2.2 miles south on the A.T., crossing two unnamed peaks on your way to Mount Bushnell (elevation 1,834 feet). At mile 3.4, reach Glen Brook Shelter. Water is available from the stream at the junction of the A.T. and the short side trail to the shelter.

From the shelter, hike .4 mile to the Guilder Pond Loop, which takes you around Massachusetts' second highest pond (elevation 2,042 feet). The loop trail for the pond uses a portion of the A.T. to complete the loop. Reach the Guilder Pond Picnic Area in .1 mile and continue following the white-blazed A.T. Climb the north slope of Mount Everett and reach the summit at mile 4.6.

From the summit of Mount Everett (elevation 2,602 feet), there is a commanding view of the Taconic and Berkshire ranges, the Housatonic River Valley and the distant Catskills. The pitch pines around the summit are said to be dwarfed by poor soil, not by altitude.

The steep and rocky .75-mile descent off Mount Everett brings you to a sag between Mount Everett and Race Mountain, and the junction with the Race Brook Trail. Continue following the A.T. for 1.1 miles, climbing to the summit of Race Mountain (elevation 2,365 feet). In another .25 mile, the trail follows a rocky ledge along the side of the mountain offering fine views of the Housatonic River Valley to the east.

At mile 8.1, cross Bear Rock Stream. On your left, find the camping area at the top of Bear Rock Falls. The campsite has established fire rings and a privy. The sunrise from the rock outcrop in the camping area can be magnificent.

One mile beyond the campsite, begin the short descent into Sages Ravine. At mile 9.5, cross Sages Ravine Brook on a footbridge. There are designated campsites and a privy on the opposite side of the brook. A caretaker is in residence during the summer but no fee is charged.

At mile 10.2, reach the junction with the Paradise Lane Trail. Continue following the A.T. for .25 mile to the steep, rocky ascent of Bear Mountain. In .25 mile, the trail reaches the summit of Bear Mountain (elevation 2,316 feet), where you'll find a good view from the ruins of a stone tower. This is not, as once believed, the highest point in Connecticut (though a monument from 1885 says otherwise). Bear Mountain is the highest mountain peak in the state, but the highpoint (elevation 2,380 feet) is on the south slope of nearby Mount Frissell, whose peak is in Massachusetts. From Bear Mountain, hike .75 mile to an old charcoal road, which the A.T. follows briefly.

At mile 11.6, reach Riga Junction, where the Undermountain Trail meets the A.T. Hike .4 mile to Bond Lean-to. Water is available from the small stream on the A.T. before the lean-to. Hike another 1.2 miles to the short side trail for Riga Lean-to, which boasts a fine view of the valley below. Water is available from a spring near the shelter.

The junction with the Bald Peak Trail is .25 mile beyond the Riga Lean-to side trail. Hike another .5 mile to Lions Head (elevation 1,738 feet). Twin Lakes can be seen far below the peak, which affords a 360° view of the surrounding countryside. In .25 mile, reach the junction with the Lions Head Trail and continue following the A.T. along a moderate then gradual

1.9-mile descent to the Plateau Campsite. Descend another .25 mile down to the trailhead on Connecticut 41.

Trailhead Directions
From Massachusetts 41, 6 miles north of the Massachusetts/Connecticut state line, turn left on Curtiss Road. Curtiss Road becomes Jug End Road and reaches the trailhead in 1.5 miles. There is adequate parking at the trailhead.

The southern trailhead is a parking lot on Connecticut 41 (Undermountain Road), .75 mile north of its junction with US 44 in Salisbury, Connecticut.

CONNECTICUT

CONNECTICUT

From the state line with Massachusetts, the A.T. climbs Bear Mountain as it enters Connecticut. The trail follows the Taconic Range to its southern end at Lions Head, where there is an outstanding panoramic view. The A.T. then crosses a few mountains and follows the Housatonic River during its 52-mile trek through western Connecticut.

Although the mountains in Connecticut are all under 2,400 feet in elevation, there are many fine viewpoints in this section from the the A.T. The highpoints—Lions Head, Rand's View, Hang Glider View and others—offer commanding views of the countryside.

Often referred to as the most photographed section of trail in the state, the red pine grove along the Houstaonic River north of Kent is dying a slow death. The trees, which are not native to the area, are being killed by a parasite and will all be dead within a few years. You should visit this special place while there is still time.

The A.T. crosses into and out of New York on the side of Schaghticoke Mountain and then crosses into New York a final time at Hoyt Road, 7 miles farther.

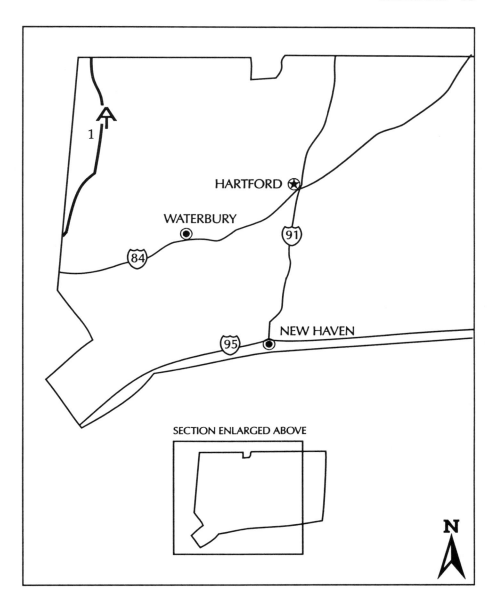

SECTION ENLARGED ABOVE

N

1. Mount Easter/St. Johns Ledges

MOUNT EASTER/ST. JOHNS LEDGES

MODERATE
23.5 mile traverse

This traverse takes you through through the Housatonic State Forest, over Sharon Mountain and Mount Easter, and includes great views of the Housatonic River Valley. The section from Connecticut 4 to St. Johns Ledges is a relocation that opened in 1988, taking the A.T. out of Cornwall, Connecticut. After climbing Silver Hill and passing the largest big-tooth aspen tree in Connecticut (just south of Swift's Bridge), the trail reaches River Road and follows the Housatonic, passing through a beautiful grove of red pine that is dying of blight. The grove was planted as an experiment in the early 1930s.

The section from St. Johns Ledges to Connecticut 341 is located in the township of Kent, Connecticut. This area was Indian territory for thousands of years but by 1752, only eighteen out of the approximately 100 families inhabiting the area remained and most of the land had been sold off. Some of the archaeological sites along the Housatonic River date back more than 9,000 years.

The Hike
From US 7 near Falls Village, follow the A.T. south, enter the woods, and cross over several stiles. In .25 mile, you will reach Belter's Bump, an outlook named in honor of Willie Belter, former landowner. Hike .1 mile to Belter's Campsite, where water is available from a spring near the trail.

In another .25 mile, the trail climbs steeply and follows the ridge, offering viewpoints both to the east and west. At mile 2.5, you will pass Hang Glider View, carved out by hang gliding enthusiasts, and offering views north to the Taconic Range. You may also see the Lime Rock Race Track below.

From here, hike just under a mile to the side trail for the Sharon Mountain Campsite, and another .1 to a brook crossing. At mile 4.4, reach the summit of Mount Easter and enjoy views to the west. In another .25 mile, you will cross a forest service road.

At mile 6, reach the side trail to Pine Swamp Brook Shelter. Water is available nearby. In .75 mile, the trail descends through Roger's Ramp, a narrow space between two huge boulders. Descend for .25 mile to West Cornwall Road.

Continue into the woods and cross Carse Brook over a log bridge in .1 mile. Nearly a mile later, cross the abandoned Surdam Road. From Surdam Road, hike 1.4 miles to the abandoned Caesar Road, an old turnpike that crossed the Housatonic on Young's Bridge in 1770. The abutments are still visible. There is a camping area on a knoll just south of the brook.

At mile 10.3, the A.T. reaches its junction with the Pine Knob Loop Trail, where a short climb to the left leads to a nice view. In another .1 mile, the two trails reach Pine Knob, an outlook with views of the Housatonic River Valley. The Pine Knob Loop Trail heads left to US 7 and the Housatonic Meadows State Campground .1 mile later.

Continue along the A.T., cross Hatch Brook in .1 mile. At mile 11.8, the trail crosses Old Sharon Road; a blue-blazed side trail (the old A.T.) heads to a trailhead and parking area on US 7. Descend to Guinea Brook and cross the brook in .1 mile. (If the water is too high, follow the dirt road left down to Connecticut 4 and turn right on Connecticut 4 to rejoin the trail.) Reach Connecticut 4 and cross it diagonally to the left to pick up the A.T. in the woods.

In .1 mile, turn right, climb very steeply to the height of the land, and enjoy good views. Reach the side trail to the former Silver Hill Shelter in a mile. The Shelter burned to the ground in 1991 because of a faulty fireplace; however the spring, which flows through a wall to a hand-pump faucet, the enclosed cooking area, and privy are still usable The area is now primarily a campsite.

At mile 14, you will reach River Road. There is a piped spring a few feet to the left. The A.T. continues along the road, and just beyond the spring, you will find the site of Swift's Bridge. The A.T. leaves the road, goes down an embankment, and picks up the old River Road, which ambles along the Housatonic River to St. Johns Ledges at mile 18.9.

The A.T. continues south, with the river on one side and hayfields on the other. The fields are locally known as Liner Farm. In 2.2 miles, you will cross Stony (Swift) Brook. Camping is permitted here.

In just under .5 mile, you will cross Stewart Hollow Brook and reach the side trail to the Stewart Hollow Shelter. Water is available from the brook, which flows out of a pasture, so make sure you treat the water. From the shelter side trail, hike .75 mile to the red pine plantation. Even though the trees are dying of blight, the walk through the grove is still eerily beautiful.

At mile 18, reach the gate at the site of the old North Kent Bridge, which was destroyed by a flood in 1936. The A.T. once crossed the Housatonic River here. In another .25 mile, you will cross Mt. Brook and reach the parking area on River Road. From here, hike just over .5 mile to the base of St. Johns Ledges.

Entering the woods at the base of St. Johns Ledges, you will ascend up ninety stone steps installed by a trail crew from the Appalachian Mountain Club. You may also see rock climbers on the nearby cliffs.

Hike about .5 mile to the top of the ledges and find wonderful views of the Housatonic River Valley and the town of Kent. Hike another .5 mile to the top of Caleb's Peak (elevation 1,160 feet).The outcropping along the ledges affords good views to the south. From here, the A.T. turns left and descends through the woods.

At mile 20.6, enjoy more good views from a ledge outcropping, and .1 mile later, cross Skiff Mountain Road. At mile 20.8, cross Choggam Brook, which is dry in late summer. Hike nearly 2 miles to another ledge that provides views of Kent and the Housatonic River Valley.

Reach the old A.T., leading straight ahead to Numeral Rock at mile 22.9. The old A.T. can be used as a bypass when Macedonia Brook floods; otherwise continue another .5 mile and cross Macedonia Brook on a log bridge. Cross a pasture and hike .1 mile to Connecticut 341 and the end of this hike.

Trailhead Directions
From Falls Village, drive 2.3 miles to the trail crossing at US 7. To reach the southern end of the hike, drive .75 mile west of Kent, Connecticut, on Connecticut 341. Parking is available at the junction of Connecticut 341 and Shaghticoke Road.

NEW YORK

NEW YORK

The 92 miles of the A.T. in New York travel from Schaghticoke Mountain on the Connecticut line to the Kittatinny Range in New Jersey, passing through Fahnestock and Harriman-Bear Mountain State Parks. Just south of the Bear Mountain Bridge, the A.T. reaches its lowest point at the Trailside Zoo in Bear Mountain Park (elevation 124 feet). Hikers are no longer charged a toll for walking across the bridge.

The trail immediately south of the Bear Mountain Bridge was the first section of trail to be built. It was cleared in 1923 by a group from the New York-New Jersey Trail Conference. That group still maintains this section of trail to this day.

New York City's skyline can be seen on a clear day from several points along the A.T. in New York, including West Mountain Shelter and Mombasha High Point. After passing through Harriman-Bear Mountain Parks, the A.T. travels west then, south leaving New York near Prospect Rock.

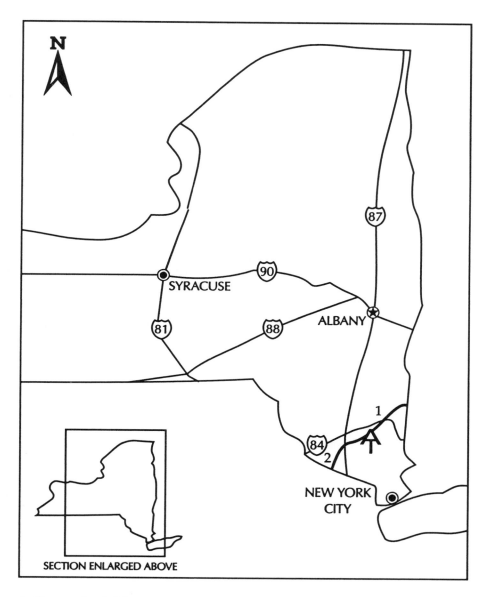

SECTION ENLARGED ABOVE

1. Shenandoah Mountain to Bear Mountain Bridge
2. Harriman State Park

SHENANDOAH MOUNTAIN TO BEAR MOUNTAIN BRIDGE

MODERATE
26 mile traverse

At the start of this two-day traverse, you will cross Shenandoah Mountain, which affords good views from the summit. You will also pass a particularly nice view of Canopus Lake. As you follow an old narrow-gauge railroad bed crossing several hills, you will pass through an area that saw a lot of activity during the Revolutionary War.

Near the end of the hike, you will follow the ridge as it descends steeply down Anthony's Nose on the way to the Bear Mountain Bridge. There are several theories on when and why the ridge was named Anthony's Nose. The *Appalachian Trail Guide to New York-New Jersey* lists three probable explantions: 1) In 1525, a Portuguese sailor, Estevan Gomez, named the ridge for the Hudson River, which he called Rio St. Antonio; 2) Diedrich Knickerbocker's *History of New York* claims it was for Anthony Corlear, also known as Anthony the Trumpeter; and 3) Some believe the ridge was dedicated to Revolutionary War General "Mad" Anthony Wayne, who led the march that successfully rested nearby Stony Point from British control. *The Thru-Hiker's Handbook* lists a fourth explantion for the ridge's name. According to that book, the ridge was called Anthony's Nose after the navigator on Henry Hudson's ship, the Half Moon.

After crossing the Bear Mountain Bridge, you will pass through the Trailside Museum and Zoo. The original idea for the Appalachian Trail, as put forth by Benton MacKaye in the 1920s, included a number of such exhibits along the route. This is the only trailside attraction ever built.

The Hike

From Horntown Road at Ralph's Peak Hikers' Cabin, follow the A.T. south. In 1 mile, cross over an unnamed peak, descend .25 mile to the level of the ridge, then begin the often steep ascent of Shenandoah Mountain. At mile 1.8, pass under powerlines in a utility right-of-way, and at mile 2.4, cross Long Hill Road. Continue climbing and reach the summit of Shenandoah Mountain (elevation 1,282) at mile 2.8. The mostly open summit has fine views to the east.

Descend .4 mile from the summit to an old woods road, and follow along the roadbed for the next .75 mile. In another .6 mile, reach the junction with a short side trail that leads to a viewpoint. At mile 4.7, reach an overlook with an outstanding view of Canopus Lake below. Descend from the viewpoint to a ridge parralleling Canopus Lake, which can be seen through the trees to the left of the trail.

At mile 6.9, reach New York 301, turn left, and follow the white-blazes along the road. Cross the road in .1 mile and walk into a grove of hemlocks. For the next .75 mile, the trail follows an old railway bed used to haul ore down from Sunk Mine. At mile 7.7, the A.T. turns to the left off of the railroad bed, and in .25 mile, reaches the junction with the Three Lakes Trail. Continue following the A.T. and climb to a ridgetop in .75 mile. In another .6 mile, the trail briefly joins Sunk Mine Road and then turns left into the woods, climbs to a high point on a ridge, and descends.

Reach Dennytown Road at mile 10.7. Water is available from a pump beside the stone building alongside the road. After re-entering the woods, the A.T. briefly shares the trailway with the blue-blazed Three Lakes Trail. At mile 11.9, reach the junction with the red-blazed Catfish Loop Trail. Continue following the A.T. for 1.6 miles, and cross a bridge over a stream. One mile after crossing Highland Road, cross the dirt Canopus Hill Road and enter the woods. Hike .75 mile to the top of Canopus Hill to enjoy limited views.

After a short, steep descent off of Canopus Hill, the trail climbs once more before descending to the intersection of Chapman Road and Albany Post Road (mile 16.2). After crossing the roads and re-entering the woods, the A.T. passes through a marshy area on bog bridges and then climbs Denning Hill. From the road, hike .75 mile to the top of Denning Hill (elevation 910). You can see New York City to the east on a clear day. In another .25 mile, reach the junction with a .1-mile side trail leading to a memorable view of the Hudson River.

The trail climbs over Little Fort Hill, and at mile 18.2, a side trail leads to Graymoor Monastery, where there are views to the east. From the Monastery side trail, hike .75 mile to Old West Point Road, which the A.T. briefly follows before re-entering the woods. In another .25 mile, cross Old Highland Turnpike (dirt), then cross a swampy area on bog bridges before reaching U.S. 9 at mile 19.5.

After crossing U.S. 9 at its junction with New York 403, continue following the A.T. south, walking through a pasture on bog bridges. Cross a fence by way of a stile, and follow a woods roads for .4 mile. One mile beyond U.S. 9, reach a junction with a short side trail leading to an excellent vista. From this viewpoint, you can see the Hudson River below. The Bear Mountain Bridge is visible to the left.

A couple of unnmarked trails join the A.T. in this area; be sure to follow the well-blazed A.T. At mile 22.2, reach South Mountain Pass, a dirt road the trail briefly follows before turning left on another dirt road. Follow the second dirt road for .25 mile before turning off and reaching the sidetrail to Hemlock Springs Campsite. Water is available from the spring. From the side trail to the campsite, hike .75 mile to another dirt road, which the A.T. follows for .25 mile. That road continues on to the summit of Anthony's Nose, affording spectacular views of the Bear Mountain Bridge and Bear Mountain on the other side of the Hudson River. Continue following the A.T. and descend rather steeply to New York 9D, which the A.T. follows for .25 mile. Turn right and cross Bear Mountain Bridge. Hikers are not charged a toll as they once were.

Turn left into the Trailside Museum and Zoo at mile 25.3 (the zoo closes at 4:30 P.M.; you must walk around it if you arrive later). The lowest spot on the entire Appalachian Trail—elevation 123 feet—is in the zoo. Pass through the zoo and hike .75 mile to the southern trailhead at the Bear Mountain Inn.

Trailhead Directions
The first exit south of Interstate 84 on the Taconic State Parkway is Miller Hill Road. Turn right onto Miller Hill Road and then take your first left onto Horntown Road. Park about .1 mile from Miller Hill Road, where the A.T. crosses Horntown Road. At this point you will see a former private residence, now maintained as the Ralph's Peak Hikers' Cabin. It is not named for a nearby mountain but for a dirt pile dubbed Ralph's Peak that once graced the lawn. The dirt pile is gone, but the name stuck. Adequate parking is available at the house.

The southern trailhead at the Bear Mountain Inn in Bear Mountain State Park on is New York 9W near the Bear Mountain Bridge and the Palisades Parkway.

HARRIMAN STATE PARK

MODERATE
18 mile traverse

On this overnight hike, you will cross New York's Harriman State Park. The park was conceived by Edward Harriman who made his fortune in railroads and dreamed of creating a park in this area. After his death, his widow helped to make the dream a reality. She donated ten thousand acres to the state for use as a park with the condition that New York abandon plans to build a prison on lands it had acquired around Bear Mountain. The state agreed, and Bear Mountain and Harriman Parks were born.

As you cross Bear, West, Black, Letterock, Fingerboard, Island Pond, and Green Pond Mountains, you will find many fine views along the way. This hike takes you past the ruins of Civil-War-era Greenwood Mine and within sight of Lake Tiorati. The trail through Harriman exhibits the trail builders' sense of humor (if not ingenuity) as you wiggle your way through the tight-fitting section of trail known as the "Lemon Squeezer."

Throughout the hike description, you will read about a number of other trails that meet, cross or share the footpath with the A.T. For more information about those trails and other hiking opportunities in the area, read *Harriman Trails: A Guide and History* by the New York-New Jersey Trail Conference.

The Hike

From the trailhead near the Bear Mountain Inn, hike south on the A.T. on the paved path along the shore of Hessian Lake, and turn left at the playground. The A.T. shares this section of trailway with the yellow-blazed Suffern-Bear Mountain Trail. As you begin climbing, cross under the ski jump in .25 mile and then briefly join a gravel road. After leaving the gravel road, hike .25 mile to where the Suffern-Bear Mountain trail continues ahead and the A.T. turns right. From this trail junction, continue on the A.T. and hike .4 mile to the now abandoned, paved Perkins Drive. Enjoy the views of the Hudson River and Bear Mountain Bridge.

At mile 1.5, turn left and use the steps as you continue climbing Bear Mountain. Cross Scenic Drive a couple of times, and at mile 2, reach the summit of Bear Mountain (elevation 1,305 feet), where there is a sweeping view to the east of the countryside and the New York City skyline. There is a stone observation tower, water fountain and restrooms on the summit.

From the summit, continue following the paved road for the first .1 mile, leave the road and descend, and reach Perkins Drive in .5 mile. Follow Perkins Drive for .5 mile and then re-enter the woods. In another .5 mile, cross Seven Lakes Drive and follow an old woods road. At mile 3.9, reach junction with the red-blazed Fawn Trail. Continue on the A.T. and begin sharply ascending West Mountain. From the Fawn Trail junction, hike .5 mile to a point offering fine views to the east. In another .1 mile, the A.T. joins the blue-blazed Timp-Torne Trail. The two trails share the same footpath for the next .75 mile. As you climb West Mountain, there are several views from the rocky ledges.

At mile 5.2, the Timp-Torne Trail turns off to the left. West Mountain Shelter is .6 mile down the Timp-Torne Trail. There is no water available at the shelter. You can see the skyline of New York City from the shelter, and if there is an event, the lights of the Meadowlands in New Jersey can be seen at night.

From the junction of the Timp-Torne Trail (to the left), hike .5 mile to the Beechy Bottom Road, which the A.T. joins for .1 mile and then turn right to enter the woods. In .25 mile, reach the junction with the red-on-white blazed Rampano-Dunderberg Trail, which shares the trailway with the A.T. for the next 3.3 miles. At mile 6.2, cross Beechy Bottom Brook, and in another .25 mile, cross the Palisades Interstate Parkway. Be particularly careful when making this road crossing; though the speed limit is 55 mph, the traffic often goes faster.

From the Parkway, hike .25 mile to the junction of the 1779 Trail. Continue following the A.T. and climb, often steeply, for .4 mile to the top of Black Mountain. Enjoy views from the open rock ledges. In .4 mile, reach a vista of Silver Mine Lake below, then continue descending for .1 mile to a cross-country ski trail.

Begin climbing Letterock Mountain. After crossing an unnamed knob on the ridge, descend to William Brien Shelter at mile 8.5. Water is available from a well on a short side trail. This well is sometimes dry and should not be depended on.

Beyond the shelter, continue climbing Letterock Mountain and reach the summit (elevation 1,195) in .25 mile. Descend .5 mile and cross a bridge over a boggy section of trail in the gap between Letterock and Goshen Mountains. The red-on-white blazed Rampano-Dunderberg Trail continues straight ahead, and the A.T. turns right to climb along the side of

Goshen Mountain. In 1.2 miles, cross Seven Lakes Drive at an angle, and in another .25 mile, cross a bridge over a stream and begin to climb the ridge. From Seven Lakes Drive, hike 1 mile to a rock outcrop with a fine view of Lake Tiorati. You will briefly follow and cross several old woods roads before descending to Arden Valley Road at mile 12.7. From this road crossing, hike .25 mile to the left to Tiorati Circle where there is a bathhouse, restrooms, water fountains, a restaurant, and a picnic area.

As you cross the road, the A.T. will once again join up with the red-on-white-blazed Rampano-Dunderberg Trail. The two trails will share the same footpath for the next 1.1 miles. In .1 mile, pass a water tank and ascend. Reach the summit of Fingerboard Mountain (elevation 1,328 feet) in another .4 mile. There is an old stone fireplace on the summit. Descend from the peak and then climb gradually again to the junction with the blue-blazed Hurst Trail (.5 mile beyond Fingerboard Mountain or mile 13.7). You can see Fingerboard Shelter just down the Hurst Trail. Though water is available .5 mile down the Hurst Trail at Lake Tiorati, you may want to pick up your water at Tiorati Circle, .25 mile from the trail crossing at Arden Valley Road: The water there is treated and the side trip is shorter.

After passing the Hurst Trail, hike .1 mile to where the Rampano-Dunderberg Trail goes straight and the A.T. turns right. Continue following the A.T. and descend sharply. In .5 mile, the trail follows Surebridge Mine Road and passes a water-filled pit. This was the site of the Greenwood Mine, a Civil-War-era iron mine. In another .1 mile, the trail turns right and climbs for .25 mile up Surebridge Mountain before descending for .25 mile from the trail's highpoint on the mountain.

At mile 15.2, reach the junction with the blue-blazed Long Path. Continue south on the A.T. and begin the .25-mile climb up Island Pond Mountain. On the summit of Island Pond Mountain (elevation 1,303 feet), the A.T. joins the red-triangle-on-white-blazed Arden-Surebridge Trail. The two trails share the same footpath for the next .25 mile as they descend to and pass through the Lemon Squeezer. Take the bypass trail if you don't want to follow the blazes down the steep descent and through the narrow passage between the boulders of the Lemon Squeezer. At the bottom of the Lemon Squeezer, the Arden-Surebridge Trail turns left and the A.T. turns right. (*Note:* The A.T. is being rerouted in this area as the book is going to press. The description that follows should be correct, however if the blazes differ from the description, follow the blazes.) Follow the A.T. as it descends briefly and then descends for some distance to an old woods road. Turn right and follow road for 300 feet, crossing an inlet of Island

Pond. Turn left off the road and climb to a viewpoint over Island Pond. Descend and cross an outlet of Island Pond on a wooden bridge. This outlet is partially channeled into a stone spillway, made of cut stones. This spillway was constructed by the CCC in 1934, as a part of a plan to dam the pond, and thereby enlarge it. However, the work was never completed and the pond remains in its natural state.

After crossing the bridge, climb and in 300 feet, cross a gravel road which provides access for fishermen to Island Pond. Continue following the A.T. and in another 250 feet, cross dirt Island Pond Road and begin climbing the eastern slope of Green Pond Mountain. After reaching the summit of that mountain at mile 17.3 of the hike, descend to the Old Arden Road, which once connected the Arden Estate with the town of Tuxedo. This road, on which the A.T. runs concurrently with the A-SB Trail, leads to the trailhead at the Elk Pen parking area.

Trailhead Directions
The northern trailhead at the Bear Mountain Inn in Bear Mountain State Park is on New York 9W near the Bear Mountain Bridge and the Palisades Parkway. The southern trailhead is at the Elk Pen parking lot on Arden Valley Road, .25 mile east of New York 17. Arden Valley Road meets New York 17, .75 mile south of the town of Arden, New York.

NEW JERSEY

NEW JERSEY

The New York/New Jersey state line runs along the ridge of Bearfort Mountain above Greenwood Lake. Passing through the Abram S. Hewitt State Forest, the first of New Jersey's 63 miles travel parallel to the New York/New Jersey state line. The trail passes through Wawan State Park before descending to Vernon, New Jersey.

Crossing the Vernon Valley, a former glacial lake, the trail soon ascends Pochuck Mountain and then descends to the Kittatinny Valley. The A.T. continues across the Kittatinny Valley to High Point State Park after passing Unionville, New York. This section of the trail is characterized by rolling farmland, pastures, fields, and open woods.

High Point is, as the name implies, the highest point in the state of New Jersey. Although the A.T. does not actually reach the summit, there is a short side trail. From High Point State Park, the A.T. follows Kittatinny Ridge to Stokes State Forest, moving along a rocky footpath through hickory and scrub oak forests.

From Stokes State Forest, the trail continues along Kittatinny Ridge to Delaware Water Gap. It passes through Delaware Water Gap National Recreation Area and Worthington State Forest. The highlight of the southern end of the A.T. in New Jersey is Sunfish Pond, a beautiful glacial pool.

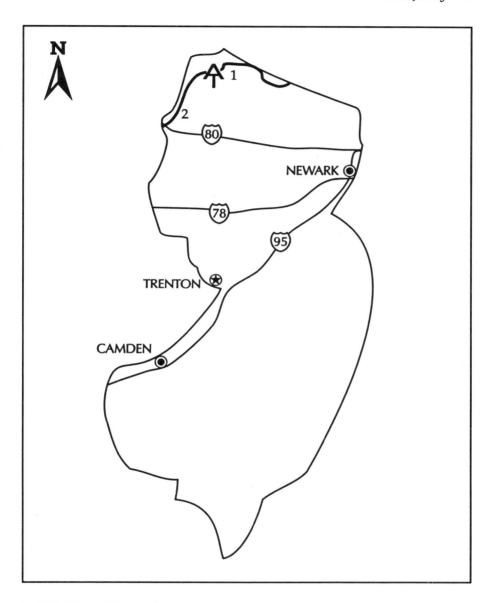

1. Kittatinny Mountains
2. Delaware Water Gap/Kittatinny Mountains

KITTATINNY MOUNTAINS

MODERATE
23.2 mile traverse

From the rolling farmlands, pastures, fields, and open woods of the Kittatinny Valley, this traverse takes you up along the ridge of the Kittatinny Mountains on a rocky footpath that passes through hickory and scrub oak forests. One of the highlights of this hike is High Point State Park, where the Appalachian Trail passes near the high point in the state of New Jersey. A short side trail (.25 mile roundtrip) leads from the A.T. to the summit (elevation 1,803 feet) with its stone monument.

The Hike
From the Appalachian Trail crossing on Lott Road (Jersey Avenue) in Unionville, New York, head south and ascend into the woods. There is a house visible to the right of the trail. In .1 mile, you will enter an open field, head right across it for .1 mile, and enter the woods. You will climb gradually while crossing a number of old quarry roads.

At mile .5, you will reach the crest of the hill, follow the left fork of the trail, and descend. About .25 mile later, you will reach Quarry Road; cross it, enter the woods on the other side, and pass an old quarry pit and a house on the right. At mile 1, reach Unionville Road (County 651). Cross the road diagonally to the left and enter the woods again.

In .1 mile, you will cross a stone wall as the trail enters an open field. After ascending a hill, cross a farm road, continue on another farm road, turn left a short distance later, and pass through a fieldbreak. You will then walk through an old apple orchard and reach Goldsmith Lane at mile 1.4.

After crossing the lane, you will enter an overgrown successional field, and a short distance later, you will head right and cross a stone wall. In .1 mile, use bog bridges to cross Vernie Swamp for .25 mile. Cross a bridge over a stream and reach Goldsmith Road. Crossing the road and entering a field, you will pass trees and a stone wall on your right marking the New York/New Jersey border.

At the crest of the field (mile 2), enjoy a good view of High Point Monument straight ahead. A view of Pochuck Mountain is on the horizon behind you. From here, descend with pines to your right, and in .1 mile, pass a pond to your left, cross a concrete dam, and enter a field. Cross the field heading left, enter the woods, and climb up a gentle hill to the crest in .1 mile. Descend.

In .1 mile, you will reach Goodrich Road, cross it, pass quickly through the woods, and enter an overgrown field. In another .1 mile, cross a small stream. Head left at mile 2.6, and then turn right to cross a log bridge over a stream. A short distance later, you will cross a second bridge over a stream, turn left, and begin to ascend for .25 mile.

Reaching the crest of the ridge, you will start to descend, passing through a muddy area at mile 3. Cross another stream, head to the right, and reach a stone wall to the left in .1 mile. Follow the wall for a short distance, and soon reach an intersection of stone walls with a fence on the right wall. Turn right here and enter a successional field scattered with cedars. Cross the field, bearing to the right.

In .1 mile, turn right, cross a brook, and then follow posts through an overgrown field. At mile 3.3, you will reach Gemmer Road; turn right, follow the road a short distance, turn left, and enter the woods. You will soon pass by a swampy area; shortly thereafter, turn left, cross a small brook, head right, and begin to climb while passing through another swampy area.

Enter an abandoned field in .1 mile; head across diagonally and to the left, following the blazed posts. Cross a stone wall and re-enter the woods in another .1 mile.

At mile 3.9, you will reach Ferguson Road. Turn right and follow the road a short distance before turning left and crossing a stile into another pasture. Follow the blazes across the pasture for .1 mile to a swampy area that you will cross on bog bridges. From there, cross over a stream on a bridge, turn left, and follow more blazed posts across a pasture while passing through another muddy area.

At an intersection of stone walls, turn right and cross a stile into a cultivated field. This land has been worked for five generations and is currently being farmed under a lease arrangement with the land's former owner. Head around the edge of the field following the treeline to the left.

At the end of the field, in .1 mile, turn right but continue to follow the treeline to the left. You will soon cross a stone wall before turning left and skirting the field again. Follow the treeline to the left. At mile 4.4, at the end of the field, turn right (still following the treeline) and then turn left, passing a pond to the right. After crossing a stile, you will turn right and follow the edge of another field. Turn right again a short distance later, pass through an electrified farm gate (make sure you shut it!), and turn left, climbing along the left side of a pasture.

After crossing a barbed wire fence near the crest of the pasture in .25 mile, descend along the left side of some cultivated fields, passing over a stile and re-entering the woods in .1 mile.

At mile 4.9, follow the blazes across and along a number of old stone walls. You will reach Courtwright Road in .25 mile. Cross the road and continue straight ahead into the woods. In .1 mile, cross a stream, and in another .1 mile, cross a grassy woods road and another stream before you enter an overgrown field.

Beyond the field, enter the woods (passing through a swampy area) and soon cross several stone walls. You will leave the woods .4 mile later and pass through fields, skirting to the right of some trees on the rise. In .1 mile, you will reach County Road 519. After crossing the road (to the left), enter the woods and begin to climb on switchbacks.

In .25 mile, you will pass through a swampy area and enter an overgrown clearing. A short distance later, turn left onto a dirt road, follow the road a short distance, and turn right, passing through a pasture. In .1 mile, you will turn right, ascend (good views to the right) and make a sharp left as you continue to climb.

In .25 mile, the trail heads left and levels off, passing through gaps in a number of stone walls. At mile 7, you will cross an intermittent brook at the head of a ravine, then head left and cross another stone wall. A short distance later, the A.T. turns right at an intersection. The old A.T. route descends along the ravine. Do not descend. Instead, turn right, hike .25 mile, turn right again, and begin to ascend. A blue-blazed side trail continues straight ahead for .1 mile to High Point Shelter. Water is available from streams just before and just beyond the shelter.

Continue along the A.T. and reach another intersection in .5 mile. The blue-blazed side trail leads to High Point Monument, a .25-mile roundtrip. Turn left to continue along the A.T. for .25 mile to reach a wooden observation platform, where there is an excellent panoramic view. Look east to view Kittatinny Valley with Pochuck Mountain in the foreground and Waywayanda Mountain on the horizon. Look southeast and you may be able to see the New York City skyline. Delaware Water Gap is to the southwest, and Lake Marcia and Highpoint Lodge with the Pocono Mountains of Pennsylvania in the background are to the west. The Catskill

Plateau is to the northwest, and High Point Monument is to the north.

The A.T. continues south along the ridge, passing through scrub oak and blueberry bushes. At mile 8, the trail heads right along the ridge, and the former A.T. route descends from the ridge. You will soon turn left and descend (the old A.T. continues straight ahead). A short distance later, descend more steeply, then gradually again.

At mile 8.8, you will leave the woods, cross a lawn, and reach New Jersey 23. Cross the road at the south driveway of High Point State Park Headquarters, and enter the woods at the south end of the parking lot. A short distance later, you will pass an unmarked trail that leads to a day-use parking area.

At mile 9.1, you will cross the red-blazed Iris Trail, which is marked by a white post to the left of the A.T. Climb slightly for .1 mile, then turn left onto an old woods road, and soon turn right, leaving the road and ascending to the ridge. When you reach the crest of the ridge, turn left and reach the junction of the Blue Dot Trail in .25 mile.

The A.T. soon reaches a viewpoint to the west over Sawmill Lake and then descends to the left into the interior valley. Once you reach the valley floor, you will begin to ascend the next ridge to the east. Reach the top of the eastern ridge in .1 mile, and enjoy the view back over the valley with the distant Pocono Mountains visible to the left. The trail crosses to the opposite side of the ridge and reaches the first in a series of viewpoints. Lake Rutherford can be seen below, as the trail continues along the ridge.

You will soon descend. At mile 10.7, turn right. At mile 11.2, enjoy another viewpoint from open rocks, and at mile 11.4, reach Dutch Shoe Rock with views to the northeast. A side trail leads left for .4 mile to the Rutherford Shelter. Water is available from a nearby spring.

The trail continues across large, open rocks before entering the woods and descending. After .5 mile, you will cross a stream and ascend. Turn right onto the red-blazed Iris Trail (a woods road) in .25 mile. To the left, the Iris Trail heads to New Jersey 23. A short distance later, you will turn left off the Iris Trail and descend into a swampy area.

Hike .25 mile and ascend slightly before descending to another swampy area. Cross a stream at mile 12.6 and begin ascending again. In .1 mile, you will climb up some rocks, turn right, and continue to climb more gradually. After crossing a cleared strip of land that contains a buried pipeline, you will reach a short side trail that leads to a view of farmland. A short distance later, the trail forks to the right away from an old road.

Sign the trail register at mile 13.2, and continue past a private home on the left. Shortly thereafter, you will cross the Iris Trail again before beginning to descend. Cross rocks over a swampy area, and in another .25 mile, pass through another swampy area. Climb again.

At mile 14.2, you will reach the parking area on Mashipacong Road (Deckertown Turnpike). A hand pump supplies water for the Mashipacong Shelter, .25 mile south. Cross the road diagonally to the left and ascend to the shelter. The shelter is in a clearing.

The trail re-enters the woods on the far side to the right. In .75 mile, you will turn left onto Swenson Road (an old woods road), walk a short distance, turn right as the road curves left, and ascend. In .5 mile, you will reach the top of the rise and begin to descend, passing through a mountain laurel thicket.

At the bottom of the descent, turn right and soon cross the outlet of a swamp to the left of the trail. A short distance later, cross a stone wall and start to climb through a stand of white birches. You will reach the top of the hill at mile 16.2. Start to descend, soon crossing a stone wall, and reach a rocky area .25 mile later.

From here, you will ascend to the top of a knoll, descend to Crigger Road, and ascend again. At mile 17.6, you will pass the parking area for Sunrise Mountain on your right. A short distance past the restrooms, a path from the parking area joins the A.T. for the climb to the summit. It is barely .25 mile to the shelter atop the summit of Sunrise Mountain (elevation 1,653 feet); enjoy good views to the east and the west. Camping is not permitted at the shelter, which has a roof but no walls.

From the southeast corner of the shelter, descend a short distance and arrive on open ledges with beautiful views to the east. On the far side of the clearing, you will re-enter the woods and descend, turning right along the rocks.

You will soon pass a viewpoint through the trees to the left as the trail levels off and continues to descend gradually. After ascending over a knoll and then descending gradually, you will reach the intersection of the yellow-blazed Tinsley Trail at mile 18.7. This trail descends to the right, crossing Sunrise Mountain Road and eventually reaching the overnight camping area at Lake Ocquittunk. The A.T. climbs a short distance before continuing along the western side of the ridge.

About .5 mile later, you will ascend and then descend gradually. Pass several ponds and swamps (when it is wet) to the left of the trail. Shortly thereafter, you will pass through several wet sections before reaching the blue-blazed Stony Brook Trail at mile 20.1. This trail leads .25 mile to the right to the Gren Anderson Shelter. Water is available from a spring a couple hundred yards beyond the shelter.

Continuing along the A.T., cross Stony Brook in .25 mile. At mile 21.1, you will reach the green-blazed Tower Trail, which descends to the right. Sign the trail register here. Following a brief climb .1 mile later, you will reach the Culver Fire Tower, which offers a wonderful 360° view for those willing to climb to the top. View Lake Owassa to the southwest, left of the Kittatinny Ridge, and view Lake Kittatinny to the right of the ridge.

The A.T. leaves the tower clearing from the southwest, soon turning right and descending. Presently, you will see Culver Lake through the trees to the left. Cross a small, grassy clearing .4 mile later, and reach a viewpoint over Culver Lake in another .5 mile.

Shortly thereafter, make a right turn and reach a viewpoint over Kittatinny Lake. The trail turns right again and continues to descend, making a sharp left turn before reaching Sunrise Mountain Road in .25 mile. Turn left and follow the road, soon passing the exit from the parking area on your right. After passing the entrance to the parking area in .1 mile, turn right on Upper North Shore Road. Follow the road to US 206 at Culvers Gap. This is the end of the traverse.

Trailhead Directions
The A.T. crossing on Lott Road (Jersey Avenue) is .4 mile from New York 284 in Unionville, New York. The A.T. crossing at Culvers Gap is 3.4 miles northwest of Branchville, New Jersey, on US 206. Park in the lot .25 mile north of the trail crossing.

DELAWARE WATER GAP/KITTATINNY MOUNTAINS

MODERATE
26.8 mile traverse

This hike begins in Delaware Water Gap on the Pennsylvania/New Jersey border, passes through the Worthington State Forest, and follows the Kittatinny Ridge to Culvers Gap. Among the highlights of this traverse are the beautiful glacier-cut Sunfish Pond and the wonderful views along

Kittatinny Ridge. A section of this hike passes through oak and hickory hardwood forests with scattered pitch pine, white pine, red cedar, hemlock, and rhododendron. During mid-summer, blueberries are plentiful along the trail.

A dam was authorized to be built in the Delaware Water Gap area in 1962. Severe opposition halted the project, but not before the government established Delaware Water Gap National Recreation Area, meant to provide recreational facilities for the now defunct lake. The recreation area now provides a protected corridor for the Appalachian Trail.

The Hike
From the Dunnfield Creek Natural Area, follow the A.T. through the parking area, pass a pump with good water (it has been tested), and enter the woods. After turning left in .1 mile, cross a wooden bridge over Dunnfield Creek, and shortly thereafter, turn right onto a woods road, following the left bank of Dunnfield Creek.

Take the left fork at mile .5 and continue along the woods road. A blue-blazed trail leads right to Mount Tammany. The trail climbs gradually to Sunfish Pond. Just over a mile later, you will reach the junction with the yellow-blazed Beulahland Trail, which heads left to Fairview Parking Area on River Road. There is also an unmarked trail to the right that leads .25 mile to Holly Spring (intermittent). The A.T. continues ahead with the Kittatinny Mountains visible to your right.

At mile 3.2, you will pass Campsite No. 2 at a trail junction. Turn right onto the woods road. (To the left, the blue-blazed Douglas Trail leads just over 2 miles to a developed campground in Worthington State Forest.)

Hike just over .5 mile to Sunfish Pond. This glacial pond has been designated a Natural Area as well as a national landmark. Camping is not permitted here. The trail skirts the pond and crosses its outlet at mile 4.1. A short distance later, turn right and pass the east end of the pond in .4 mile. Within .1 mile, you will pass a blue-blazed side trail that leads left 200 yards to a spring.

After .25 mile, turn left, descend .75 mile to a brook, then ascend .4 mile to a view to the west toward Pennsylvania. Reach a powerline cut-through providing views from both sides of the ridge. At the crest of the ridge, you should be able to see the storage ponds for Yard's Creek pump-storage hydroelectric development to the right and the Delaware River to the left. A view of Catfish Firetower lies ahead between the ridges.

Leave Worthington State Forest in .25 mile and enter the Delaware Water Gap National Recreation Area. After .5 mile, you will come to the overgrown Kaiser Road. Follow it to the left and bear right in .25 mile; Kaiser Road continues to the left, passing old copper mines.

Hike .5 mile to reach another viewpoint where you can get another eyeful of the Yard's Creek storage ponds. At mile 7.9, the trail turns left, descends, and crosses a stream. Pick up water from the stream if you intend to camp along the first couple of miles atop the ridge. Reach Mohican Road 1 mile later. From the far side of Mohican Road, begin to ascend into the Kittatinny Range.

Climb .75 mile to the top of Kittatinny Ridge, and enjoy good views to the right. In another .5 mile or so, the trail reaches the rim, follows the ledges a short distance, and re-enters the woods. The ledges offer good views to the right. The trail joins the rim again in another .1 mile.

The orange-blazed Rattlesnake Swamp Trail heads left for .5 mile to Catfish Pond. Hike another 1 mile to the Catfish Fire Tower, which offers a panoramic view from sixty feet above the ground. From the tower, you will begin your descent to Millbrook-Blairstown Road.

Follow the gravel road from the tower for .25 mile. Turn left off the road, then left again onto another gravel road in .1 mile. The trail follows the gravel road for a short distance and then enters the woods to the right. At a powerline .25 mile later, turn right onto an old woods road, pass through a rhododendron thicket, and turn right onto a gravel road. A short distance to the left (on the gravel road) find Rattlesnake Spring.

Less than .25 mile later, the road makes a sharp left and continues to the Millbrook-Blairstown Road at mile 12.2. Go left, following the paved road a short distance, and turn right onto an old woods road. Take the left fork in .1 mile. In .25 mile, you will pass a swamp to the left of the trail; descend and cross the outlet to the swamp. The trail turns left away from the road, skirts the northern edge of the swamp, and then curves to the right. Take the right fork after .25 mile and begin to ascend steeply.

In .1 mile, reach a powerline cut-through with views to the left of the Wallkill Valley and Pocono Plateau. Follow the cut-through to the right for .1 mile, turn left at the second powerline tower, and enter the woods. Below, you should be able to see Sand Pond of Camp No-Be-Bo-Sco, which belongs to the Bergen Council of the Boy Scouts of America. The trail follows the crest of the ridge through the woods and for the next 1.5 miles offers views to the east.

Following a slight descent at mile 14.4, hike along overgrown dirt road for the next 1.6 miles to Flatbrookville Road, passing several clearings that make good camping spots. Just under 1 mile to the right, find a clearing with views of Fairview Lake. In another .4 mile, a road to the right leads a short distance to another viewpoint overlooking the northern end of Fairview Lake. There is a trail register to the left just beyond the road.

Reach Flatbrookville Road in .25 mile. Turn right and follow the paved road for a short distance, then turn left, cross the road, and enter the woods. A blue-blazed side trail leads to a pump with tested water.

At mile 16.2, you will cross a dirt road, and at mile 17.2, descend steeply to the left of a smooth rock. You will pass a rock-strewn bog on the right in .25 mile, and you will cross an old gravel road diagonally to the right in another .25 mile. Enter the woods, hike a short distance, turn sharply left, and climb steeply up the face of an escarpment.

Just beyond the top of the escarpment, you will cross a gravel road and reach a viewpoint to the west. The trail joins the gravel road a short distance beyond the viewpoint and then meets a short side trail that leads to a viewpoint overlooking Crater Lake. The trail follows gravel roads for the next 1.4 miles before returning to the woods. As you continue along the ridge, there are occasional views to the west of the Pocono Mountains.

In .25 mile, make your first left onto an intersecting gravel road. Follow the road for .9 mile before turning left onto another gravel road. Shortly beyond, a blue-blazed trail heads left for 1.5 miles to Buttermilk Falls. In .25 mile, you will turn off the gravel road and head back into the woods, and in another .25 mile, you will reach a viewpoint to the west from open rocks.

At mile 20, a blue-blazed trail heads left a short distance to a viewpoint; the A.T. begins to descend. After .5 mile, bear right at a fork and then cross a stream. Just past the stream, a blue-blazed side trail leads right to a water source. Ascend Rattlesnake Mountain (elevation 1,492 feet), passing a burned out area with good views to the left.

Reach a rocky outcrop, the summit of Rattlesnake mountain, at mile 20.8. Descend for the next .4 mile, cross a swampy area on rock, and begin to climb again. Reach a rocky, cleared area in .5 mile, and turn right on an old dirt road and descend.

Turn right off the dirt road .25 mile later, and begin to ascend, passing several rock ledges with views to the left. At mile 22.3, you will reach a cleared area at the crest of the ridge. There are sweeping views of the Wallpack Valley on your left. In .1 mile, you'll enter the woods again.

Descend for .1 mile before ascending, leveling off, and descending more steeply. In just over .5 mile, you will reach Brink Road, which can be followed to the right for .5 mile to Lake Owassa and 2.5 miles to Wallpack Center. The Brink Road Shelter is 300 yards to the left of the trail crossing. The shelter was remodeled in 1990. Water is available from a dependable spring about 100 yards beyond the shelter.

From Brink Road, the trail enters the woods on the right and begins to ascend, leveling off and following the crest of the ridge in .4 mile. In .1 mile, an unmarked side trail leads to an overlook, and a short distance later, you will pass a field of rocks and boulders to the right of the trail.

There is a trail register at mile 23.8, and another unmarked side trail at mile 24.3. The side trail leads to an overlook of Lake Owassa. Shortly thereafter, the A.T. ascends then descends before leveling off and descending again. The Jacob's Ladder Trail (blue-gray blazes) leads left for .25 mile to the junction of Cross Road and Woods Road at mile 24.7. From here, the A.T. climbs, descends, then levels off.

Reach a viewpoint in a large, cleared area .7 mile later. You can see Culver Lake and US 206 (your destination) to the right, and Culver Fire Tower straight ahead. The trail enters the woods, descends for .1 mile, then rollercoasters along the ridge.

Hike .5 mile beyond the viewpoint to reach a clearing with a view of US 206 to the right. The trail turns right and descends steadily to Culvers Gap. At mile 26.2, the trail crosses a gravel road, which is the route of the Acropolis Trail (brown and gold blazes), and levels off for .25 mile before descending steadily again. At mile 26.6, turn right, leave the old woods road, and descend another .1 mile to US 206, the end of the traverse.

Trailhead Directions
The A.T. crossing at the Dunnfield Parking Area can be reached by taking the first exit on Interstate 80 after crossing the bridge into New Jersey. Parking is available at the Dunnfield Creek Natural Area through which the trail passes.

The A.T. crossing at Culvers Gap is 3.4 miles northwest of Branchville, New Jersey, on US 206. A parking area is .25 mile north of the trail crossing on US 206.

PENNSYLVANIA

PENNSYLVANIA

With more than 230 miles to traverse, the A.T. in Pennsylvania is both the one of the easiest and the hardest to hike. The trail is often characterized as a tough climb up a ridge followed by a level but rocky walk. The A.T. in Pennsylvania begins at Delaware Water Gap in the Kittatinny Mountains where it climbs more than 1,000 feet to the summit of Mount Minsi. This rough and rocky trail traverses the ridge from gap to gap (Totts, Fox, Wind, Smith, Little, and finally the rocky face of Lehigh Gap).

For the next 30 miles (after you climb out of Lehigh Gap), the trail follows the ridge, passing Bake Oven Knob, The Cliffs, and Blue Mountain Summit before reaching the area of Hawk Mountain Sanctuary near Eckville. From here, the trail climbs once again to the ridge, passing The Pinnacle, an outstanding viewpoint over the Pennsylvania countryside.

From The Pinnacle, the A.T. drops down to Windsor Furnace, the site of an old iron stove plant. Glassy slag can still be seen along the trail. The A.T. continues to Port Clinton where it regains the ridge once again, following it for more than 30 miles. From Swatara Gap, the trail leaves Blue Mountain, crosses St. Anthony's Wilderness, and passes the sites of Rausch Gap and Yellow Gap Villages. After ascending Second Mountain, Sharp Mountain, and Stony Mountain, the trail climbs to the ridge of Peters Mountain and follows it for 15 miles before descending to the Susquehanna River at Duncannon, Pennsylvania.

The A.T. heads southwest at the Susquehanna, crossing Cove and Blue Mountains before falling to the Cumberland Valley. This area was once famous for its road walk, but the trail has now been re-routed off-road, through woods and rolling farmland. At the end of the valley, the trail climbs South Mountain, which it follows all the way through Maryland.

The southern section of trail in Pennsylvania passes through several interesting locations before it reaches the Pennsylvania/Maryland state line: Boiling Springs with its beautiful Childrens Lake; Pine Grove Furnace State Park with its model furnace and Ironmasters Mansion; and Caledonia State Park with the Thaddeus Stevens Museum.

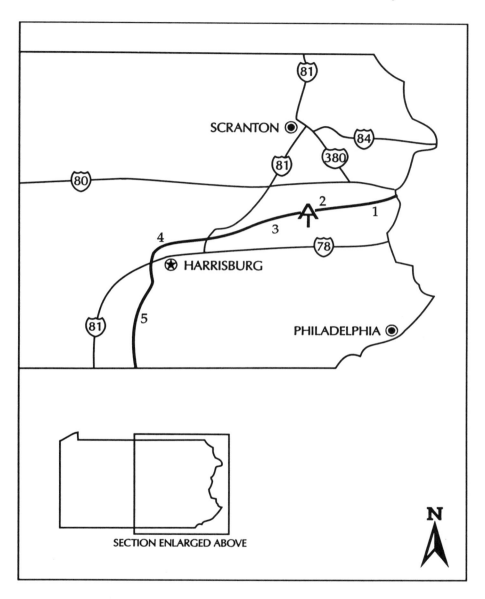

1. Delaware Water Gap/Kittatinny Mountains II
2. Blue Mountain
3. Blue Mountain II
4. Peters Mountain/Sharp Mountain
5. South Mountain

Delaware Water Gap/Kittatinny Mountains II

MODERATE
15 mile traverse

This hike features a number of good views as it rambles over the Kittatinny Ridge in Pennsylvania. From Wind Gap, it is a rocky but beautiful hike to Delaware Water Gap. The club members that maintain this section joke that they sharpen the rocks each spring in anticipation of the year's hikers. Make sure you're wearing sturdy boots with lots of ankle support! And, if you're hiking during late summer, remember that water is scarce in this section, so bring plenty with you.

Highlights of this hike include Wolf Rocks, Lookout Rock, Winona Cliff, Council Rock, and Lake Lenape. Keep an eye out at Wolf Rocks for the white blazes that mark the A.T. because the mountain is nearly a mile wide at this point, and it is easy to get lost amid the massive, tumbled boulders that cover the area. These huge boulders, covered with rock tripe and lichens, offer great views of the surrounding countryside. At Winona Cliff, look for the profile of Chief Tammany on the opposite mountain.

The Hike

An official A.T. sign board marks the beginning of the trail. From the road at Wind Gap, climb steeply up through the woods. At mile 1.9, cross the Blue Mountain Water Company Road (good views), and continue to the top of the ridge.

Follow the ridge for another 3.4 miles, and reach the junction with a blue-blazed trail on the right that leads .25 mile to an intermittent spring. At mile 6.5, reach Wolf Rocks, where there is a view ahead to Fox Gap along Blue Mountain to Delaware Water Gap; on clear days you can see the Kittantinny Ridge in New Jersey. The trail turns right onto Wolf Rocks before turning left and dropping off the north side of the rocks.

Continue along the ridge for another .25 mile, and reach an old road on the left that comes up the mountain from Cherry Valley. Take a right on this road and pass under a powerline. At mile 7.4, the trail turns left off the road and re-enters the woods. Pass under a telephone cable and enjoy a good view of Stroudsburg to the north at mile 7.9.

Reach Fox Gap at Pennsylvania 191 in .25 mile. Cross the road, hike another .6 mile, and reach the blue-blazed side trail to the Kirkridge Shelter, where there are excellent views to the south. Water is available beyond the shelter a short distance down the blue-blazed trail. This faucet is the property of the Kirkridge Retreat; hikers are allowed to use the spigot. Make sure to turn the water off when finished.

Continue on the A.T. for .1 mile to a gravel road, then cross it. For the next 1.6 miles, you will follow the ridge, crossing under two sets of powerlines at mile 10.4. Descend a rocky trail for .25 mile to Totts Gap.

At the gap, the trail heads right into the woods and passes several communications towers. At mile 10.9, the trail turns left before turning right onto a gravel road. The A.T. follows the road for 1.8 miles to the summit of Mount Minsi (elevation 1,480 feet). From the summit, descend on a series of switchbacks, where you'll have wonderful views of Delaware Water Gap.

You will reach Lookout Rock at mile 13.6, and .1 mile later, you will cross a brook in a rhododendron grove. From here, you will return to the edge of an escarpment and reach Winona Cliff in .1 mile. Across the river, view the exposed rock face of Mount Tammany, which forms the shape of Chief Tammany's profile.

At mile 14.4, you will reach Council Rock. Take the left fork at the hemlock grove, and reach a gravel road .25 mile later. From here, turn right downhill, arriving at pretty Lake Lenape at mile 15. There is a parking lot here where you can either leave a vehicle or be picked up.

Trailhead Directions

The beginning of this hike is at the junction of Wind Gap/Saylorsburg Road and Pennsylvania 33. Wind Gap is just north of the town of Wind Gap.

The end of the hike is the parking lot at Lake Lenape, which can be reached from Pennsylvania 611 in Delaware Water Gap. Take Mountain Road, and the first fork to your left passes the parking area at Lake Lenape.

BLUE MOUNTAIN

MODERATE
13.4 mile traverse

This is one of the more scenic hikes in Pennsylvania. The trail traverses Blue Mountain from Pennsylvania 309 at Blue Mountain Summit to Lehigh Gap. There are a number of highlights, including views from The Cliffs and Bear Rocks, and birdwatching from Bake Oven Knob. In the fall, the vantage point from Bake Oven Knob is great for those interested in following the hawk migrations. At the end of this hike, the North Trail (at its northernmost junction with the A.T.) leads a short distance to Devil's Pulpit and views overlooking the Lehigh River.

The Hike
From Pennsylvania 309 at the summit of Blue Mountain (elevation 1,360 feet), you will turn left (north on the A.T.) onto an eroded footpath. A short distance later, turn right and then head left again.

At mile .9, you will reach the ridge and continue following the A.T. along an old woods road. In another .9 mile, you will come to a powerline cut-through. On the other side of the cut-through, the road becomes a rocky footpath. A blue-blazed side trail to the left descends .25 mile to the base of the valley and then beyond to New Tripoli Campsite. Water is available from a spring.

Continue along the A.T. and turn left at mile 2.6, following the knife-edged ridge called The Cliffs, where there is a view ahead to Bear Rocks. Reach the blue-blazed side trail to Bear Rocks in another .9 mile. The side trail climbs a short distance to Bear Rocks, offering a 360° view of the Pennsylvania countryside.

Hike 1 mile and take the right fork at a grassy road. Reach Bake Oven Knob road at mile 4.9. This cross-mountain gravel road is passable by vehicles, and there are often a number of cars parked in the game commission parking lot—people out day hiking or birdwatching.

In another .4 mile, you will pass over the summit of Bake Oven Knob (elevation 1,560 feet). The summit still bears the remains of an old airplane beacon. Look right for an outstanding, 180° view to the south, and left for views to the north. In the fall, this vantage point is great for birdwatchers interested in following the hawk migrations.

Continue along the A.T. and reach a rock slide on the mountain's north end. Cross with care. At mile 5.9, you will reach the Bake Oven Knob Shelter to the right of the trail. A blue-blazed side trail at the shelter leads downhill to a spring (often dry) on the right, and a couple hundred yards farther to a more reliable spring, also on the right. The side trail continues another .75 mile to Bake Oven Knob Road. This road leads (to the left) another 1.1 miles to a paved road in the valley.

From the Bake Oven Knob Shelter, hike .75 mile to a good view to the north. The trail follows a rock outcropping here and crosses a rocky crest on the north side of the mountain in .25 mile. At mile 8.4, cross a transmission line and head right on the road at Lehigh Furnace Gap. A short distance later, you will pass a woods road that heads left to a radio tower and turn left into the woods. The trail turns right .75 mile later and follows a boundary line for the Pennsylvania Game Lands (the boundary is also marked with white blazes, but unlike A.T. blazes, they are irregular in shape, size and location).

At mile 9.8, the trail turns left, away from the game lands boundary, and crosses an abandoned telephone line cut-through. You will pass a large rock outcropping to your right just over .25 mile later. Follow a rough trail to the top of some rocks, and enjoy superb views of the area. One mile after turning away from the game lands, you will pass over the Northeast Extension of the Pennsylvania Turnpike, which passes through a tunnel far below your feet.

You will meet the southernmost junction of the North Trail at mile 11. The North Trail heads to the left before rejoining the A.T. 2.4 miles later. This is the more scenic route of the two trails, but is vulnerable to winter storms. From here, the North Trail leads 2 miles to another side trail that takes you downhill for .4 mile to the Devil's Pulpit, a rock outcropping with great views of Lehigh Gap, and .4 mile farther to the A.T.

From the southern junction of the North Trail, continue along the A.T., and hike along the southeast side of the mountain, reaching the northernmost junction of the North Trail in 1.6 miles. From here, it is .4 mile to the side trail that leads another .4 mile downhill to Devil's Pulpit.

Hike .1 mile past the junction with the North Trail, and reach the George W. Outerbridge Shelter, and one of the best springs in Pennsylvania (especially appreciated on this water-scarce ridge!). The piped spring is on the A.T. a short distance past the shelter and nearly always gushes forth cold water. The trail passes to the left of the shelter and descends past the spring. Just .5 mile after leaving the shelter, pass under powerlines, where there are views of Lehigh Gap.

Hike .25 mile and reach the west end of the highway bridge (Pennsylvania 873) over the Lehigh River, the end of the traverse.

Trailhead Directions
The hike begins on Pennsylvania 309 at Blue Mountain Summit (a sign marks the spot), located south of Snyders and Tamaqua. The hike ends at Pennsylvania 873/248 on the south side of the bridge, 2 miles south of Palmerton. Limited parking is available.

BLUE MOUNTAIN II

MODERATE
14.4 mile traverse

This traverse follows the ridge of Blue Mountain from Hawk Mountain Road near Eckville to The Pinnacles, Pulpit Rock, and down to Windsor Furnace and the town of Port Clinton. Views of the Pennsylvania farmland are spectacular from The Pinnacles, and Pulpit Rock offers splendid views of Blue Rocks, a stretch of jumbled boulders more than a block wide and a mile long. Deposited during the glacial period, this 40,000-year-old sandstone rock gets its name from the quartzite and other minerals that give the stones a bluish tinge in early morning light and on moonlit evenings.

At Windsor Furnace, the site of an early pig iron works, glassy slag can still be seen in the pathway. Look for the remains of the old engine foundation in the undergrowth. Iron stoves were once manufactured at this furnace, and, more interestingly, an iron replica of the Last Supper. The furnace was fueled by charcoal, and many charcoal hearths, thirty to fifty feet in diameter, can be seen on this hike, including a hearth at Pochohontas Spring.

The Hike
From the parking area off Hawk Mountain Road, a blue-blazed side trail leads .25 mile to the A.T. Turning left and heading south on the A.T., you will reach Panther Spring in 1 mile as you ascend the ridge. The spring to your right is a reliable water source.

One mile past the spring, at the junction of a woods road, the A.T. turns left. At mile 2.9, you will pass Gold Spring. This, too, is a reliable water source and is a short distance off the trail to your right. Because it is part of the Hamburg Borough Watershed, camping and fires (unless otherwise noted) are not allowed in this area.

Continue along the A.T. and keep to your left where the woods road bears right, .25 mile past the spring. In another .75 mile, bear left as the woods road bears right. In another .25 mile, when you reach a clearing, keep to the left again.

At mile 4.6, you will pass a charcoal hearth. In another .25 mile, you will reach the side trail leading to The Pinnacles. This short trail heads left to one of the most outstanding views in Pennsylvania. The Pinnacles (elevation 1,635 feet) looks out over the quilt-like landscape of Pennsylvania farmland. There are two caves to explore below The Pinnacles as well as many sheer cliffs. Keep an eye out for copperheads. No camping or fires are allowed here.

Continue along the A.T. to the sidetrail (yellow blazes) that leads to Blue Rocks at mile 5.3. The side trail heads left, often steeply, downhill for 1.3 miles to Blue Rocks, and another .25 mile to Blue Rocks Campground, which is privately owned. Continue along the A.T. for another 1.1 miles, and cross a rock field, passing through a cleft in a rock formation in another .1 mile. Pass a rock field to your right in another .1 mile where there are good views to the north.

Enjoy excellent views to your left from a rock outcropping in .25 mile, and pass a tower to your right in another .1 mile. Reach Pulpit Rock (elevation 1,582 feet) .1 mile later. From Pulpit Rock, look left for wonderful views of The Pinnacles with Blue Rocks in the foreground.

Continue along the A.T. and pass the Astronomical Park of the Lehigh Valley Amateur Astronomical Society at mile 7.1. Hike another .1 mile along the A.T. to where the trail heads left and descends the mountain along an old woods road.

At mile 8.9, you will reach the side trail to Windsor Furnace Shelter. The blue-blazed trail heads right a short distance to the shelter and camping area. Water is available from a questionable creek.

After .25 mile, the trail, now on a road, crosses Furnace Creek. Swimming and bathing are not allowed in the creek. Reach Windsor Furnace .1 mile past the creek. The Borough of Hamburg has provided a camping area about 500 yards south on a blue-blazed trail. The sites are just beyond the reservoir buildings on a dirt road to the left. A stream at the campsites provides water.

From the furnace, the A.T. continues to the left on an old woods road. At mile 9.7, take the right fork away from the woods road. In another .75 mile, you will pass an intermittent spring (almost always dry in the summer), and just over a mile later, you will reach Pochohontas Spring, which runs year round. Camping is allowed in the vicinity of the spring. A blue-blazed trail here heads left 1 mile to the YMCA Blue Mountain Camp.

From Pochohontas Spring, hike .25 mile to the ridge and head left. In .75 mile, you will cross a telephone line cut-through, and in another .25, a boundary line designating game lands. One mile after crossing the telephone line cut-through, you will reach the top of the ridge, where there are views of the Schuylkill River Valley and Dam.

In another .25 mile, you will begin to descend the ridge on switchbacks. Reach the road crossing and parking area at mile 14.4, the end of the traverse.

Trailhead Directions

Just .5 mile south of Eckville, the unimproved Pine Swamp Road heads south to a Game Commission parking area on the right. A blue-blazed trail leads to the A.T. To reach Eckville, on Hawk Mountain Road, travel on Pennsylvania 895 from Drehersville or on Pennsylvania 143 near Kempton and Albany.

Coming from Hamburg on Pennsylvania 61, parking is available a half-mile south of Port Clinton on a macadam side road to your right.

PETERS MOUNTAIN/SHARP MOUNTAIN

MODERATE
24.1 mile traverse

The first half of this hike traverses Peters Mountain, which offers several fine viewpoints over the Susquehanna River, particularly from Shikellimy Rocks and Table Rock. The second half of this hike follows a variety of old pathways as the A.T. passes through the ruins of two old mining towns: Rausch Gap and Yellow Spring Villages. Both towns were thriving coal mining towns during the mid to late 1800s.

In Rausch Gap, the only notable remains of the old village include the community well (about twenty feet to the left of the trail), and some ruined building foundations and stone walls. In its heyday, the village was large enough to support a Catholic Mission, which was probably located near the cemetery. It is tricky to locate the only three tombstones that are still in evidence because they lie about 150 feet off the A.T.

Near the old village of Yellow Springs, the A.T. passes by an inclined plane used by the mining industry. It leads nearly 1 mile down the mountain to the site of the long abandoned Yellow Springs Station. In these historic areas, the trailway crosses or follows, on different sections, an old railroad bed, a stone arch railroad bridge, a mine road, and a stage road.

The Hike

From the trailhead on Pennsylvania 225, hike north on the A.T., climb to a high point on the ridge, and reach a radio tower in .25 mile. In another .25 mile, cross under a powerline cut-through, and enjoy fine views of the valley below. Hike 1.4 miles to the side trail to Zeager Shelter, where there is an excellent view from the rocks in front of the shelter. No water is available at the shelter.

From the shelter, hike .5 mile to Table Rock, which is just to the right of the trail. Table Rock affords an excellent view of the Susquehanna River and the surrounding countryside. In another .1 mile, reach the junction with a yellow-blazed trail (it leads to a church camp). Continue following the A.T. for .9 mile, and reach Peters Mountain Shelter at mile 2.1. Water is available down a steep, .25 mile side trail to a somewhat reliable spring, but your best bet is to bring water to the shelter.

Hike .6 mile to the junction with the blue-blazed Victoria Trail, and another 2 miles to a second blue-blazed trail, which leads a short distance to a viewpoint. Hike .75 mile to Shikellimy Rocks, where there are fine views of the river valley below. At mile 7.1, reach the junction with the blue-blazed Shikellimy Trail. The A.T. then descends to a gap, climbs once more, and begins the steep descent off Peters Mountain at mile 8.4. During the descent, you will pass a short side trail leading to a spring. At the base of the descent, cross Pennsylvania 325 at mile 9.2.

Cross the highway and climb Stony Mountain. For the next 3.3 miles, the trail follows an old road to the firetower on the summit. At mile 13.2, reach the junction with the blue-blazed Horseshoe Trail. Continue following the A.T., and in 3.1 miles, pass the yellow-blazed Yellow Springs Trail, and soon reach the remains of Yellow Springs Village. The trail in this section follows the old stage road.

From the site of Yellow Springs Village, hike 2.3 miles to the junction with the blue-blazed Cold Spring Trail. In another 2.3 miles, reach the .25-mile side trail to Rausch Gap Shelter. This shelter is a popular camping spot and can be crowded on the weekends. Water is available at the shelter, and there are good camping spots nearby if you prefer to sleep in your tent.

After passing the shelter, hike .6 mile to where the A.T. turns left and then follow the old railroad bed for the Susquehanna and Schuylkill Railroad. In .25 mile, cross Rausch Creek on an old stone arch railroad bridge. This rail line was last used in the 1940s. After crossing the creek, the trail turns right onto an old road. In .1 mile, reach the ruins of Rausch Gap Village. No camping is allowed in this historic area, which is located in Saint Anthony's Wilderness. The area was first named Saint Anthony's Wilderness on a map dating from the time of the Revolutionary War. In .25 mile, cross Haystack Creek and climb up and over Second Mountain. Like all of the mountains crossed on this traverse, Second Mountain is actually a ridge.

At mile 23.4, reach a short side trail to "Hotel Bleu-Blaze" Hostel. The hostel is open to longdistance hikers only, but parking for overnight hikers is sometimes allowed. To make arrangements, call the hostel-keepers Dick and Ann Tobias, at (717) 866-9093. To finish the trip, hike .75 mile to Pennsylvania 443 at Larry's Green Point Grocery, where parking is sometimes available. Ask inside the store before you leave your car.

Trailhead Directions
The parking area on Pennsylvania 225 is at the summit of Peters Mountain north of Dauphin, Pennsylvania. The northern trailhead on Pennsylvania 443 is at Larry's Green Point Grocery in Green Point, Pennsylvania.

SOUTH MOUNTAIN

EASY
20.3 mile traverse

The highlights of this hike include the preserved ruins of the iron furnace and the former Ironmaster's mansion at Pine Grove Furnace State Park and the iron furnace and museum at Caledonia State Park. From Pine Grove Furnace State Park, the A.T. ascends the ridge of South Mountain and follows the ridge until the descent to Caledonia State Park.

Pine Grove Furnace, which was owned by the same family (the Eges) that owned the furnace at Boiling Springs (also on the A.T.) produced firearms for the revolution in the late 18th century. The furnace was later purchased by the Watts family and by the mid 1800s included the furnace, a forge, coal house, brick mansion house, smith and carpenter shops, 30 log dwellings, and grist and saw mills. The 35,000 acres surrounding the furnace were mined to get charcoal to fuel the furnace. All structures except the mansion and furnace were destroyed in a 1915 fire. A small museum features the natural and industrial history of the area.

George and Martha Washington are said to have stayed at the Ironmaster's mansion during the wedding of the Ironmaster's daughter. The Ironmaster's daughter, upon the birth of twins (male and female) gave the president and his first lady the honor of naming her children. They graced the pair with the names of George and Martha. The iron works was finally shut down in 1893, having operated since 1762.

The railroad that once serviced the furnaces in the area is now a roadbed, part of which is used by the Applachian Trail. While sharing the old railbed, the A.T. passes Fuller Lake. The lake, which is about ninety feet deep, was the ore hole for the furnace. When the pumps broke down at the turn of the century, the mine was flooded and abandoned; the lake remained.

The A.T. also passes the mansion, which is now an American Youth Hostel. And, all along the trail in this area, you'll find traces of the old charcoal hearths, thirty to fifty feet in diameter, and the bluish-green glassy slag from the furnace.

Caledonia State Park also features one of the ten iron furnaces in the South Mountain area. Caledonia's furnace was built in 1837, and was owned by abolitionist Thaddeus Stevens at the time of the Civil War. His iron works was destroyed by the Confederate Army enroute to the Battle of Gettysburg. Only the furnace and the old blacksmith shop remain. The blacksmith shop, which sat along the former A.T. route, is now a museum. The old A.T. route is now a blue-blazed trail that leads to the museum as well as a swimming pool and concession area.

You will also pass the site of the former Camp Michaux. Take the time to locate the ruins of a large stone barn. The Keystone Trails Association used to hold its fall meeting at this former church camp. The site was also once a prisoner-of-war camp for captured German submarine crews. Before the war, it served as a CCC camp.

The Hike
The trail crossing at Pine Grove Furnace State Park can be picked up in the park near the store and mansion, or from Pennsylvania 233 (about 500 yards west of the park). The trail heads south on a gravel road. The gravel road ends in .1 mile, and the A.T. turns left onto an old woods road.

At mile .7, you will leave the woods road and pass several charcoal flats. In another .25 mile, you will pass the intersection of the blue-blazed Sunset Rocks Trail to your left. The trail heads 2.4 miles to the Toms Run Shelters.

Hike .1 mile, cross Toms Run on a foot bridge, then turn left onto the Old Shippensburg Road. The Pine Grove Furnace Cabin, belonging to the Potomac Appalachian Trail Club (PATC), is uphill to your right. Behind the cabin, the Wildcat Rocks Trail leads 2.1 miles to Ridge Road and Wildcat Rocks.

At mile 1.5, you will reach a side trail that leads a short distance to Half Way Spring. From here, hike .5 mile to a clearing, which is the site of the former Camp Michaux. Locate the ruins of a large stone barn.

At the former camp site, the trail turns right onto High Mountain (Michaux) Road. Hike .25 mile and turn left onto an abandoned road. At mile 3.4, you will reach Toms Run Shelters, twin shelters replaced in 1992. Water is available from a spring behind the old chimney. You will cross Toms Run again and reach the southern junction of the Sunset Rocks Trail to your left. From here, the A.T. climbs steeply up Antmire Hill.

At mile 4.5, you will cross Woodrow Road, and .5 mile later, you will turn right at the boundary of the privately-owned Tumbling Run Game Preserve. The trail parallels Ridge Road, a short distance to your right.

You will cross the entrance to the game preserve in .75 mile, and in another .75 mile, reach the junction with a blue-blazed side trail that leads to the Anna Michener Memorial Cabin, also belonging to the PATC, the Dead Woman Hollow Trail and the Blueberry Trail. At mile 7.3, after arriving at the crest of the hill, the A.T. turns left and crosses the old roadbed of Dead Woman Hollow Road, which is now a winter snowmobile trail.

Just over a mile later you will cross the Arendtsville-Shippensburg Road. To enjoy wonderful views from Big Flat Tower, turn right on the Arendtsville-Shippensburg Road and right again on to Ridge Road. Big Flat Tower is a short distance beyond the radio tower to your left.

From Arendtsville-Shippensburg Road, hike 1.2 miles to Birch Run and the Birch Run Shelters at mile 9.6. Cross Birch Run. Water is available from a spring to the right of the shelters. Continue along the A.T., cross the old Fegley Hollow Road in .75 mile and then pass beneath a powerline. Hike another .5 mile to Michaux Forest's Rocky Knob Trail on the left. Ridge Road is a short distance to the right; you will cross it a mile later and begin to descend steeply.

You will cross Milesburn Road at mile 12.1. The PATC's Milesburn Cabin is just ahead. A blue-blazed trail leads right downstream and across Milesburn Road to a spring. Begin to climb steeply.

In another .4 mile, you will reach the intersection of Canada Hollow Road, Means Hollow Road, and Ridge Road. The blue-blazed Rhododendron Trail heads right on Means Hollow Road for a 1.75-mile loop hike that returns to the A.T. After crossing the roads, hike .4 mile to the second junction of the Rhododendron Trail. The trail comes in on your right, and .1 mile later, you will cross Middle Ridge Road. Once again, the trail parallels Ridge Road, this time for 1.4 miles before crossing a TV cable line. Hike .4 mile to a powerline cut-through.

At mile 15.6, you will reach the intersection of Ridge Road and Stillhouse Road (Sandy Sod). The trail follows Ridge Road for .1 mile, turns left into the woods, and descends through Quarry Gap. In another .75 mile, you will reach the junction of the Hosack Run Trail on your left. The Hosack Run Trail connects with the Locust Gap Trail in 1.1 miles.

The A.T. turns left after .5 mile where a stream comes in from the right, and follows the stream downhill, arriving at Quarry Gap Shelters in .25 mile. The two shelters at Quarry Gap were rebuilt in 1993. Water is available from a small spring that feeds the creek.

Continue along the A.T. and pass another spring on your right in .25 mile. The spring is near the site of the former Antlers Camp. There is a gate here to control access to the Quarry Gap Shelters. In another .1 mile, the A.T. leaves Quarry Gap Road to the right.

After .25 mile, the blue-blazed Locust Gap Trail enters from the left on Greenwood Road.The trail leads left 1.8 miles to Milesburn Road and continues with the A.T. for another .25 mile. Continue along the A.T./ Locust Gap Trail and take the left fork at a former rifle range, then climb steeply up Chinquapin Hill. The Locust Gap Trail continues ahead 3 miles to Houser Road and Fayetteville near US 30. Follow the A.T. left and pass the blue-blazed Caledonia Park Three Valley Trail.

You will pass two parking lots. A year-round restroom adjoins the second lot. The road goes to the park office. Hike another 1.4 miles and cross Conococheague Creek on Caledonia Park bridge. Follow the A.T. right (where the former A.T., now blue-blazed, went left and passed the park swimming pool and museum). The new A.T. crosses a bridge over a former canal in .25 mile and reaches US 30, only .1 mile later. Walk .6 mile east (left) to the parking area off Pennsylvania 233 at Caledonia State Park, which is the end of the traverse.

Trailhead Directions
Parking is available at Pine Grove Furnace State Park off Pennsylvania 233. Caledonia State Park is also located on Pennsylvania 233.

MARYLAND

MARYLAND

The Applachian Trail follows the ridge of South Mountain through Maryland for more than 40 miles and descends to the Potomac River at Harpers Ferry, West Virginia. From Pen Mar Park in the north to Weverton Cliffs in the south, the trail in Maryland is steeped in history, particularly concerning the Civil War era.

The Appalachian Trail passes High Rock, Buzzard Knob, Black Rock Cliffs, Annapolis Rocks, Monument Knob, White Rocks, Crampton Gap, and Weverton Cliffs. Of particular historical note are Washington Monument State Park, Turners Gap with the South Mountain Inn, Crampton Gap with Gathland State Park, and the town of Weverton.

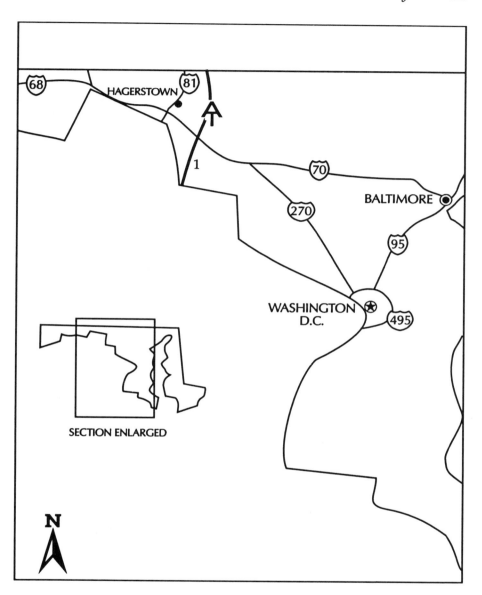

1. South Mountain II

SOUTH MOUNTAIN II

MODERATE
18.9 mile traverse

This hike traverses the ridge of South Mountain, passing a number of notable features including the Washington Monument, the historically important Turners Gap, Gathland State Park, and Weverton Cliffs. The first point of major interest that you will pass is the Washington Monument in Washington Monument State Park. This native-stone monument, reminiscent of an old cream bottle, was the first tower to be erected in honor of George Washington. The thirty-foot-high tower was built in 1827 by the citizens of Boonsboro, Maryland, and dedicated by an elderly survivor of the Revolutionary War. The monument is about three miles into the hike, and picnic tables, restrooms, and telephone are all available in the park.

Continuing along the ridge, the next point of interest is Turners Gap, a key area in both the Civil War and the Battle of South Mountain. The battle, fought on September 14, 1862, was the opening act for the Battle of Antietam/Sharpsburg. The three days of fighting, beginning on South Mountain and moving to Antietam Creek, led to the highest casualty rate of the war. It was in Turners Gap that Union forces met strong resistance from the small Confederate encampments along South Mountain. More resistance was met at Fox, Crampton, and Brownsville Gaps (also on this hike on the A.T.). Located in Turners Gap is the South Mountain Inn, used as the Confederate command post during the Civil War. The inn is a couple of hundred years old and has been frequented by several Presidents. Opposite the inn is a Gothic stone chapel built by the widow of Admiral John A. Dahlgren, creator of the Dahlgren rifled cannon. He was commandant of the Washington Navy Yard during the Civil War, and in 1876, his widow purchased the South Mountain Inn as a summer home.

From Turners Gap, the hike continues along South Mountain to Reno Monument Road. Here, the Federals, under Major General Jesse L. Reno, enveloped the Confederates, who were led by Brigadier General Samuel Garland. Reno and Garland were both killed in battle. Future President Rutherford B. Hayes was wounded. A monument to Reno was erected just under .25 mile (steep climb) down this road to the left on September 14, 1889 (the 27th anniversary of the battle) by veterans of the 9th U.S. Army Corps.

In Crampton Gap, at Gathland State Park, there is a memorial to Civil War correspondents and artists. Framing the Catoctin Valley, the fifty-foot-high memorial faces the battlefields of Winchester and Gettysburg. Inscriptions cover the arch and mythological figures are carved into its stonework. The discussion continues as to the architectural origins of the arch. It remains a mystery as to whether the arch is a cross between a Moorish arch and the old Frederick Fire Company building or a reproduction of the front of the former Antietam Fire Company building.

The arch was designed by Civil War Correspondent George Alfred Townsend, who never explained the origin of the design. Townsend, who used the pen name Gath, built his estate on South Mountain in 1884 with the proceeds from his war fiction and newspaper articles. He built a home, a hall, a library, a lodge, a guest house, a house for his wife, servants' quarters, a stable, and a tomb for himself (although he was not buried in it). He named the estate Gathland after his pseudonym. Since 1884, all the buildings, though built of stone, have been vandalized to such a degree that only one wing of Gath Hall could be restored.

The memorial arch is now administered by the National Park Service, whereas the 135-acre park is maintained by the Maryland Department of Natural Resources. A museum is now housed in the restored wing of Gath Hall. Restrooms, water, picnic tables, and a telephone are all available at the park.

The hike continues to Weverton Cliffs (with its spectacular views of the Potomac River Gorge) and the drops down to Weverton. The town of Weverton was the product of an unsuccessful industrial venture by Casper W. Wever, an otherwise successful highway and railroad engineer. Using his savings to purchase land and water rights as well as build the necessary industrial housings, he founded the town of Weverton. But he immediately began to make mistakes. He favored the railroad over the C&O Canal, opposing a canal right-of-way through his property. The railroad survived longer but his opposition was ill-timed as the canal was the main mode of transporting goods at the time. He ostracized the community, refusing to lease space for a temporary hospital in his empty buildings (the canal workers contracted Asiatic Cholera in the epidemic of 1833). And, he overestimated the power of the Potomac, believing the drop of fifteen feet at Weverton was sufficient to power the 300,000 to 600,000 spindles in his textile mills. With his too-high leases and his barely up-to-code buildings, he was able to lease only two—one for marble cutting, the other for the construction of files for the national armory in Harpers Ferry. The town failed miserably, and by World War II, even the railroad disappeared.

The Hike
From the parking area off US 40, follow the blue-blazed trail to the A.T. (.1 mile). Follow the footbridge (south) over Interstate 70. At the end of the bridge, begin to climb, turn left, head up stairs, turn right and follow an easement between two houses.

After crossing the bridge, reach Boonsboro Mountain Road in .1 mile. Cross the road and climb Bartman Hill on an old road. You will pass through hickory, oak, dogwood, maple, and sassafras. At mile .5, you will begin to descend, reaching the intersection of an old road to your right .25 mile later.

At mile .8, you will cross Old Wolfsville Road and start to climb again, soon reaching a telephone line cut-through. In .1 mile, you will turn right at the fork, head off the road and onto a footpath. Soon, descend through a forest of laurel, chestnut, oak, and American chestnut shoots.

The trail levels off at mile 1.2 and crosses a dirt road .1 mile later. Shortly thereafter, you will turn left onto a dirt road. When an old road intersects the trail to the left, continue straight ahead and begin to climb. At mile 2.1, an unmarked path heads left a short distance to a rock outcropping with a good winter view. The trail levels off, descends steeply, then levels off again in .4 mile.

You will soon cross a high-tension powerline cut-through and climb steeply up Monument Knob. As you climb, you will reach a large talus slope that has good views to the right. Rocks may be loose, so tread carefully. In another .1 mile, you will cross a graveled path, continue straight uphill, and reach Washington Monument shortly thereafter. You can climb the monument for good views to the west.

From the monument, descend steeply along a graveled path and soon reach the parking area. Restrooms and a water fountain are to the right, downhill. Camping is permitted in the park but only at designated sites. From the parking area, turn left, descend a paved road, and shortly thereafter, turn right into the woods. At mile 3.3, you will cross a campground road and then Zittlestown Road before climbing straight ahead on Monument Road, passing houses and fields.

In .1 mile, just before the crest of the hill, you will turn left off the road onto a footpath that leads through a forest of mostly maple. This is private land, so remain on the trail. Take note, as you pass through an area of profuse poison ivy; this was the locale of intense fighting during the Battle of South Mountain. Here, under Hooker, the Federals closed in on the Confederates led by Rhodes. Dahlgren Road, to the south, was the focal point of the attack. (*NOTE:* A relocation is planned for the A.T. in this area. Keep an eye out for the blazes.)

At mile 3.8, descend, and soon pass through a stone fence and then another, and climb again. Just over .1 later, a trail to your right heads a short distance to a small cliff with good winter views. The A.T. remains level for the next .25 mile before descending and passing through a fence at mile 4.4. After .1 mile, you will reach the gravel Dahlgren Road, where there is a spectacular 180° view. You should be able to see Lambs Knoll (closed firetower on summit).

Hike another .5 mile to US Alt. 40 at Turners Gap. The South Mountain Inn is .1 mile to the right. Continue along the A.T., cross US Alt. 40, and descend on an old road opposite Dahlgren Road. You will soon turn left at a junction with a dirt road and then take a left off that road shortly thereafter. At mile 5.3, you will pass the Dahlgren Backpack Camping Area to your right where there is water, restrooms, hot showers, picnic tables, and campsites.

The A.T. continues straight ahead, climbing an old road through a woods with profuse dogwood, which is spectacular in the spring. Turn right off the road in .4 mile, continue along a footpath, and soon descend over rocks. You will cross an old trail .1 mile later and head through a forest of mostly chestnut oak. At mile 5.9, you will reach the Reno Monument Road just west of Fox Gap, the site of heavy fighting during the Battle of South Mountain. The monument to Reno is down the road to the left.

The trail begins to climb beyond Reno Monument Road. In .25 mile, you will cross a high-tension powerline cut-through where there are good views to the west. In another .25 mile, you will turn right onto an old road as the trail levels out. At mile 6.7, you will turn left at the fork and climb steeply up to a blue-blazed trail, which heads right .25 mile to Rocky Run Shelter (there is a swing in front). *Note:* A relocation is planned for the A.T. between here and Lambs Knoll. Keep an eye out for new blazes and directions.

From the side trail to the shelter, it is .25 mile to the crossing of an old road, then just over .1 mile to the crossing of a paved road. The paved road heads right to the summit of Lambs Knoll and left to Reno Monument Road. From here, hike another 1.4 miles to the summit of Lambs Knoll (elevation 1,772 feet), where there is profuse laurel. The tower is closed. Descend for .25 mile to the side trail to White Rocks. The blue-blazed side trail leads a short distance to the left to small quartzite rock cliffs with excellent winter views of the South Mountain. (This directional illusion is a result of Lambs Knoll being offset to the east of the ridge.)

Continue along the A.T. for less than .1 mile, and turn right at the fork onto a recent relocation. Descend through azaleas, red maples and chestnut shoots, pass a rock outcropping to your left, and rejoin the old A.T. to the left, which is the end of the relocation (mile 9.1). In just under .25 mile, you will turn right at another junction where a blue-blazed trail heads left .25 mile to Bear Spring and .75 mile to Bear Spring Cabin, which can be rented from the Potomac Appalachian Trail Club (PATC). See appendix for information on how to rent.

Continue along the A.T. on a rocky path through woods with dense undergrowth. In .6 mile, you will reach a winter view to the left and begin to descend moderately. In .25 mile, you will arrive at a large rockpile that affords a limited view of Elk Ridge and Pleasant Valley to your right. The path improves as you continue toward an interesting knoll to your left that features an evenly fractured pile of boulders, offering another excellent winter viewpoint.

At mile 11.6, a blue-blazed side trail heads left .25 mile to Crampton Gap Shelter. Water is available from an intermittent spring. The trail continues ahead, forking right off an old road onto a footpath, and rejoining the road again in another .1 mile. From here it is a very short distance to Gathland State Park. Facilities include water, restrooms, phone, museum, and picnic tables. Camping is allowed at designated sites. As you head toward Crampton Gap, you will pass a field, picnic tables, and the ruins of a large stone barn built in 1887.

The barn marks the site of intense fighting during the Battle of South Mountain. The Federals, under Franklin, overwhelmed McLaws' Confederates. Passing through a gap in a stone fence, you will reach Gapland Road (Maryland 572). Locate historical markers and a memorial arch to your left. Cross Gapland Road and continue up the park driveway, straight ahead.

Turn left at the parking lot, ascend a gravel road, and pass Gath's empty tomb to the right and the park office on the left. A short distance later, you will reach a point where an earthworks from the Civil War can be seen straight ahead. You will turn right, then right again at the fork just ahead. The left fork goes to designated campsites (camping by permit only). The trail continues along the ridge of South Mountain.

At mile 13.3, you will pass a dark red granite memorial on your left, dedicated to Glenn R. Caveney. Caveney, who co-maintained this section of trail with his father, was killed in an auto accident. A fund, established by his father, was used to purchase the four-acre tract of land surrounding Glenn's memorial. In 1.5 miles, you will pass an impressive knoll (like the one north of Crampton Gap) that exhibits an evenly fractured rock pile.

Hike .25 mile to Brownsville Gap, cross the road and bear right where the old road intersects on the left. As you pass numerous beech trees, another road intersects from the right. Continue straight ahead on the A.T., shortly crossing a buried coaxial cable line.

At mile 15.1, you will pass an impressive knoll with squarely stacked rocks that are oddly balanced. Less than .5 mile later, you will reach a blue-blazed side trail that heads a short distance to the right to another limited view of Elk Ridge and Pleasant Valley. In .6 mile, turn left at the junction of an old road, and shortly thereafter, reach a giant beech that has the oldest graffiti markings on the ridge—1892 and 1899! Hike another .6 mile to an old road that intersects from the right, and continue straight ahead on the A.T.

You will go right at the fork at mile 17.3 and descend, steeply at times, along a rough path for .75 mile. Turn right and continue to descend steeply, then more moderately, down switchbacks. There is a blue-blazed sidetrail that heads straight ahead .1 mile to Weverton Cliffs, which affords spectacular views of the Potomac River Gorge. A plaque set in the stone at the cliffs memorializes Congressman Goodloe E. Byron (1928-1978), a strong supporter of the Appalachian Trail.

At mile 18.9, following the descent off South Mountain, you will cross paved Weverton Road and follow another road ahead to the parking area on the left at the shoulder of the road.

Trailhead Directions
From Hagerstown, take US 40 to its first crossing over I-70. The parking area is immediately to your right after you cross the interstate. To reach the A.T., hike .1 mile on the blue-blazed side trail.

From US 340, take Maryland 67 to Weverton Road, which is the first right after exiting US 340. There is a parking area alongside the trail where it crosses Weverton Road a mile from Maryland 67.

WEST VIRGINIA

VIRGINIA

WEST VIRGINIA/VIRGINIA

The A.T. in West Virginia is limited to a short section of trail (about 3 miles) centered in the town of Harpers Ferry, which is also the home of the Appalachian Trail Conference Headquarters. The A.T. visits West Virginia farther south when the trail travels along the border of the two states. Here, the trail traverses Peters Mountain north of Pearisburg, Virginia.

The longest stretch of A.T. is in Virginia, host to more than a quarter of the A.T.'s length. From the Potomac River near Harpers Ferry, the A.T. ridge hops westward along the Blue Ridge until it reaches Shenandoah National Park. After traversing the park for more than 100 miles, the trail leaves the park behind at Rockfish Gap. Picking up the Blue Ridge Parkway, which the A.T. more or less parallels for 100 miles until the Roanoke area, the trail traverses Humpback Mountain, Three Ridges, The Priest, Spy Rock, Punchbowl, and Bluff Mountains. After descending to the James River, the trail climbs to Apple Orchard Mountain, the highest point on the Blue Ridge Parkway in Virginia.

In Troutville/Cloverdale, the A.T. leaves the Parkway and heads west toward the border of West Virginia, passing the remarkable features of Tinker Cliffs, MacAfee Knob, Dragons Tooth, and the Audie Murphy Monument. The stretch along the crest of Peters Mountain is on the Virginia/West Virginia border. After Peters Mountain, the A.T. descends to Pearisburg and climbs Angels Rest on Pearis Mountain. For the next 85 miles, the A.T. slowly winds its way back toward Interstate 81, crossing Interstate 77 near Bastian, Virginia, first.

From Atkins, Virginia, the A.T. heads south into the Mount Rogers National Recreation Area, passing through Grayson Highlands and within half a mile of the summit of Mount Rogers, Virginia's highest peak. From Mount Rogers, it is 30 miles to the Virginia/Tennessee state line. In this southern section of Virginia, the trail traverses White Top Mountain, Buzzard Rock, and Straight Mountain before descending into the hiker-friendly town of Damascus, Virginia. Damascus holds an annual Trail Days Festival each May. The state line is three miles south of Damascus.

Shenandoah National Park

Of special note is Shenandoah National Park, which the A.T. traverses through Northern Virginia. Established by President Coolidge in 1926, Shenandoah National Park took ten years to complete. Most of the work was done by President Roosevelts's CCC; it was dedicated by President Roosevelt in 1936. The parkway—Skyline Drive—was also part of the original concept, and took eight years to complete. Beginning construction in 1931, the southern, central and northern sections were opened as they were completed (1939, 1934 and 1936, respectively).

Although the Appalachian Trail was first constructed in the 1920s and opened in 1929, much of the trail was relocated as Skyline Drive was built. The CCC was also put to work rebuilding the A.T.—note the laborious rock work that shores up much of the trail.

Anyone hiking long distance through the Shenandoahs is required to pick up a backcountry camping permit at the entrance station. The permit allows you to use the huts monitored by the Potomac Applachian Trail Club (PATC), the group is also responsible for the maintenance of the trail in the Shenandoahs.

The history of the Shenandoahs—natural, geologic, cultural—can and does fill books. For additional information, books on the park are sold at the park's visitor centers. The flora and fauna of the park is varied and includes everything from black bear and white-tailed deer (the latter extremely prevalent) to the less often seen mountain lions and bobcats. Areas of intense defoliation have been caused by the gypsy moth (make sure this nasty pest hasn't attached itself to your camping equipment). The deer tick is also present in the Shenandoahs, so search your body carefully for this carrier of Lyme Disease. As for flora, everything from hemlock-hardwood forests to boreal forests can be found in the Shenandoahs. The tiny island of boreal trees is found at Skyland-Big Meadows, both of which you'll pass on this traverse. Flowers and flowering shrubs also abound, making the park a fairyland walk from late spring through mid-summer.

Note: The only overnight hike given for West Virginia is the Peter's Mountain hike which follows the West Virginia/Virginia border for twelve miles.

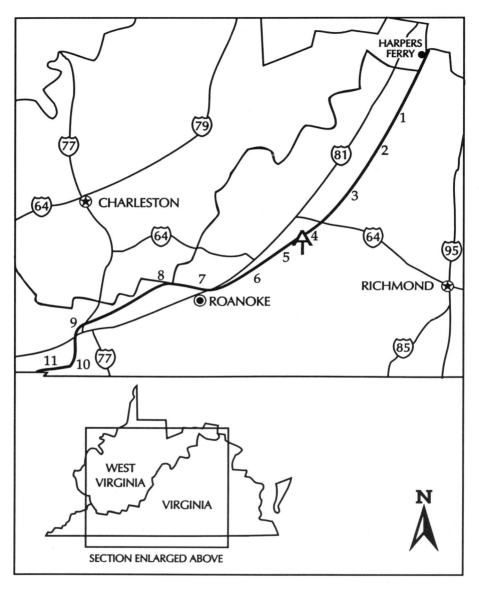

1. South & North Marshall Loop
2. Stony Man/Big Meadows
3. Southern Shenandoahs
4. Three Ridges Loop
5. Tar Jacket Ridge/The Priest
6. James River Face Wilderness
7. Catawba Valley Loop
8. Peters Mountain
9. Garden Mountain
10. Virginia Highlands
11. Mount Rogers Loop

SOUTH & NORTH MARSHALL LOOP
Shenandoah National Park

EASY
13 mile loop

On this loop, you will follow the Mount Marshall, Bluff, and Appalachian Trails as you hike through Shenandoah National Park. There are some moderate climbs along the way, but with only 13 miles to cover in two days, this is a nice, easy weekend hike. This short loop offers several fine views from North and South Marshall Mountains.

North and South Marshall Mountains were once known locally as Bluff Mountain. They were re-named for John Marshall (1755-1835), who served as Chief Justice of the United States for the last thirty-five years of his life. North and South Marshall Mountains were once owned by the renowned jurist.

The Hike
From the trailhead at Jenkins Gap, hike east on the yellow-blazed Jenkins Gap Trail. Almost immediately, cross Skyline Drive, and in .1 mile, reach the junction with the Mount Marshall Trail. Turn left onto this yellow-blazed trail, and soon cross two small streams—Bolton Branch and Waterfall Branch—on your way to the junction with the Bluff Trail, 3.5 miles beyond Skyline Drive.

Turn right onto the yellow-blazed Bluff Trail and follow the trail along the eastern, then southern slopes of North and then South Marshall, experiencing little change in elevation. At mile 6, reach the junction with the blue-blazed Big Devils Stairs Trail. Continue following the yellow-blazed Bluff Trail, and reach a junction with the Harris Hollow Trail, which shares the same footpath with the Bluff Trail for the next .1 mile. As the Harris Hollow Trail turns off to the left, follow the Bluff Trail, which becomes blue-blazed.

In .1 mile, cross a gravel road leading downhill to Gravel Springs Hut. The shelter is for use by long distance A.T. hikers only. Water is available from a spring at the shelter. Continue following the Bluff Trail for .25 mile to the junction with the A.T. Turn right on the A.T., hiking north for .25 mile to where the A.T. crosses Skyline Drive at milepost 17.7., where the

Browntown Trail meets the Drive. Climb the west slope of Mount Marshall for the next mile. Just before the summit, enjoy fine views from rock outcrops to the left of the trail.

Reach the summit of South Marshall (elevation 3,212 feet) at mile 8.6, and descend to a gap between South and North Marshall, where you'll cross Skyline Drive at milepost 15.9. Begin climbing North Marshall on switchbacks. During the climb, there are distinct cliffs to the right of the trail with outstanding views of Skyline Drive and the surrounding mountains and countryside. At mile 9.8, reach the summit of North Marshall (elevation 3,368 feet).

The trail descends gently from North Marshall and passes a short side trail, which leads to a piped spring in .9 mile. In another .6 mile, cross Skyline Drive at milepost 14.2 (Hogwallow Gap). Climb from Hogwallow Gap to the top of an unnamed mountain (elevation 2,882 feet), and in 1.7 miles, reach the end of the hike at Jenkins Gap.

Trailhead Directions
There is parking for more than a dozen cars at Jenkins Gap. The parking lot is at Skyline Drive milepost 12.3.

Stony Man/Big Meadows
Shenandoah National Park

MODERATE
26.3 mile traverse

Shenandoah National Park of Virginia is one of the most popular areas to hike along the Appalachian Trail. This traverse takes you south from US 211 at Thornton Gap to Lewis Mountain Campground, passing Marys Rock, Stony Man, Skyland, and Big Meadows.

The Hike
From the A.T. crossing at US 211 (elevation 2,307 feet), follow the A.T. south and head through the woods to the west of the Panorama Restaurant. The A.T. climbs steadily up the mountain, reaching a side trail at mile 1.7. The side trail heads .1 mile to the right to Marys Rock, which probably has the most spectacular views in the park. The huge rock outcropping of

granodiorite (elevation 3,514 feet) is dated by geologists at more than one billion years old.

Continue along the A.T., following the crest of the ridge (with occasional views to the west) before descending gradually. In another .75 mile, you will reach a sag where Meadow Spring Trail intersects the A.T. from the left. Meadow Spring is .25 mile downhill on this side trail. Continue along the narrow crest of the ridge, and enjoy a good view to the west at an outcropping in .1 mile.

At mile 2.7, reach another viewpoint, head left, and descend to the base of The Pinnacle. In another .25 mile, reach a service road and follow it a short distance to Byrds Nest #3, a day-use shelter with piped water. The service road leads another .25 mile to Skyline Drive (milepost 33.9). The A.T. continues, climbs moderately, and reaches a side trail in .75 mile.

The side trail leads a short distance to the right to a view north. In another .1 mile, you will see the jagged rocks (a short distance to your right) that form the north peak of The Pinnacle. The trail continues for .1 mile along the crest of the ridge, which has spectacular views of the mountain's sheer western slopes. At mile 4, you will reach the highest point of The Pinnacle (elevation 3,730 feet) and begin a descent through mountain laurel. In another .75 mile, you will reach the junction with the blue-blazed Leading Ridge Trail, which leads left .1 mile to Skyline Drive. The A.T. continues to descend through white pine.

In .1 mile, you will pass below the Jewel Hollow Overlook (elevation 3,335 feet) at Skyline Drive (milepost 36.4). In another .25 mile, you will reach a side trail that heads back a short distance to the Jewel Hollow Overlook. The trail continues, climbing moderately along the crest of the ridge, where there are views to the west across Jewel Hollow. Hike .1 mile past the side trail that reaches and then parallels the entrance road to the Pinnacles Picnic Area (milepost 36.7). The A.T. follows the right fork (unpaved) and skirts the picnic area through laurel.

Pass restrooms and a water fountain in another .25 mile, then enter the woods, climbing briefly and descending again. At mile 5.7, pass a notable white pine to your left, and in another .1 mile, cross under powerlines. Climb to the knob at the head of Nicholson Hollow, and in another .4 mile, turn sharply to the right and descend to a good viewpoint of Nicholson Hollow and Old Rag Mountain.

In .1 mile, you will reach an abandoned trail to your right that will take you .25 mile downhill to a spring near the former site of the Shaver Hollow

Shelter. From the side trail, hike .6 mile to the blue-blazed Crusher Ridge Trail, which crosses the trail on an old woods road (Sours Lane). At mile 7, reach the junction with the blue-blazed Nicholson Hollow Trail. The side trail leads .1 mile to Skyline Drive. You will reach another side trail in .25 mile that heads left a short distance to the southern end of the Stony Man Mountain Overlook (milepost 38.6). This is also Hughes River Gap (elevation 3,097 feet). Water and restrooms are provided at this overlook. The trail continues around Nicholson Hollow, parallels Skyline Drive, and ascends.

Reach the side trail to Little Stony Man Parking Area in .4 mile. The short side trail heads left to Skyline Drive (milepost 39.1). The A.T. climbs Stony Man moderately on switchbacks and reaches another trail junction at mile 8. Follow the A.T. left at the fork (the right fork, the Passamaquoddy Trail, heads 1.4 miles to Skyland Lodge and is a former A.T. route). The left fork continues another .25 mile to the cliffs of Little Stony Man and ascends .6 mile to another trail junction.

You have two options—you can follow a .4-mile loop trail to the summit of Stony Man, or continue along the A.T., descending .4 mile to the Stony Man Nature Trail Parking Area. Don't follow the horse trail to the nature trail. The parking area is .25 mile to the left of Skyland Lodge and Dining Hall, and .1 mile to the right of Skyline Drive (milepost 41.7).

From the parking lot, cross the paved road that leads to Skyland, climb gradually through the woods, and reach the service road to Skyland in .25 mile. From here, it is .25 mile to the right to Skyland Lodge and Dining Hall. Continue to climb, and soon reach an open field with a large green water tank. Descend .6 mile to Skyland Road. The road heads left to Skyline Drive and right to Skyland Development. Continue on the A.T. and hike along the cliffs under Pollock Knob (elevation 3,560 feet) in another .25 mile. Pollock Knob and the Passamaquoddy Trail (which means "abounding in Pollock") were named for George Pollock, the founder of Skyland.

The trail begins to descend via switchbacks at mile 10.9, with great views of Hawksbill Mountain and Ida Valley. Paralleling Skyline Drive, you will pass through a thicket of laurel and reach an open area in .5 mile. A side trail to the left heads a short distance uphill to the Timber Hollow Parking Overlook at Skyline Drive (milepost 43.3).

In .1 mile, the trail ascends a small ridge and then descends the western slopes of Blue Ridge, passing some interesting trees with contorted limbs. An oak, in particular, offers the tired hiker a seat on an extended limb. In .6 mile, you will reach a concrete post that marks a side trail that heads right

.1 mile uphill, just north of Crescent Rock Parking Overlook (milepost 44.4) to good views at Bettys Rock. The trail continues under the Crescent Rock cliffs. Enjoy great views of Nakedtop and Hawksbill Mountain.

At mile 12.6, you will reach Hawksbill Gap. A side trail turns right downhill and reaches a spring in a short distance. To the left, a short distance away, is Hawksbill Gap Parking Area on Skyline Drive at milepost 45.6 (elevation 3,361 feet). From the gap, the A.T. climbs up the northern side of Hawksbill Mountain (site of a peregrine falcon release program) and continues along under cliffs. Look behind you for good views of Crescent Rocks, Stony Man, and Old Rag Mountain, and ahead for views of Ida Valley and Luray.

At mile 13.6, you will reach the sag between Hawksbill and Nakedtop; there is a side trail that heads left .9 mile to the summit of Hawksbill. The A.T. continues for another .25 mile through deep woods before it arrives in an old orchard that is rapidly becoming overrun by other trees. A service road enters from the left that looks like a grassy meadow. (No camping allowed.) The road heads left for .25 mile to Skyline Drive (milepost 47.8). Continue along the A.T. and reach the side trail (with signpost) that heads right .25 mile to Rock Spring Cabin, which can be rented through PATC, and Rock Spring Hut, where you can stay overnight. From late May through June, A.T. long-distance hikers are likely to fill the shelters in the Shenandoahs, but there is still room to camp in the area.

At mile 14.5, you will reach another side trail (with signpost) that heads a short distance uphill to Skyline Drive at Spitler Knoll Parking Overlook (milepost 48.1). The A.T. continues along the slopes of Blue Ridge before passing a concrete post marking the side trail to the left, which heads uphill .25 mile to the north end of Franklin Cliffs Overlook. In another .25 mile, the A.T. passes another side trail, also marked by a post, that heads left .25 mile to the south end of Franklin Cliffs Overlook.

At mile 15.8, you will reach the intersection with Red Gate Fire Road in Fishers Gap (formerly Gordonsville Turnpike). The road heads right to Virginia 611 and left to the north end of Fishers Gap Parking Overlook. After passing below the overlook, you will pass another post marking a side trail that heads left a short distance to the Fisher Gap Parking Overlook. In another .1 mile, you will pass to the right of a split rock, climb up to a hemlock grove, and cross a small stream twice.

At mile 16.8, locate David Spring a short distance to the right of the A.T. where a trail enters from the left. The A.T. skirts the north edge of Big Meadows Campground. Pass several unmarked trails that lead to the campground. Camping and lodging along with food, and water, are all available at Big Meadows. Enjoy views along here of Hawksbill Mountain, Stony Man Mountain, Knob Mountain, and Neighbor Mountain.

Cross a small, rocky knob called Monkey Head in .25 mile, then skirt the western edge of the ridge, and pass below the open-air amphitheater in Big Meadows in another .25 mile. In .1 mile, you will pass a concrete post that marks the intersection of the A.T. with the trail to Lewis Falls (1.2 miles to the right) and the Lodge Trail (left to the amphitheater parking area). The A.T. continues straight ahead, passing under the sheer cliffs of Blackrock in .25 mile. From the rocks at the right, there are outstanding views of the Shenandoah Valley, the Massanuttens, Great North Mountain, with the Alleghenies rising in the distance.

At mile 17.9, a side trail heads left for .1 mile to a view at Blackrock, and at mile 18.1, another trail leads to Big Meadows Lodge. The A.T. descends down the ridge for .4 mile to a service road, which leads .25 mile left to Skyline Drive (milepost 51.4). The service road reaches the Drive .1 mile south of Big Meadows Wayside, where you'll find meals and supplies, and the Harry F. Byrd, Sr. Visitor Center. Just past the service road, the A.T. reaches the outlet of the boxed Lewis Spring and continues to descend through the woods for another .6 mile before reaching Tanners Ridge Cemetery on the right.

The A.T. continues along a level footpath from here to Milam Gap, just over a mile away. About .25 mile after leaving the cemetery, you will pass a spring a short distance to the left of the A.T. Reach Skyline Drive (milepost 52.8) at mile 20, south of Milam Gap (elevation 3,257 feet). The A.T. continues east through a field before reaching a concrete post marking the intersection with the Mill Prong Trail to the left. From here, the trail climbs the north ridge of Hazeltop, bearing right at the crest in .4 mile and climbing moderately to the north end of Hazeltop at mile 21.5.

In another .4 mile, you will cross the tree-covered crest of Hazeltop (elevation 3,812 feet), the highest point on the A.T. in the Shenandoahs. Note the red spruce and balsam on the summit that is marked by a sign. After .5 mile, you will reach the intersection of the blue-blazed Laurel Prong Trail, which heads 2.8 miles left to Camp Hoover. In another .4 mile, you will reach Bootens Gap (elevation 3,243 feet) and the gate across Conway River Fire Road. Skyline Drive (milepost 55.1) is a short distance to the right. The A.T. descends moderately for .25 mile before paralleling Skyline Drive with little change in elevation for the next .5 mile.

Begin to climb again along the western slope of Bush Mountain before reaching another trail junction in .5 mile. The blue-blazed side trail heads right for .1 mile to Bearfence Mountain Parking Area on Skyline Drive (milepost 56.4). For excellent views, follow the side trail left over some rough boulders. You will pass a loop trail over Bearfence Mountain in .25 mile, which makes a figure eight with the A.T.

Continue along the A.T. and reach the loop trail noted above in .25 mile, where it leaves the A.T. to the left. The loop is only a short distance longer than the length of the A.T. between the trail junctions of the loop, and the loop offers outstanding views. But if you continue on the A.T., you will reach the second junction with the loop in another .25 mile. From here, the trail descends by switchbacks for .6 mile to a gap where it intersects the yellow-blazed Slaughter Trail. The side trail heads left .1 mile to the access road to Bearfence Hut, then right a few feet to Skyline Drive (milepost 56.8).

At mile 25.3, another side trail leads left for .1 mile to Bearfence Mountain Hut, which is designated for long-distance hikers. There is a spring a short distance south of the hut that is often dry in the summer. From the hut, the A.T. climbs moderately up Lewis Mountain, leveling off at 3,400 feet. You will pass several paths that lead right to Lewis Mountain Picnic Area and Campground (open May through October), but don't leave the A.T. until you reach the post marking the side trail that leads right 100 yards to the campground at mile 26.3. Take this side trail to the campground and its parking area.

Trailhead Directions
The Applachian Trail crossing at Thornton Gap (US 211) is .1 mile west of Skyline Drive. US 211 can be reached via Interstate 81 at New Market or via US 15/29 at Warrenton near Washington, D.C.

Lewis Mountain Campground is off Skyline Drive at milepost 57.5.

SOUTHERN SHENANDOAHS
Shenandoah National Park

MODERATE
21.9 mile traverse

Shenandoah National Park of Virginia is one of the most popular areas to hike along the A.T. This traverse takes you south from Loft Mountain Campground over the southern Shenandoahs to Beagle Gap. In September, Calf Mountain, just north of Beagle Gap, is an excellent site for watching the hawk migrations.

The Hike

Begin at Loft Mountain Campground, just past milepost 79 on Skyline Drive. Take the short side trail to the A.T. that begins just south of the Ranger's residence and camp store. The campground has supplies, a laundromat, a phone, and showers. At the junction with the A.T., turn right and begin a moderate ascent of Big Flat Mountain.

In .25 mile, you will begin to circle clockwise around the campground along the summit of Big Flat Mountain (elevation 3,387 feet). Concrete posts at mile .6 and mile 1.1 indicate side trails that lead to the campground. Reach a third concrete post .25 mile later that marks the .25-mile trail heading to the Loft Mountain Amphitheater. In .5 mile, you will reach an outstanding 360° view of Rockytop, Brown Mountain, Rocky Mountain, Rocky Mount, and to the far right, east of Skyline Drive, Loft Mountain.

The A.T. descends for another .25 mile until it reaches the junction of the Doyles River Trail. A short distance to the right is Skyline Drive (milepost 81.1). Big Run Parking Overlook is a short distance south on Skyline Drive. To the left, it is .25 mile to Doyles River Cabin and spring. The cabin can be rented through the PATC. See the appendix for more information on how to rent. For the next .9 mile, the A.T. parallels Skyline Drive.

At mile 3, the A.T. passes through Doyles River Parking Overlook (milepost 81.9 on Skyline Drive). Follow the ledges (with good winter views) and cross to the right of Skyline Drive (milepost 82.2). From Skyline Drive, enjoy a good view of Cedar and Trayfoot Mountains. At mile 3.7, you will reach the intersection of the Big Run Loop Trail and then begin a moderate descent.

In another .6 mile, you will arrive at the concrete post marking the junction with the Madison Run Fire Road a short distance to the right of Skyline Drive (milepost 82.9). This is Browns Gap (elevation 2,599 feet), which was used by General Stonewall Jackson during the Civil War. The A.T. crosses Skyline Drive diagonally to the left and begins to ascend. At mile 5.1, the A.T. skirts to the east of Dundo (a developed area at milepost 83.7) for the next .25 mile. Water is available at Dundo from May through October.

When a trail heads right to the Dundo Campground Area, follow the A.T. left and reach the junction with the Jones Run Trail in .6 mile. Jones Run Parking Area is a short distance to the right. The A.T. continues ahead, soon passing through an old apple orchard and then crossing Skyline Drive (milepost 84.3) at mile 6.1. The trail begins a moderate climb for .75 mile until the A.T. and the Trayfoot Mountain Trail come within a few feet of each other but do not cross. The trails parallel each other for about .1 mile before the A.T. turns right and circles the sides of Blackrock (elevation 3,092 feet) with its tumbled, lichen-covered boulders.

In another .25 mile, you will reach the blue-blazed Blackrock Spur Trail, which heads right along the ridge to Trayfoot Mountain. In another .1 mile, the A.T. crosses Trayfoot Mountain Trail and begins a descent to Blackrock Gap. At mile 7.7, you will reach the side trail to Blackrock Hut (.25 mile away in a deep ravine with a spring a short distance in front of the hut), where you can stay overnight. From late May through June, A.T. long-distance hikers are likely to fill the shelters in the Shenandoahs, but there is still room to camp in the area.

The A.T. continues ahead and crosses an old road a short distance later. It then parallels the road for .25 mile, then joins it and follows the road to its junction with Skyline Drive (milepost 87.2). Cross the Drive, continue along its east side for .25 mile, and reach Moormans River Fire Road (yellow blazes) at Blackrock Gap (milepost 87.4). The fire road is the former A.T. route, and heads 9.4 miles to Jarman Gap. The new A.T. ascends a small knob and then descends to a sag at mile 9.5, where Skyline Drive is a short distance to the right. From here, the trail ascends a second small knob.

At mile 10.2, the trail crosses Skyline Drive (milepost 88.9) in a sag and ascends again, reaching the intersection with the blue-blazed Riprap Trail in .75 mile at the summit of a knob (elevation 2,988 feet). From here, descend steeply, and in .4 mile, reach a graded trail that heads left to the Riprap Parking Area on Skyline Drive (milepost 90). Descend steeply for another .1 mile and then more gradually. Follow a path that rolls gently up and down for 2 miles. Keep an eye out for the Catawba rhododendron in this section.

You will reach the junction of the Wildcat Ridge Trail at mile 14. The Wildcat Ridge Parking Area on Skyline Drive (milepost 92.1) is a short distance to the left. The A.T. climbs moderately, crosses Skyline Drive (milepost 92.4) in .25 mile, then continues to ascend, reaching a summit (elevation 3,080 feet) in .5 mile. The trail then descends to a slight sag before regaining the lost elevation, then descending steeply again toward Turk Gap.

At mile 16.3, the A.T. reaches a concrete post marking the beginning of the Turk Branch Trail, which leaves the A.T. to the left. The A.T. crosses Skyline Drive at Turk Gap (milepost 94.1) and joins the Turk Mountain Trail for .25 mile before the Turk Mountain Trail leaves the A.T. to the right. Continue ahead on the A.T., reaching the crest of the ridge a short distance later, and beginning a long, moderate descent.

At mile 17.9, in a deep sag at the northern edge of the Sawmill Run Parking Overlook, the A.T. crosses Skyline Drive (milepost 95.3) and begins to ascend. While ascending, look over your shoulder for views of Turk Mountain, Sawmill Ridge, and the city of Waynesboro. Hike .6 mile to the summit of an unnamed hill (elevation 2,453 feet), and as the trail begins to descend, enjoy views to the east of Bucks Elbow Mountain. In another .4 mile, cross a grass-covered pipeline cut-through and continue to descend.

You will reach the South Fork of Moormans River .25 mile later, which is just a small creek here. Follow the west bank of the creek to its source, and continue along the A.T. another .25 mile to the Moormans River Fire Road. The road heads left .1 mile to Skyline Drive at Jarman Gap (milepost 96.8). A short distance later, after crossing the road, you will pass a spring to your left and begin to ascend.

At mile 19.8, you will reach the Bucks Elbow Mountain Fire Road, which is a short distance east of Skyline Drive (milepost 96.9), and begin to climb toward the south. In another .4 mile, you will pass a spring to your left, and .1 mile later, you will cross a powerline cut-through. At mile 20.8, you will reach a side trail that heads right .25 mile to a spring, and another

.1 mile to Calf Mountain Shelter. This is a shelter, not a hut, and can be used by short-distance hikers as well as long-distance hikers.

Hike .25 mile to an open area, where the trail follows a pasture road through grass and staghorn sumac, and reach the summit of Calf Mountain (elevation 2,974 feet) in another .25 mile. In September, this is an excellent site for watching the hawk migrations. The A.T. continues along the ridge before descending through pines and crossing a stone fence. At mile 22, the A.T. passes to the left of Little Calf Mountain and descends .25 mile to Beagle Gap at Skyline Drive (milepost 99.5). Beagle Gap Parking Overlook, which is the end of this traverse, is less than a .5-mile walk to the south along Skyline Drive.

Trailhead Directions
Loft Mountain Campground is between mileposts 79 and 80 on Skyline Drive. Parking is available at the campground. Beagle Gap Parking Overlook is just north of milepost 100 on Skyline Drive. Hike approximately .5 mile north to pick up the A.T. at Beagle Gap.

THREE RIDGES LOOP

STRENUOUS
11.8 mile loop

You will follow the A.T. and Mau-Har Trails on this short overnight hike. There are several fine viewpoints on the A.T. portion of this hike, which climbs to the summit of Three Ridges. The Mau-Har Trail boasts a forty-foot waterfall and creates an easier descent back to the Tye River. Also of note is the 100-foot-long suspension bridge over the Tye River, which was built by the U.S. Forest Service.

All in all, this is an outstanding weekend hike, but it is not to be under estimated. Although the hike is less than 12 miles long, there is a 3,000 foot change in elevation from the Tye River (elevation 920 feet) to the summit of Three Ridges (elevation 3,970 feet) and most of the change comes in 3 miles of climbing.

The Hike
From Virginia 56, follow the A.T. north and descend gradually. In .1 mile, cross the 100-foot suspension bridge over the Tye River. The A.T. begins

climbing on switchbacks, and in 1.6 miles, reaches the junction with the Mau-Har Trail. Continue following the A.T. and cross Harper Creek in .75 mile. In another .1 mile, a blue-blazed side trail leads to Harpers Creek Shelter. Water is available from the creek.

The climb gets steeper beyond the side trail to the shelter. In 1.6 miles, enjoy a view of The Priest, and in another .1 mile, cross the lowest of the ridges that make up the mountain. Beyond the crest of that ridge, hike .25 mile to Chimney Rock, a boulder pile to the left of the A.T. Just beyond the boulders, at mile 4.6, pass a viewpoint on the right side of the trail and then cross the crest of the second ridge.

The last of the three ridges is the toughest climb. After 1.3 miles, the climb eases, and in another .25 mile, at mile 6.3, reach the wooded summit of Three Ridges (elevation 3,970 feet). Hike a moderate .5 mile, descending to Hanging Rock, which provides views of The Priest and the valley below. Continue descending Three Ridges, and in .5 mile, begin climbing again. In .9 mile, reach summit of Bee Mountain (elevation 3,034 feet) and descend. In another .4 mile, reach the junction with the blue-blazed Mau-Har Trail. Pick up the Mau-Har Trail, and in .1 mile, pass Maupin Field Shelter at mile 8.8. There is a caretaker at the shelter during the summer, but no fee is charged. This is a good point to break up the hike. Although the first day is long and hard, it allows for a shorter second day with time to enjoy the waterfall and get home for dinner.

In 1.5 miles, reach the forty-foot falls on Campbell Creek, the highlight of this trail. Continue following the Mau-Har Trail, and in another 1.5 miles reach junction with the A.T. Turn right on the A.T. and hike south 1.6 miles to the suspension bridge over the Tye River. From there it is a short climb to Virginia 56, the end of this hike.

Trailhead Directions

The A.T. crosses Virginia 56, 1.4 miles west of Tyro, Virginia, and 11.3 miles east of the Blue Ridge Parkway.

TAR JACKET RIDGE/THE PRIEST

MODERATE
24.9 mile traverse

At the beginning of this hike, you climb to the wooded summit of Bald Knob. The name may seem innapropriate, but the knob was once a cleared mountain. Summertime hikers might think that the rest of the hike will be through a tunnel of green, but as you will soon see, this overnight hike has a lot of magnificent views to offer. As you climb across the grassy summits of Cole Mountain and Tar Jacket Ridge, you are afforded spectacular panoramic views. Both highpoints were once used as pasture land; the cleared highlands are the result of years of cattle grazing. Tar Jacket Ridge is now mowed by George Washington National Forest to maintain the ridge as a bald.

This hike will also take you to Spy Rock, whose name dates back to its use as a Confederate lookout point in the Civil War. The last mountain you will climb is The Priest whose wooded summit towers over the Tye River Valley. The descent down sometimes steep switchbacks takes you from The Priest to the highway nearly 3,000 feet below.

This hike is described as moderate, but be prepared for a couple of short strenuous sections at each end of the hike—ascents and descents. *Note:* the Forest Service map and some guidebooks refer to Cole Mountain as Cold Mountain. This inaccuracy has wormed its way into many publications, but the mountain has always been known as Cole Mountain.

The Hike

From US 60, follow the A.T. north and begin climbing Bald Knob. In 2.8 miles, reach the tree-covered summit of Bald Knob (elevation 4,059 feet). Descend from the Knob, and in 1 mile, pass a .6-mile side trail to Cow Camp Gap Shelter. Water is available from a nearby spring.

Following the A.T. north, climb .75 mile to the grassy summit of Cole Mountain (elevation 4,022 feet). Hike another .25 mile to the northern summit of Cole Mountain. All along the top of the mountain there are a number of interesting rocks jutting from the grass. From Cole Mountain, enjoy a tremendous panorama of the surrounding mountains including a view of the remainder of your hike. In the foreground to the northeast, you can see the grassy top of Tar Jacket Ridge. Farther away and a bit to the east, view the peaks of the Religious Range. The closest mountain is the

Cardinal, and in the distance, you can see Little Priest and The Priest, which you will cross at the end of the hike.

Descend Cole Mountain on the A.T., reach USFS 48 in Hog Camp Gap at mile 5.9, and in .5 mile, reach a highpoint along Tar Jacket Ridge (elevation 3,840 feet). Like Cole Mountain, the grassy ridge offers a noteworthy panoramic view. Continue north, descend Tar Jacket Ridge, and reach USFS 63 in Salt Log Gap at mile 8.1.

The trail climbs out of Salt Log Gap, crossing USFS 246 in 1.2 miles. Reach USFS 1176A, locally known as Greasy Spring Road, .5 mile beyond Salt Log Gap. Continue north on the A.T. and climb to Wolf Rocks Overlook in another .9 mile. Rocky Mountain is the peak to the southwest with antennas on top. To the northeast, view The Priest. After a short descent, the trail is evenly graded along sidehill until the .1-mile side trail to the Seeley-Woodworth Shelter at mile 13.3. Camping here breaks the hike up into two roughly equal sections. Water is available from a spring near the shelter.

After passing the side trail to the shelter, the trail passes through an open meadow with views of Spy Rock and The Priest during the 2.2 miles to Virginia 690 (locally known as Fish Hatchery Road). Climb, somewhat steeply, for .4 mile to the junction with the side trail leading .1 mile to Spy Rock. Spy Rock is the best viewpoint on this hike, and is well worth the short stroll; the dome-shaped Spy Rock offers a spectacular view of the entire Religious Range as well as other surrounding peaks.

In .25 mile, cross the summit of Maintop Mountain (elevation 4,040 feet). Descend Maintop for the next 2.2 miles, and reach the dirt Cash Hollow Road at mile 18.6. The trail climbs over an unnamed highpoint and descends to Virginia 826 (locally known as Crabtree Farm Road) in .75 mile. In .75 mile, during the climb up The Priest, reach the junction with an unblazed trail that leads 1.5 miles to Little Priest. Continue to follow the A.T. for .25 mile to reach The Priest Shelter. Water is available from a nearby spring. From the shelter, hike another .5 mile to the wooded summit of The Priest (elevation 4,063 feet). Descend The Priest on switchbacks, crossing Cripple Creek in 3 miles, and descend another 1.3 miles to Virginia 56, the end of the hike.

Trailhead Directions

The southern end of this hike is at US 60, which the A.T. crosses just over 8 miles east of Buena Vista, Virginia. The northern end of the hike is at the Tye River on Virginia 56. The trailhead is 11.3 miles east of the Blue Ridge Parkway and 1.4 miles west of Tyro, Virginia.

JAMES RIVER FACE WILDERNESS TRAVERSE

STRENUOUS
21.7 mile traverse

Nearly half of this hike is in the 8,093-acre James River Face Wilderness Area. Along the way, you will see a variety of geographic features and diverse plant life that make this hike outstanding. Be prepared for extreme changes in elevation as you descend 2,700 feet from Bluff Mountain to the James River, and again, as you ascend 2,500 feet to Highcock Knob.

The most outstanding feature on this hike is the water gap cut into the Central Blue Ridge by Virginia's longest waterway—the James River. Enjoy tremendous views of the water gap near the summit.

The Hike

From the unmarked parking area at Blue Ridge Parkway mile 51.7, hike south on the A.T. and begin climbing the northeast slope of Punchbowl Mountain. In .4 mile, reach the .25-mile side trail to Punchbowl Shelter. The shelter has an idyllic setting on the banks of a small pond. Water is available from a small spring nearby.

Continue hiking south on the A.T. for .5 mile to the tree-covered summit of Punchbowl Mountain (elevation 2,848 feet). Descend .25 mile to a gap and begin climbing Bluff Mountain. In .9 mile, reach the summit of Bluff Mountain (elevation 3,372 feet), and enjoy limited views from the spruce grove at the summit. Locate the unique plaque in memory of Little Ottie Cline Powell, also on the summit. Descend steeply on switchbacks, then more gradually, and in 1.5 miles, reach the junction with the blue-blazed Belle Cove Trail in Salt Log Gap at mile 3.5. The A.T. continues south along sidehill trail as it skirts Silas Knob, reaching the junction with the blue-blazed Saddle Gap Trail in 1.1 miles at Saddle Gap.

From Saddle Gap, the trail ascends to a highpoint on the ridge, Big Rocky Row (elevation 2,992 feet), in 1.4 miles. Don't miss the short side trail at mile 7 leading to Fullers Rocks, which offers a spectacular view of the James River water gap. In .25 mile, reach the junction with the blue-blazed Little Rocky Row Trail. Continue descending and reach Johns Hollow Shelter in 2 miles. Water is available from the creek. Although this shelter is only a mile or so short of being the halfway point of the hike, the best way to break this hike up into two sections is to camp at Matts Creek Shelter, 4.9 miles south.

Continue south for .6 mile and cross USFS 36/Virginia 812. Re-enter the woods, and cross USFS 36E twice in the next .75 mile. After the second crossing, hike .6 mile to US 501/Virginia 130 at mile 11. Turn left on the highway, follow the white blazes as you turn right at the fork, and cross the Snowden Bridge over the James River (elevation 660 feet). After crossing the bridge, continue following the highway for .1 mile and then re-enter the woods. Hike another .1 mile to a self-registration point for the James River Face Wilderness. You will be in the wilderness area for the next 10 miles.

The A.T. follows an old road for just over a mile during the climb up to Matts Creek Shelter. From the entrance to the wilderness area, hike .6 mile to a good spring along the trail. Water for the shelter is available from the creek, but you may want to pick up some from the spring. Either way, you will need to treat it. At mile 14, reach Matts Creek Shelter. The wooden footbridge that crosses the creek between the trail and the shelter is dedicated to Henry Lanum, a hiker who volunteered thousands of hours to maintain trails in this area. A staunch supporter of trails, Lanum died in 1991 on a trip to build a new trail in Idaho.

Continue following the A.T. south as it climbs up to Highcock Knob. Cross Big Cove Branch 1.9 miles past the shelter. This area, between Matts Creek Shelter and Marble Springs, shows signs of a recent infestation by the southern pine beetle, a native pest. The Forest Service predicts that the worst of this outbreak is over. In another 3.6 miles, reach Marble Spring Campsite (elevation 2,300 feet). The spring itself is on a .1-mile side trail. In the next mile, the trail climbs more than 700 feet to the wooded summit of Highcock Knob (elevation 3,073 feet) at mile 20.5. The A.T. descends .9 mile from the Knob to Petites Gap (USFS 35), the end of this hike.

Trailhead Directions
The northern end of this hike is at the small parking area on the Blue Ridge Parkway (milepost 51.7). The southern end of this section is at Petites Gap on USFS 35 just off the Blue Ridge Parkway (milepost 71.0). The nearest access to the Parkway at this point is US 501 on the James River (Parkway milepost 63.6).

CATAWBA VALLEY LOOP

MODERATE
28.7 mile loop

This hike encompasses a circuit of Catawba, Tinker, and North Mountains. From McAfee Knob and Tinker Ridge, the A.T. follows a series of sandstone outcroppings with wonderful views of the farms and orchards below in the Valley of Virginia, Roanoke Valley, and Catawba Valley. Catawba Mountain was created by the collision of continental plates more than a billion years ago.

The North Mountain Trail (former route of the A.T.) completes the loop around the Catawba Valley. Joining the A.T. at Scorched Earth Gap, the North Mountain Trail crosses the Catawba Valley, rolls up and down the wooded crest of North Mountain for 9 miles, and descends to Virginia 311 and 624, where it rejoins the A.T.

The Hike

From the parking area on the south side of Virginia 311, cross the highway (carefully because there is limited visibility for southbound traffic) and head north, soon passing beneath two utility lines. You will turn left here and begin to climb along switchbacks to the crest of the ridge.

Once reaching the crest of the ridge, you will bear right, climb along an old woods road for .1 mile, and follow the rocky crest of the ridge. You will soon descend, bear right again, and rejoin the woods road for a short distance before turning right once again at the bulletin board to the left of the trail.

Continue along the A.T., turn left, and parallel the crest of the ridge, with small ups and downs, for the next 1.5 miles. In the fall and winter, enjoy views to the right of Fort Lewis Mountain. At mile 1, pass the Boy Scout Shelter, which is a short distance off the trail to your right. The spring in front of the shelter is often dry in the summer.

At mile 1.9, turn right on an old woods road and begin to descend. Soon thereafter, you will reach the intersection with a blue-blazed trail that heads left to a spring. After crossing a stream, you will reach the junctions of a couple more blue-blazed trails that head right to the Catawba Mountain Shelter. The spring you just passed is the water source for the shelter.

From the shelter turn-off, hike .1 mile, turn left off the woods road, and begin to climb. A primitive campsite lies a short distance off the trail to your right. Within .25 mile, you will cross a road and pass through an area of thick laurel growth, and in another .25 mile, you will pass under powerlines. Shortly thereafter, turn right and begin your ascent up McAfee Knob. The outcroppings of rock to your left offer good winter views of the Catawba Valley, Gravelly Ridge, and North Mountain.

At mile 3.3, turn left onto an old road and continue to climb past large boulders. There are many trails criss-crossing this area so keep an eye out for the white blazes that mark the A.T. In another .25 mile, you will reach the side trail (in a small clearing at the end of the road) that heads left to the cliffs at McAfee Knob. The side trail is short, and the views of the Catawba and Roanoke Valleys from this overhanging rock ledge are not to be missed.

Back on the A.T., you will descend along rock steps to Devil's Kitchen, an area of large boulders. Once again, there are many trails criss-crossing the area so keep an eye out for the blazes. Soon descend along steep switchbacks to an old road, upon which you will continue your descent.

At mile 4.1, you will reach the Pig Farm Campsite equipped with picnic tables and a fire grate. Water for the site is available from a spring .1 mile away on a blue-blazed side trail. To your right are views of Roanoke Valley. Shortly after the campsite, you will turn left, leaving the old road and soon reaching the side trail that heads right to the Campbell Shelter. Water is available from the spring to the left, just before the shelter.

Continue along the A.T. for .75 mile to an old road to the left. Follow the road for .75 mile, then head left away from the road, and climb. At mile 5.9, you will pass between two boulders called Snack Bar Rock, and .25 mile later, pass Rock Haven, an overhanging outcropping. You will soon begin to climb along a rocky ridge that can be a bit treacherous in icy and wet conditions. Another rock outcropping at mile 6.5 affords splendid views to the left of McAfee Knob and to the right of Carvin Cove, Tinker Mountain, Peaks of Otter, and Apple Orchard Mountain.

In another .75 mile, you will leave the ridge and descend along an old road, reaching Brickey's Gap in a large, open field at mile 7.3. The blue-blazed trail here heads 1.7 miles to Lamberts Meadow and rejoins the A.T. in another 3.2 miles. The old road to the left will take you to Virginia 779. From the gap, descend steeply and reach the southern end of Tinker Cliffs in 1.3 miles. The last .5 mile along the cliffs offers excellent views of

Dragon's Tooth, McAfee Knob, North Mountain, and other mountains in the distance. This area is also treacherous in icy and wet conditions.

At mile 9.1, you will reach the end of the cliffs at The Well, a natural hole in the rocks, and at mile 9.2, you will reach Lunch Box Rock, which offers views of Purgatory Mountain and the Blue Ridge. Turn left and descend along switchbacks to Scorched Earth Gap (elevation 2,360 feet) at mile 9.6. Pick up the yellow-blazed North Mountain Trail, which heads left 2.3 miles to Virginia 779 and then continues for another 13.2 miles to rejoin the A.T. at Virginia 624.

Descend steeply on the North Mountain Trail into the Catawba Valley, crossing an intermittent stream just below a huge rock tooth within .25 mile. In another .1 mile, pass an old homesite to your left (the chimney is still standing) and continue to descend to the left of the stream for the next .75 mile. In .25 mile, you will pass to the left of a logged area, cross a stream, and continue to descend along it.

In another .1 mile, you will cross the stream again, descend along a dirt road for .25 mile, head right along a dirt road, and cross the stream for the third time. Then pass an open area to your left, the site of a sawmill, and pass the remains of an old log cabin.

At mile 10.7, you will cross a fence on a stile and continue to descend through the woods, emerging into the valley in another .25 mile. After another .1 mile, you will cross a log bridge with handrails over the twenty-foot-wide Catawba Creek. (If recent high water has washed out the log, follow the creek downstream (right) to the edge of the pasture.)

At mile 11.2, cross another fence on a stile next to a big, double-trunked sycamore. Turn left here and follow the fence through the pasture, crossing Little Catawba Creek in .1 mile. After passing through a wooden gate (or cross fence on platform stile), you will begin to climb uphill through woods. In another .25 mile, you will descend a short distance through an open area before heading right, uphill again.

At mile 11.7, you will reach the top of the hill and begin to descend to Virginia 779. After crossing this road, you will climb along an old logging road before entering a dense stand of hardwoods .5 mile later. In .25 mile, you will climb up rock steps (with a small stream at their base) before ascending steeply up a rough and rocky footpath. In another .6 mile, you will turn left and follow the crest of North Mountain for the next 9 miles, alternately ascending and descending. A side trail here heads 4.5 miles to Stone Coal Gap.

You will reach a side trail at mile 14.9 that descends a short distance (steep!) to an intermittent spring. In another .75 mile, descend a short distance down natural rock steps, and continue to a sag where you will intersect the Turkey Trail. The Turkey trail heads right 1.5 miles to USFS 224, but is often blocked by undergrowth.

At mile 18.9, you will reach another sag and the intersection of the Grouse Trail, which heads right about a mile to USFS 224. One mile later, in another gap, reach the Deer Trail, which heads right 1 mile to USFS 224. This trail is also often obscured by undergrowth. In another 1.2 miles, you will pass a small rock outcropping that affords views to the right of Sinking Creek Mountain and Craig Creek Valley, and to the left of Cove Mountain.

Just over .25 mile later, descend from the northern end of North Mountain, and pass a rock outcropping with limited views in .1 mile. After crossing the sloping summit, you will continue to descend along switchbacks. Reach Virginia 311 at mile 22.3 (elevation 1,780 feet), and pass through the narrow gap between North and Cove Mountains. Turn left onto Virginia 311, passing a gas station and grocery store on your right in .1 mile.

Turn right onto Virginia 624 after another .1 mile, reaching the intersection with the A.T. at mile 22.8. The A.T. (for your purposes) heads left and crosses a stream on a culverted driveway. Begin climbing to the left, then turn sharply to the right, following switchbacks for the next .4 mile. After awhile, you will turn left, crossing a stile near the top of Sandstone Ridge, and begin to descend through an overgrown pasture. In .1 mile, you will cross a barely recognizable old road and enter a wooded area before following another woods road to your right. In .1 mile, you will rejoin and follow the woods road, descending through pines.

At mile 23.7, you will cross a bridge over a stream, then follow the stream, left, downhill, and pass the remains of an old dam in another .25 mile. Climb the bank of the stream to the right, leave the road, and pass through another pasture, where you'll have views of Sawtooth Ridge to your left. You will then climb .1 mile before descending to the right of a small sinkhole. Reach the top of an open hill with a blazed post in another .1 mile, and a short distance later, pass the fence corner and descend along an electric fence.

You will reach an intermittently wet area at mile 24.3; turn left below it and follow an intermittent stream to Virginia 785. Cross a stile, then Virginia 785, and another stile, before climbing to the left of a hilltop.

Descend to the floodplain of Catawba Creek, cross the creek on a bridge, turn left, and cross a stile a short distance later.

Within .25 mile, cross another stile, and a short distance later, an intermittent stream (on a bridge). From here, you can see Beckner Gap to your right. You will soon leave this open area and begin to climb. Look to the rear for views of Cove Mountain and Dragon's Tooth. In .1 mile, turn right and climb five switchbacks and four sets of log steps in the next .25 mile.

After crossing another stile, you will reach outcroppings of rock in .25 mile as you reach the crest of Sawtooth Ridge. A rolling walk (ups and downs) for the next 2.9 miles takes you along the knolls that give the ridge its name. As you traverse the ridge, Fort Lewis Mountain is to your right, Cove Mountain and North Mountain to your left. You will reach the end of Sawtooth Ridge at mile 28.3. From here, hike .4 mile, descending to Virginia 311 and the parking area, the end of this loop hike!

Trailhead Directions
Virginia 311 can be reached from Interstate 81 near Roanoke-Salem. The trail crossing is 8 miles north of Salem and 12 miles north of downtown Roanoke.

PETERS MOUNTAIN

MODERATE
18.8 mile traverse

This hike features a walk along Peters Mountain, which straddles two states—Virginia and West Virginia. The A.T. skirts the Virginia/West Virginia border as it traverses the crest of Peters Mountain for more than 12 miles. Symms Gap Meadow and Rice Field afford excellent views of the Appalachians to the east and of West Virginia to the west. Symms Gap Meadow, a cleared area at the site of an old orchard, offers especially good views of West Virginia near the mid-point of the hike. The extensive pastureland of Rice Field also affords views of West Virginia, and it is made especially memorable by the numerous rock outcroppings that dot the area. Rice Field is at the southern end of the hike.

Note: Water is scarce along the crest so make sure you carry enough to get you through the night if you plan to camp on the ridge.

The Hike

From the small (two-car) parking area on Virginia 635 near the bridge over Stony Creek, take the A.T. north, heading right, uphill along an old woods road. Hike .4 mile to the only shelter in the section—Pine Swamp Branch Shelter (elevation 2,530 feet) to your left. The right fork in the trail leads to an "iffy" water source. Make sure you treat the water before using it. Continue ahead on the A.T., switchback at an old road bed, and climb more steeply along a stream.

In another .4 mile, the A.T. heads right across a rock and gravel path, and climbs the ridge of Peters Mountain along switchbacks. One mile later, the trail levels and descends into the sag of Pine Swamp, which features a pretty hemlock grove. At mile 2.1, reach the junction with the yellow-blazed Allegheny Trail to the right. You will reach the crest of Peters Mountain (elevation 3,740 feet) in .1 mile. The trail turns southwest and passes to the west of a 3,956-foot knob.

The trail tops the crest of the ridge again at mile 3.9 and descends toward Dickinson Gap. Locate a stone marker to your right as you pass through Dickinson Gap .4 mile later. A blue-blazed trail heads left 1.4 miles to Virginia 635, 7.4 miles north of U.S. 460. Continue along the crest of the ridge, rollercoastering over knobs.

At mile 5.2, reach the junction of the blue-blazed Groundhog Trail to the right, which heads 2 miles northwest to West Virginia 219/24. Reach Symms Gap Meadow at mile 6.8. Climb along a grassy path and enjoy views to your right of the rolling woodland, pastures, and high ridges of West Virginia. After passing through the meadow, you will follow the wooded crest of the ridge along old roads for the next 4.2 miles.

You will reach an access road for a powerline cut-through at mile 11; turn right. Shortly thereafter, you will reach the cut-through, where there are views to the south of Pearis Mountain. You will pass a television antenna on your right .5 mile later before beginning your descent to Rice Field. At mile 12.9, you will pass through another powerline cut-through; at mile 13.2, a pipeline right-of-way; and at mile 13.4, another pipeline right-of-way.

Turn left at mile 14.7 and descend along the eastern edge of Peters Mountain, passing two intermittent springs, and reach an open, level area suitable for camping in .1 mile. Follow a rocky trail for 1 mile, turn right, and shortly thereafter, turn left across a stream. Just past the stream, you will turn right, head downhill, and soon turn onto an old woods road for .25 mile.

At mile 16.1, you will turn off the woods road and begin to climb over knobs along the spur of the mountain. In .1 mile, you will descend steeply via switchbacks from the knobs, and .25 mile later, turn right off the spur. Head left downhill when you reach a fork, and join a dirt access road.

You will join another access road at mile 16.6, and shortly thereafter, turn off the road and cross another powerline cut-through. In .1 mile, you will cross a tributary of Stillhouse Branch, which you cross several more times as you continue to descend off Peters Mountain. At mile 17, turn left onto another access road, and a short distance later, cross Stillhouse Branch Road (Virginia 641). After crossing Stillhouse Branch for the last time, climb the high bank beyond it, and turn right at the top of the bank.

In another .25 mile, you will head right off the spur; and descend steeply into a gully and cross gullies and small spurs continuously for the next .4 mile. At mile 17.6, you will cross a small creek (with sulfurous and unsafe water) and climb up another spur. From this spur, turn left, descend, cross a .25-mile series of spurs and gullies, and descend again by switchbacks.

At mile 18.1, you will cross a dirt road, turn right, and climb another spur. Turn right again and gradually descend to a gravel road. Turn right onto a paved road, and shortly thereafter, cross all four lanes of US 460. Follow this highway to the left and cross the New River on the Senator Shumate Bridge, the end of this hike.

Note: Damage caused by Hurricane Hugo in 1989 has left portions of the trail at the southern end of this hike in a rough and broken state. Major relocations for this section of the Appalachian Trail are in the planning stages. Keep an eye out for the white blazes and signs posted on the relocations if the balzes differ from this description, follow the blazes.

Trailhead Directions
The trailhead at the northern end of the section is on Virginia 635, 9 miles northeast of US 460 at an intersection about 5 miles east of Pearisburg. The intersection is marked with a sign indicating the way to White Rocks USFS Recreation Area.

At the southern end, parking is available in the commercial lot across US 460 from the trail. Ask permission from the grocery store before you leave a car. The hike ends on the eastern side of the Senator Shumate Bridge where US 460 crosses the New River near the Hoescht Celanese Plant.

GARDEN MOUNTAIN TRAVERSE

MODERATE
17.1 mile traverse

Virginia 623, where you begin this hike, is the only paved road into this National and Virginia Rural Historical District. For the first 5 miles, you will follow the crest of Garden Mountain on the south side of Burkes Garden. Consisting of more than 20,000 acres, the Garden is an oval-shaped bowl that looks like a volcanic crater. It was actually formed by water eroding the underlying limestone rock.

From Chestnut Knob, which you cross at the southwest corner of the bowl, there is a commanding view of Burkes Garden and the surrounding countryside. Perhaps the best view on the mountain is from the three-sided privy for Chestnut Knob Shelter, a stone cabin on the summit. After descending Chestnut Ridge, you will cross over several ridges and drop into a few hollows on your way to Rich Valley.

The Hike
From the parking area on Virginia 623 on top of Garden Mountain (elevation 3,900 feet), hike south on the A.T. for .25 mile to a highpoint on the ridge. For the next 3.5 miles, follow the edge of a cliff that rises more than fifty feet above Burkes Garden. Enjoy occasional views into Burkes Garden in the summer (although the best views are after the leaves have fallen for the winter). This section of the trail is often rough and rocky with several short climbs and descents along the ridgeline.

At mile 4.9, reach Walker Gap (elevation 3,460 feet) where a small gravel road leads down into the community of Burkes Garden, Virginia. Water is available from a good spring a short distance to the left, down a blue-blazed side trail.

From Walker Gap, climb 1.3 miles up to Chestnut Knob (elevation 4,409 feet). Chestnut Knob Shelter is the stone cabin on the summit. Enjoy outstanding views from the open summit of the knob. Descend the knob on a broad path. In .25 mile, re-enter the woods on a woods road, and in .5 mile, emerge from the woods along the treeless spine of Chestnut Ridge. At mile 8, you will see a spring-fed pond to the right of the trail.

Follow the white blazes carefully as you descend Chestnut Ridge. The trail follows and crosses several old logging roads. Be sure to follow the well-marked trail instead of the equally well-worn roads. At mile 10.8, cross USFS 222/Virginia 625. After crossing the road, the trail follows an old railroad grade for about .25 mile. Climb over an unnamed highpoint and cross Lick Creek on a bridge at mile 12.1.

Beyond the creek, the trail follows an old road bed for .25 mile, and climbs up rocky Lynn Camp Mountain on switchbacks. In another .9 mile, reach a wooded highpoint on the mountain (elevation 3,000 feet) at mile 13.3. Descend more gradually on the southern slope of the mountain, cross USFS 632 in another .9 mile, and immediately cross Lynn Camp Creek on a footbridge. There are three more creek crossings in the next .75 mile. The third crossing is the closest available water for Knot Maul Branch Shelter, which is .25 mile further at mile 15.2.

Beyond the shelter, the trail continues climbing for 1 mile to a highpoint on Brushy Mountain (elevation 3,000 feet), and then descends gradually for .9 mile, often on switchbacks, to Virginia 42, the end of this hike.

Trailhead Directions
To get to the northern trailhead, turn left off of Virginia 42 onto Virginia 623 and drive about 10.5 miles west of Interstate 77. Then drive just over 10 miles up to the crest of Garden Mountain and the trailhead, where parking is available. Some vandalism has been reported at this parking lot.

The southern trailhead is on Virginia 42, 18.4 miles west of I-77. Parking is available at the O'Lystery Community Picnic Area, which the trail passes through.

VIRGINIA HIGHLANDS TRAVERSE

STRENUOUS
23.8 mile traverse

Mountain peaks and high meadows are the highlights of this traverse on the "rooftop of Virginia." By taking a 1-mile side trip to the fir and spruce-covered summit of Mount Rogers, you can hike to the top of Virginia's three highest points on this trip (Rogers, Whitetop, and Pine Mountains). The mountain was known as Balsam Mountain until 1883, when it was named for William Barton Rogers (1804-1882). Rogers was Virginia's first state geologist. Mount Rogers' summit is covered with red spruce and the northernmost stand of fraser fir. There are no views from the wooded peak.

The open fields at Grayson Highlands, Wilburn Ridge, Rhododendron Gap, Pine Mountain, and Buzzard Rocks offer many sweeping panoramas that are without peer in the southeast United States.

This popular area attracts many hikers, particularly in mid-June to the first week in July, when the hundreds of acres of rhododendron along the trail burst into bloom. The awesome spectacle of the vast fields in bloom is a must-see event. These same meadows are filled with ripe blueberries in late August, but fewer hikers attend that event.

Three miles of this hike pass through Grayson Highlands State Park, where ponies roam free along the trail. The ponies aren't actually wild. They are herded together every fall; some of these horses are sold at auction during a fall festival in the park during the last weekend in September. Although the ponies may approach you, it is best that you neither approach nor attempt to ride them.

This traverse is crossed many times by other trails that form a number of possible loop hikes for both hikers and horseback riders. Be careful and follow the white-blazed A.T. at all times. In the high meadows, the trail is marked with blazes on fence posts.

Much of this hike is over 4,000 feet in elevation, and the temperature can be cool even in the summer. Be prepared for extremes in weather, particularly as you hike or camp in open areas.

The Hike
From the trailhead on Virginia 603, hike south and enter the woods, and begin climbing along the northern slope of Pine Mountain. In .25 mile, you will enter the Lewis Fork Wilderness Area. At mile .9, cross the Old Orchard Horse Trail, and at mile 1.6, cross the Lewis Fork Horse Trail. In another .1 mile, reach Old Orchard Shelter. Water is available from a nearby piped spring.

Beyond the shelter, the trail continues to climb Pine Mountain. In .5 mile, leave the wilderness area. At mile 3.4, reach the highpoint on the open crest of Pine Mountain (elevation 4,900 feet), where a blue-blazed trail leads off to the right. Enjoy the magnificent views here.

Descend gradually from Pine Mountain to a rail-fenced corral known as "The Scales" at mile 4.8. The name comes from this spot's historical use as a weighing and loading station for cattle. Cross the fences on stiles and begin climbing the northwest slope of Stone Mountain. In .25 mile, reach the open summit of Stone Mountain (elevation 4,800 feet).

Descend .9 mile to a fence and reach the junction with the Bear Pen Horse Trail at the entrance to the Little Wilson Creek Wilderness Area, which the trail passes through for the next 1.2 miles. In .4 mile, pass a spring on the left side of the trail.

At mile 7.3, cross the East Fork of Big Wilson Creek on a bridge. At mile 7.5, cross Little Wilson Creek on a bridge, then a stile as you enter Grayson Highlands State Park. Campfires are not permitted in the park. This section of the trail crosses a meadow on the way to Wilburn Ridge where ponies are often seen roaming free. In another mile, cross a stile over a fence and then cross Quebec Branch. In 1.3 miles, reach the junction with the blue-blazed Rhododendron Trail. Hike .25 mile beyond this trail junction to the rail fence marking the boundary of Grayson Highlands State Park. Cross a stile and enter Jefferson National Forest. In .25 mile, reach the junction with an unnamed blue-blazed trail leading straight across Wilburn Ridge (mile 10.5).

Continue following the A.T., and at mile 11.9, reach Rhododendron Gap (elevation 5,440 feet) at the heart of hundreds of acres of rhododendrons. Two blue-blazed trails intersect the A.T. in the Gap. Follow the white blazes and cross two fences on stiles in the next .9 mile. The second fence marks the boundary of the Lewis Fork Wilderness Area, which the trail enters for a second time. The A.T. passes through the wilderness area for the next 3.5 miles.

At mile 13, reach Thomas Knob Shelter. Water is available from a nearby spring. Beyond the shelter, hike .1 mile to the junction with the .5-mile side trail that leads to the summit of Mount Rogers (elevation 5,729 feet), Virginia's highest peak.

The trail skirts around Mount Rogers, about 400 feet from the summit. In 1 mile, cross a fence on a stile, and in another .75 mile, reach the junction with the blue-blazed Elk Garden Trail and the Virginia Highlands Horse Trail. At mile 15.1, reach the former site of Deep Gap Shelter, which is still on many maps. The shelter is now on display in a park in Damascus, Virginia. In 1.2 miles, cross a fence that marks the wilderness area boundary, and in .5 mile, cross Virginia 600, where there is a small parking area. There is also a junction with the Virginia Highlands Horse Trail. Climb along the east slope of Whitetop Mountain.

At mile 19.3, reach the gravel Whitetop Mountain Road, and follow the road briefly. If you would like to make a side trip to the summit of White-top (elevation 5,520 feet), continue on the gravel road when the A.T. turns left off of it. It is about .25 mile to the top.

Leave Whitetop Mountain Road, and cross a high meadow on the way to Buzzard Rocks at mile 20.1, which offer a commanding view of the valley below. Descend from Buzzard Rocks steeply, often over switchbacks, and cross the gravel Virginia 601 at mile 22.6. Continue, with a few small uphill sections, on this mostly downhill hike to US 58. Reach the highway .4 mile south of Summit Cut, the end of this hike.

Trailhead Directions

The northern trailhead is a parking area on Virginia 603 about 4 miles west of Troutdale, Virginia. The southern trailhead is on US 58, .4 mile east of Summit Cut, and 14 miles east of Damascus, Virginia.

MOUNT ROGERS LOOP

MODERATE
18.3 mile loop

This loop hike covers some of the most varied terrain in the Southern Appalachians—fields and forests, open meadows covered with rhodo-dendron and blueberries, and spruce and fir atop Mount Rogers. Mount Rogers, whose summit is visited via a side trail on this loop, is the highest point in Virginia (elevation 5,729 feet). Mount Rogers boasts the northern-most natural stand of Fraser fir. An annual rainfall average of sixty inches and average snowfall of fifty-seven inches is not unusual. Snow can still be seen atop the summit as late as March. In addition to Mount Rogers, this hike features Pine Mountain (elevation 5,050 feet), a high plateau of open meadows dotted with trees, rock outcroppings, rhododendron, and aza-leas.

The Hike

From the parking area at Virginia 603 (elevation 3,480 feet), head south along the A.T. into the woods. In .25 mile, cross a log footbridge over a stream and climb the forested slope of Pine Mountain, where you will enter the Lewis Fork Wilderness Area. At mile .9, you will cross the Old

Orchard Horse Trail, and .75 mile later, the Lewis Fork Horse Trail (as you enter an old orchard). Within .1 mile, you will reach the Old Orchard Shelter and a good view of Iron Mountain. Water is available from the spring a short distance to right in the woods.

Continue climbing along switchbacks and leave the Lewis Fork Wilderness Area. At mile 3.4, reach the crest of Pine Mountain (elevation 5,000 feet) at the edge of a meadow dotted with trees. Pick up the Rhododendron Gap Trail (former A.T. route), and hike 2.1 miles to Rhododendron Gap, where you will pick up the A.T. again.

At Rhododendron Gap (elevation 5,440 feet), you will also reach the junction of the Wilburn Ridge Trail, which follows the cliffs along the ridge back toward the A.T. and The Scales on Stone Mountain. The gap also offers a high rock cliff (right) with outstanding views.

Follow the A.T. left and continue south through rhododendron and blueberries. At mile 5.9, cross a stile and enter the Lewis Fork Wilderness Area again. In .25 mile, turn left and descend around the summit of Mount Rogers. A blue-blazed side trail leads .5 mile to the summit of Mount Rogers (elevation 5,729 feet), the highest point in Virginia. Pass the new (in 1991) Thomas Knob Shelter .1 mile before you reach the side trail to the summit. Water is available from a spring a short distance behind the shelter.

In .25 mile, enter the woods again, cross several small streams (the headwaters of Helton Creek), and turn right at mile 7.7 at a fence on the edge of a field where there are good views. In another .75 mile, cross the Virginia Highlands Horse Trail, and reach the junction with the Elk Garden-Mount Rogers National Recreation Trail. Follow this blue-blazed trail 4 miles down to the USFS Grindstone Campground at Virginia 603. After crossing 603, continue climbing, using the blue-blazed Elk Garden-

Mount Rogers Trail, until you reach Cherry Tree Shelter and the yellow-blazed Iron Mountain Trail. Water is available from a spring just in front of the shelter.

Cross the dirt road behind the shelter, pass a toilet, and continue along a woodland trail for.25 mile to the junction of a dirt road. Turn right on the dirt road, descend, and in .1 mile, turn left off the road. Climb .5 mile to the crest of Flat Top Mountain (elevation 4,451 feet), and then descend 1 mile to the junction of the Iron Mountain Trail with the A.T. at Chestnut Flats (elevation 4,200 feet).

From Chestnut Flats, follow the A.T. south, reaching the crest of Iron Mountain (elevation 4,320 feet) in .25 mile. Descend 1.9 miles to Fox Creek, cross the creek on a log footbridge, and in .1 mile, reach the parking area at Virginia 603, the end of this hike.

Trailhead Directions
The trailhead can be reached at the parking area where the A.T. crosses Virginia 603, 4 miles west of Troutdale and 8 miles east of US 58 at Konnarock.

TENNESSEE
NORTH CAROLINA

TENNESSEE/NORTH CAROLINA

Because so many miles of the A.T. traverse the Tennessee/North Carolina border, these two states are usually placed together in trail guides. Combined, the two states offer more than 370 miles of trail. Heading south, the trail begins in Tennessee (heading north, it begins in North Carolina).

For the first 37 miles, the trail traverses the ridgeline as it makes its way to Wautaga Lake near Hampton, Tennessee. From Hampton, the trail heads through Laurel Fork Gorge, where there are spectacular waterfalls, and continues up White Rocks Mountain before it descends to Elk Park, North Carolina.

From Elk Park, a strenuous climb up to the Hump Mountains brings you to Grassy Ridge (a 6,000-foot grassy bald), Roan Highlands, Roan High Knob, and Roan High Bluff. Roan High Bluff, over 6,000 feet high, is known for its spectacular rhododendron gardens that bloom profusely each June. From Roan, the trail continues along the Tennessee/North Carolina border for nearly 100 miles as it makes its way to Hot Springs, North Carolina, and heads into the Great Smoky Mountains National Park. In this section, the trail passes Little Rock Knob, Unaka Mountain, and Beauty Spot. It descends to Erwin, Tennessee, and then to Hot Springs.

From Hot Springs, it is just over 30 miles to Davenport Gap, the northern entrance of the A.T. into the Smoky Mountains. In the Smokies, the trail traverses Mount Cammerer, the Sawteeth, and Charlies Bunion, reaches Newfound Gap, and proceeds to Clingmans Dome, the highest point on the entire A.T. (elevation 6,643 feet).

The A.T. continues across Silers Bald to Thunderhead and Rocky Top, heads down to grassy Spence and Russell Fields, continues to Shuckstack, before descending to Fontana Dam at the Little Tennessee River, the southern boundary of the Great Smoky Mountains National Park.

From the Smokies, the A.T. ascends into the Nantahalas with its 4,000- and 5,000-foot peaks. The area between Fontana and Wesser is said to be one of the toughest sections on the A.T. From the Nantahala Outdoor Center at Wesser, the A.T. climbs up to Wesser Bald, Wayah Bald, and Silers Bald, then heads up to the ridge along Standing Indian Mountain. Albert Mountain is also a notable climb in this section. From Albert, it is not far to the North Carolina/Georgia border at Bly Gap.

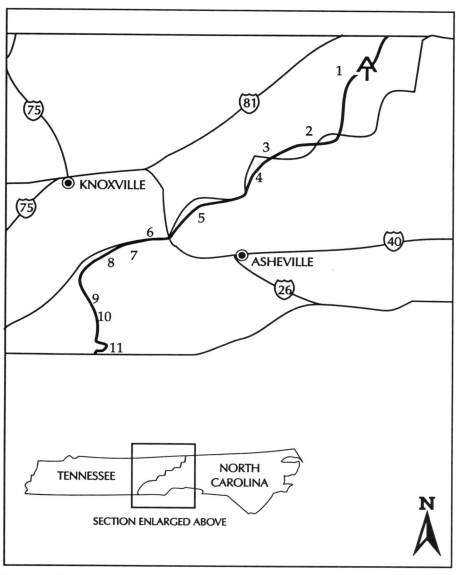

1. Iron Mountain
2. Roan Mountain
3. Bald Mountains
4. State Line Trail
5. Max Patch/Hot Springs
6. Mount Cammerer Loop
7. Mount Collins/ Clingmans Dome
8. Russell Field/Spence Field/ Rocky Top Loop
9. Northern Nantahalas
10. Wayah Bald/Siler Bald
11. Standing Indian Loop

IRON MOUNTAIN TRAVERSE

EASY
19.1 mile traverse

This traverse follows the narrow ridgeline of Iron Mountain, passing through nearly 6 miles of the Big Laurel Branch Wilderness Area. The trail offers many fine views of Watauga Lake, which is located just below the steep southern slope of Iron mountain.

On this hike, you will also pass a monument to Nick Grindstaff (1851-1923). He was a local hermit who, as noted on his monument, "lived alone, suffered alone, died alone." The marker is made from the remains of the chimney to his cabin.

The last part of this hike can often be overgrown by midsummer. The volunteer trail maintainers have difficulty keeping up with the quick-growing weeds. Iron Mountain is particularly nice when the leaves have fallen in preparation for winter because it offers many more views. Although rated as easy, remember that no 20-mile hike on the A.T. is without significant climbs and descents.

The Hike
From the trailhead on Tennessee 91, hike south and begin a moderate ascent. Cross a logging road at mile .4. The trail in this section crosses a couple of wet areas on bog bridges. Continue to ascend Iron Mountain steadily, reaching a highpoint at mile 2.7.

At mile 3.2, locate the Nick Grindstaff Monument. It is the stone chimney a short distance to your right. The inscription does not face the trail. In another 1.3 miles, reach Iron Mountain Shelter. Water is available from a small stream about .25 mile beyond the shelter. Reach another highpoint on the ridge about .5 mile beyond the shelter.

At mile 5.2, cross under powerlines in a utility right-of-way, and enjoy year-round views. In .4 mile, cross over another highpoint on the ridge, and in another .25 mile, reach the junction with an unnamed blue-blazed trail. Continue following the A.T. and reach Turkeypen Gap at mile 6.2. For the next mile, there are several unblazed trails leading off the ridge. Continue following the white blazes across the ridgetop. At mile 8.2, reach the junction with the Horselog Ridge Trail, and at mile 9.9, enter the Big Laurel

Branch Wilderness Area. The remainder of the hike is in this wilderness area.

Reach Vandeventer Shelter at mile 11.2. Water is available from a spring located down a blue-blazed trail, which branches off the A.T. a short distance beyond the shelter. The blue-blazed trail leads .5 mile down the mountain to a spring, so it is a good idea to bring water with you to the shelter, if possible. Behind the shelter, a rock outcrop offers a particularly good view of Watauga Lake.

About 1.5 miles past the shelter, the trail begins its descent from Iron Mountain. It is a steady descent from here to the lake. At mile 12.8, pass the junction with the blue-blazed Iron Mountain Trail on your right, and at mile 15.6, reach Watauga Dam Road.

Climb the stone steps, re-enter the woods, and ascend to a highpoint at mile 15.9. Then descend sharply for .25 mile to join the access road that leads to the dam. Follow the road as it descends to and crosses Watauga Lake Dam. At mile 16.9, re-enter the woods, and in .6 mile, reach the short blue-blazed side trail to Watauga Lake Shelter. Water is available from the creek that the trail crosses on the way to the shelter.

At mile 18.8, cross a gravel road leading to the lake, and in another .25 mile, cross a stream and another access road. At mile 19.1, reach the USFS Shook Branch Recreation Area, the end of this hike.

Trailhead Directions
Locate the northern trailhead on Tennessee 91, 19 miles north of Elizabethton, Tennessee, and 4 miles south of US 421 in Shady Valley, Tennessee. Locate the southern trailhead at the USFS Shook Branch Recreation Area on US 321, about 3 miles east of Hampton, Tennessee.

ROAN MOUNTAIN TRAVERSE

STRENUOUS
23.5 mile traverse

This hike features a walk along the crest of the Iron Mountains. The A.T. winds its way over knolls and balds from Indian Grave Gap to the spectacular summit of Roan Mountain. Unaka Bald (elevation 5,180 feet) and Little Rock Knob (elevation 4,919 feet) are also notable features on this overnight hike.

If this hike is taken in mid to late June, the highlight of this hike will be the Cloudland rhododendron gardens atop Roan Mountain. Every year, the beautiful Catawba rhododendron burst into bloom, carpeting the mountain with their purple flowers. Don't be surprised, though, to find the mountain socked in with fog. The elevation of Roan—6,285 feet at Roan High Knob—means the summit is often capped by clouds. Fraser fir and red spruce also abound atop Roan.

The hike ends at Carvers Gap, opposite Grassy Ridge, the only 6,000-plus-foot bald on the A.T.

The Hike

From Indian Grave Gap (elevation 3,360 feet), enter the woods on the north side of the road. In .75 mile, you will reach a powerline cut-through and then join an abandoned road. As you continue, other abandoned roads will cross the trail.

Nearly .5 mile later, cross the gravel USFS 230 and begin to climb along the right side of the ridge. Reach the crest of the ridge in .1 mile, turn left, and continue to climb. At about mile 2, enter an open field, continue along a road track, and turn right. You will soon head left around a knoll and follow the A.T. through a sag.

Almost .5 mile later, you will reach the summit of Beauty Spot (elevation 4,437 feet). This grassy bald has great views of Roan Mountain to the east, the Black Mountains to the south, Big Bald and the Flattop Mountains to the southwest, and the Toe River Valley below. You might also catch several glimpses of the Nolichucky River to the south and west.

The A.T. continues along an old road track then leaves the field and road, entering the woods. In .25 mile, you will reach Beauty Spot Gap (elevation 4,300 feet) at a gate in a fence where USFS 230 enters from the left. The blue-blazed trail leads a short distance through the gate and across the road to a spring. There is a good campsite on a small knoll to the east. Continue to the right on the A.T., keeping to the left of the fence. A short distance from the end of the fence, head straight downhill a short ways, then head left and continue to descend.

Hike .1 mile to where the trail levels out and turns left, then cross a small bog in .25 mile. A side trail, just before the bog, leads a short distance to a spring and campsite, and further to USFS 230. Climb along the ridge, cross an old woods road, and enter the woods again. In .5 mile, you will see a field to your right and a road to your left. Head away from the road and soon cross a small summit.

Reach Deep Gap (elevation 4,100 feet) at mile 3.8. There is a good campsite in the meadow to your left. Just across the road, an old, graded trail leads to a spring boxed with concrete. A trail at the western end of the gap heads right 1.2 miles to Upper Poplar. When the road heads left to skirt left of the summit of Unaka Mountain, leave the road and begin to climb the ridge toward the summit of Unaka.

In .5 mile, at a switchback on the crest, USFS 230 is only a few feet to the left. Continue up the trail along switchbacks. In another .25 mile, you will reach the crest and continue to climb gradually through the woods, crossing a quartzite ledge as you reach the broad summit area.

Reach the benchmark on the summit of Unaka Mountain (elevation 5,180 feet) at mile 5.4. From this evergreen woods with its rare stand of red spruce, descend to hardwoods, then steeply off the mountain. You will pass a spring and continue your steep descent. Hike 1.5 miles to a trail junction (the trail is unmarked but leads about .5 mile to USFS 230; it is also the former route of the A.T.). Turn sharply to the right on the A.T., and skirt the to the left of the ridge.

At Low Gap (elevation 3,900 feet), just over .25 mile later, a poorly defined side trail leads a short distance to a spring (just to the right of the trail at the base of a hemlock tree). The A.T. follows the Tennessee/North Carolina border for the next 4 miles. The trail continues from Low Gap, climbing to the east.

Reach Cherry Gap Shelter at mile 8.1. Water is available from a good piped spring on a blue-blazed trail. From the shelter, continue along the ridgecrest for nearly .5 mile to Cherry Gap (elevation 3,900 feet). A woods road passes through the gap heading left to USFS 230 and right to Pigeonroost, North Carolina. The trail climbs out of the gap, and in .25 mile, skirts the southern slope of Piney Bald. The open summit affords good views. To reach the summit, you must bushwhack through the woods.

Continue along the A.T., head right into a narrow gap within .25 mile, and climb steeply up the ridge. In just over .25 mile, cross the left shoulder of a small knob, turn left, and descend through the woods. The A.T. then mostly follows the ridgecrest with gentle ups and downs. At mile 9.6, you will reach the summit of Little Bald Knob (elevation 4,459 feet).

From the summit, descend the ridge with a fence to your left. At the edge of the woods, you should be able to see Roan Mountain. In .25 mile, cross an old logging road, pass to the left of a big rock outcropping, descend steeply, and cross a graded trail. Hike .1 mile to a sag where underbrush may slightly obscure the trail. Begin to climb again, closing in on the fence to your right. You will then head right, away from the ridgecrest, and descend along the footpath.

Reach an old woods road in .25 mile, and turn left onto a gravel road in another .25 mile. The A.T. follows the gravel road for a short distance and returns to the woods, heading along the right side of the ridgeline. The gravel road parallels the trail, above, on the crest. At mile 10.8, reach Iron Mountain Gap (elevation 3,723 feet) at Tennessee 107/North Carolina 226. A grocery store with limited supplies for hikers is .5 mile to your right.

From here, the A.T. passes through a gate and climbs along a gravel road, along the left side of the ridgecrest, for the next 1.5 miles. In nearly .5 mile, a fence and tree farm border the road to the left. There are good views here back toward Unaka Mountain. In another .5 mile, the woods on your right end just below the summit, and afford spectacular views of Unaka to the west, Roan to the southeast, and Little Rock Knob to the east. Leave the crest and head downhill along the road.

Soon, an old track will come in from the right; keep to the left and continue to descend along the road. At mile 12, enter an old orchard, continuing along the road, and pass through a slight saddle, skirting the right side of a knoll. Take care to note when the A.T. turns off the road. While the road continues ahead, descending the Tennessee side of the mountain, the A.T. heads east through the woods, turning right and descending into a weedy gap.

After the gap, enter the woods, begin to climb again, and shortly thereafter, turn left uphill. A blue-blazed side trail descends steeply to the right for .1 mile to a stream. In .25 mile, reach the crest of the ridge, which the trail follows for the next 2 miles. Continue to climb beside a fence and enjoy occasional views to your left. In just under .5 mile, top the first major summit of the ridge, and .25 mile later, reach the second summit (elevation 4,426 feet). From here, continue along the ridgetop and soon pass an overhanging rock (good shelter in inclement weather).

Hike another 1.25 mile to the summit of a knob (elevation 4,332 feet), and then head left. Descend along the inside edge of the woods with a wire fence and field to your right. From the field, view Roan High Bluff and Grassy Ridge to the south and southeast. In just over .25 mile, reach the corner of the old field and begin to descend gradually along the ridgecrest. At mile 14.6, reach a blue-blazed side trail that descends steeply to a spring and campsite. The side trail continues past the campsite and joins the A.T. again at Greasy Creek Gap.

The A.T. reaches Greasy Creek Gap (elevation 4,034 feet) in another .25 mile. To the right, a dirt road descends to Buladean, North Carolina, and to the left, 2.5 miles to Tiger Creek. From the gap, the A.T. continues straight ahead along an old woods road, climbing the ridgecrest for the next 1.8 miles. Nearly a mile from the gap, reach the foundation of old homestead with a row of six maple trees in front. There is a spring a short distance down the hollow to the left. Continue between the homestead and the row of trees.

At mile 16.5, reach a shallow gap; the trail runs parallel to an old road on the right. In .25 mile, a road to the left leads a short distance to a spring. The A.T. heads away from the road and becomes a treadway. In another .1 mile, you will reach the blue-blazed side trail that heads left a short distance to the Clyde Smith Shelter. Water is available from a spring a short distance behind the shelter. The sign for the shelter is hard to see, and the shelter is not visible from the trail.

From the side trail for the shelter, the A.T. continues to climb through trees and a grassy area, eventually skirting the left side of a knoll near the edge of the woods, just below the summit. The partly open summit (elevation 4,640 feet) can be reached by hiking a short distance to your right. Begin to descend along the ridgecrest, reaching a gap in another .25 mile. A side trail in the gap heads left for .1 mile to a spring. From the gap, begin to climb again through a hardwood forest.

In just over .25 mile, you will enter a rhododendron and laurel grove and continue to climb steeply along a narrow path as you ascend toward Little Rock Knob. Reach the cliffs of the knob in .1 mile. Little Rock Knob (elevation 4,918 feet) offers spectacular views to the west and north. The A.T. continues through rhododendron and laurel just below the summit before heading right and descending steeply off the southern slope.

Enter a field in a gap with young tree growth .75 mile later. Climb steeply with a new fence to your left. On the other side of the fence is a wooded area with lots of blowdowns (chestnuts). In another .25 mile, pass over a summit, and beyond a slight gap, the trail widens into an old woods road. Pass over a second summit in another .25 mile, and reach the road crossing at Hughes Gap (elevation 4,040 feet) at mile 18.9. The A.T. continues across the road to the left.

On the north side of the road, the A.T. climbs steeply up the left side of the ridge along an old road. Hike .5 mile to where the trail returns to the ridgecrest and begin to climb to Cloudland. At mile 20.2, reach a side trail that heads right to an overlook with good views. From the side trail, hike .1 mile to the summit of Beartown Mountain (evelation 5,481 feet), and then descend through a beech wood. Hike nearly .5 mile further to Ash Gap (elevation 5,340 feet) where there is a good campsite. A very faint trail leads .1 mile to a small spring.

Continue along the A.T. for just over .5 mile to an area of dense spruce and rhododendron. Turn left off the old trail .1 mile later, begin to climb steeply, and reach a summit (elevation 6,150 feet) in another .1 mile. Turn right and enter a grassy meadow that leads to an open area. Look straight ahead to locate the former site of the Cloudland Hotel. There are excellent views of the Black Mountains from here. Next to the former hotel site is a small forest service parking lot, and to the right, a larger forest service parking lot. Beyond these parking lots are the Cloudland rhododendron gardens and drinking water from fountains. To the west, view Roan High Bluff (elevation 6,267 feet).

From here, descend a rocky bank to the left of the path to the parking lot, and follow an old road track to the large spruce tree at the left front corner of the hotel site. At mile 21.6, you will turn left and enter the woods. Not long thereafter, you will reach an old cabin site. Head right, cross toward the opposite corner, head left beyond the site, and descend through the woods.

In .1 mile, pass a picnic table at the edge of a road. Keep left and follow the old road (don't cross the paved road) through Fraser fir and rhododendron. The A.T. follows this road nearly all the way to Carvers Gap.

In .5 mile, reach a blue-blazed trail to your right that leads .1 mile to the summit of Roan High Knob (elevation 6,285 feet). The summit of Roan High Knob boasts the highest shelter on the A.T. Formerly a fire warden's cabin, the shelter was renovated in 1980 for hiker use. Water is available from a spring behind the cabin on a blue-blazed trail.

The A.T. continues along the old road, skirting the left side of a knob. Beyond the knob, descend along several switchbacks. Just over a mile later, turn left off the road onto a footpath and descend. Head to the right through weeds and open firs. In .1 mile, you will reach the paved USFS Cloudland Rhododendron Garden Road near a large rock. The trail heads left downhill to the left of a pole fence.

At mile 23.5, reach Carvers Gap (elevation 5,512 feet), the end of this hike. To your left, locate a parking lot and a picnic area with spring and toilets.

Trailhead Directions

From Erwin, Tennessee, reach Indian Grave Gap via Tennessee 395 (10th Street in Erwin; Rock Creek Road outside the city limits). The A.T. crossing is 6.6 miles southeast of Erwin. At mile 3.3, you will reach the USFS Rock Creek Recreation Area.

Reach Carvers Gap via Tennessee 143, 14 miles south of Roan Mountain, Tennessee, or via North Carolina 261, 14 miles north of Bakersville, North Carolina.

BALD MOUNTAINS

MODERATE
12.7 mile traverse

The summits of High Rocks and Big Bald are the highlights of this short traverse over the Bald Mountains. High Rocks is on a short side trail off the A.T. and affords great views of Little Bald, Temple Hill, and No Business Knob. Big Bald offers spectacular 360° views of the Southern Appalachians, including an excellent view of Mount Mitchell only 20 miles distant. Mitchell (elevation 6,684 feet) is the highest peak east of Mississippi River and lies in the Black Mountains of North Carolina. Mount LeConte in the Great Smoky Mountains can also be seen from Big Bald. To the southwest, between the Black Mountains and the Smoky Mountains, view the Nantahala Mountains; to the northwest,view Coldspring Mountain with its two peaks, Camp Creek Bald and Big Butt; and to the northeast, view the Unaka Mountains.

After ascending from Sams Gap, the A.T. crosses extensive open pastures and follows the ridgecrest to Street Gap where the A.T. begins a long, gradual climb up Big Bald (elevation 5,516 feet). From the extensive meadows at Big Bald, the A.T. descends to the Bald Mountain Shelter, makes the short climb up the wooded summit of Little Bald, descends to Whistling Gap, and then climbs to High Rocks. The traverse ends at Spivey Gap, just north of US 19W.

Note: Because of planned highway construction in the Sams Gap area, relocations may be in place. Keep an eye out for signs indicating any changes. If the blazes differ from this description, follow the blazes.

The Hike

From Sams Gap (elevation 3,800 feet), ascend a ramp, follow the eastern embankment of US 23 for a short distance, and head right into the woods. You will then ascend for the next .25 mile or so and reach the summit of a wooded knob. Pass through a wire fence and follow the fence along the crest.

At mile 1, in a slight sag, find an intermittent spring to your left. A short distance later, you will pass a dirt road that heads left to US 23 in Tennessee. In another .1 mile, pass an abandoned talc mine to your right, and continue to climb to the right of a barbed wire fence. Reach the top of a knob (elevation 4,440 feet) in just over .25 mile, and leave the woods for open meadows. View Big Bald to the northeast. The trail continues across the meadow, descending to the left of the fence.

In another .25 mile, the fence (and the trail) heads right. You will skirt a small knob to the left and return to following the fence. At mile 2.1, reach the road at Street Gap (left to Flag Pond; right to a paved road and the first house on Puncheon Fork Road). On the other side of the road, follow a dirt road through the fence and begin to climb along the ridgecrest. View Big Bald to your left.

Hike .5 mile to where the trail heads right and the dirt road continues straight up the ridge. Following this graded trail, switcback to your left, and reach the ridgecrest in .25 mile. Turn right and descend steeply into the Cherokee National Forest.

At mile 3, the A.T. leaves the road and ridgeline, heading left along the Tennessee side of the ridge. In .1 mile, reach a blue-blazed trail that heads left a short distance to a spring. In another .1 mile, reach Low Gap.

From Low Gap, climb through hardwoods and a spring wildflower garden for about a mile, passing a spring in just over .5 mile. One mile from Low Gap, pass ruins to the left of the trail, skirt the left slope of the ridge, and climb moderately. Climb gently for a mile and reach a blue-blazed side trail that heads left a short distance to a spring. In another .1 mile, reach a blue-blazed trail that leads a very short distance to a spring. The side trail can also be used in bad weather because it follows the southeastern slope of Big Bald on graded trail, turns left on Wolf Laurel Road, and rejoins the A.T. at mile 6.2 at Big Stamp. Big Bald can be nearly impossible to navigate in foggy and stormy weather.

In another .25 mile, begin to climb steeply up a rocky slope, crossing several small streams. A short distance later, enter a rhododendron grove as you continue to climb, and reach more level trail in another .25 mile. The trail bears right and continues up the east slope of Big Bald, soon passing through scattered mountain ash, serviceberry, and hawthorn before entering the open, grassy meadows of the bald.

At mile 6, reach the highest point on Big Bald (elevation 5,516 feet), which is marked by a post. From the summit, descend the treeless saddle of Big Stamp. In .25 mile, reach the junction with the "bad weather" trail at mile 6.2. Reach a campsite with double springs in just over .25 mile by following the road to the left and taking the right fork. The left fork leads to a grassed over parking lot near the summit.

From this trail junction, climb along the ridgecrest and across meadows with great views. Nearly .5 mile later, pass over a small rise with scattered trees and large rocks. To the southwest, enjoy an excellent close-up view of Big Bald. In .25 mile, descend through an open meadow with a view of Little Bald ahead. Enter the woods, and soon thereafter, cross a dirt road and re-enter the woods.

At mile 7.1, reach a blue-blazed side trail on your left that leads .1 mile to Bald Mountain Shelter. Water is available from a spring down another short side trail between the trail and the shelter. Camping is not encouraged here because the area around the shelter is very fragile (Bald Mountain Shelter is one of the highest shelters on the A.T.) If you're interested in camping, a good spot is located at mile 7.5.

Cross a small stream in .25 mile, and a short distance later, a spring to your right. In another .25 mile, reach the junction with another blue-blazed trail that heads left to Big Bald Creek. There are good campsites along the ridge and a good spring less than .25 mile down the trail near the head of Tumbling Creek. The A.T. continues ahead, alternately following an old woods road and a footpath through the woods.

Reach the end of the road in .75 mile. The trail begins to climb up the ridge to the left of a fence. At mile 8.5, reach the wooded summit of Little Bald (elevation 5,185 feet). The A.T. leaves the Tennessee/North Carolina state line and descends into North Carolina for the last 4.2 miles of this hike. A vista opens to the left a short distance from the summit of Little Bald with views of No Business Knob and Temple Hill to the north. The A.T. continues steeply down the mountain with several switchbacks and steps.

In another .75 mile, pass a spring to your left, and .25 mile later, the former route of the A.T. enters from the right, leading to the summit of Little Bald. A new switchback (to the south) is being planned here. Watch the blazes. Continue to descend down the ridge with a barbed wire fence to your right. In .5 mile, after climbing a slight rise, pass a huge boulder to your left blazed with the A.T. symbol.

At mile 10.4, reach Whistling Gap (elevation 3,840 feet). The far end of the gap can be used as a campsite. A trail to the left leads .1 mile to a spring. Beyond it, the old A.T. heads to US 19W, just west of Spivey Gap. The A.T. continues ahead, climbing the crest and soon crossing a small knob. Reach a sag in just over .25 mile, and begin to climb toward High Rocks.

Near the summit of High Rocks, reach the junction of a blue-blazed trail that heads steeply right to the peak of High Rocks (elevation 4,280 feet). This blue-blazed trail goes beneath the northern rim of High Rocks, rejoining the A.T. at mile 11.1.

Continue on the A.T. and head left. Skirting the base of a rocky cliff, climb to a small saddle with the peak of High Rocks to your right. At mile 11.1, the blue-blazed trail rejoins the A.T., which heads left, steeply descending along steps and switchbacks. At mile 12.1, cross a stream and turn right, and .1 mile later, reach an area used as a campsite with a stream to the right. You will descend along log steps and then continue descending along an old road.

Enter a stand of white pine and hemlock, and pass to the right of a clearing in another .25 mile. Soon thereafter, cross Big Creek and climb up the bank to the highway. At mile 12.7, reach Spivey Gap at US 19W, the end of this hike.

Trailhead Directions

The A.T. crossing at Sams Gap is on US 23, 12 miles north of Mars Hill, North Carolina, 31 miles north of Asheville, North Carolina, and 6 miles south of Flag Pond.

Spivey Gap, on US 19W, is 8 miles south of Erwin, Tennessee, and 43 miles north of Asheville, North Carolina.

STATE LINE TRAIL TRAVERSE

EASY
20.2 mile traverse

The A.T. shares a treadway with the forest service State Line Trail from Devil Fork Gap to Allen Gap. This circuitous traverse follows mostly ridgecrest from Green Ridge to Camp Creek Bald. The crest is partially cleared in many places and offers especially good views from Ballground and Blackstack Cliffs. Bearwallow Gap features a dense rhododendron thicket.

Also of note on this hike is the grave of William and David Shelton atop Coldspring Mountain. David Shelton, and his nephew, William, left their mountain farms in Shelton Laurel, North Carolina, to join the Union cause. While returning for a rendezvous with their families in a cabin atop Coldspring Mountain, the two men and a boy lookout were ambushed by Confederates and killed. They were buried in a single grave atop the mountain. In 1915, two preachers petitioned the federal government for grave markers. They hauled them up the mountain on an ox sled and erected one at each end of the grave. Because the boy lookout was not a soldier, the government did not supply a tombstone for the youth.

The Hike

From North Carolina 212 at Devil Fork Gap (elevation 3,107 feet), head south, climbing up steps and turning right into a field. Climb, with a switchback to the right, and reach the ridge. In .1 mile, you will turn right and shortly thereafter pass through a fence. The trail continues ahead through a slight sag and across a ridge, and then descends steps to an old railroad grade.

After following the railroad bed for a short distance, reach a view of Camp Creek Bald (west) and a sweeping panorama of the Bald Mountains to Green Ridge Knob (north). Continue along the railroad bed, descend for just over .5 mile, and climb again.

At mile 1.4, reach the ridge and the former route of the A.T., which heads right to Devil Fork Gap. The A.T. continues along the ridgecrest, reaching the site of the old Locust Ridge Shelter (removed in 1982) in nearly .5 mile. Water is available in a ravine to the left. The A.T. continues beyond the next rise and then skirts the western side of Flint Mountain. Nearly a mile later, you will pass a spring and two streams and then the Flint Mountain Shelter.

Continue along the A.T., cross a ridge in another .5 mile, and descend along a narrow path that widens into an old logging road. At mile 3.5, reach Flint Gap (elevation 3,425 feet) and begin to ascend along a graded trail. Nearly .5 mile later, turn right onto a dirt road, and shortly thereafter, turn left as you begin to climb the ridge. The trail follows the road for about 3 miles, climbing steeply up the ridge crest for a short distance before turning off the crest to the left.

Return to the crest of the ridge at mile 4.5, where the old road comes in from the right. Turn left and climb steeply up the slope of Cold Spring Mountain. In .25 mile, at the top of the rise, view Green Ridge Knob to your left as you cross the crest of the ridge on Cold Spring Mountain, and then descend into the woods, following an old road and passing through a stand of white pines.

Pass the graves of David and William Shelton and their 15-year-old relative in .5 mile. The markers read, "Wm. Shelton, Co. E, 2 N.C. Inf." and "David Shelton, Co. C, 3 N.C. Mtd. Inf." Continue along the crest, passing alternately through overgrown fields and woods, and in .25 mile, reach a blue-blazed dirt road that leads downhill to a spring. The road curves left .1 mile later, and there is another spring to the right in a ravine. Pass to the left of the summit of Gravel Knob, and skirt another low summit on your right.

At mile 6.7, the trail abruptly turns southwest, and shortly thereafter leaves the road and enters the woods. On the other side of the road, the blue-blazed Squibb Creek Trail heads east to Ball Ground on the ridge of Rich Mountain and then to Horse Creek Campground in 4.5 miles. Continue along the A.T. for a short distance, and pass a side trail to your right that leads to the rocky outcropping of Big Rock (elevation 4,838 feet), which offers panoramic views of the valley below. You can also see Camp Creek Bald, Big Bald, and Gravel Knob from here.

The A.T. continues along a rocky footpath, eventually descending on big rock steps. At mile 7, cross a dirt road, and shortly thereafter, reach a small knoll with a cleared view. On the right side of the A.T., locate the a small stone memorial to Howard E. Bassett of Connecticut. Bassett, a 1968 thru-hiker, died in late 1987 and his ashes were later scattered here (April 27, 1988). Cross the road and pass a large rock to the left of the trail in .25 mile. In another .25 mile, cross a cleared field along the left side.

Just over .5 mile later, leave the field and enter the woods, turning left and descending into North Carolina along switchbacks. In Chestnut Gap (elevation 4,150 feet), the trail rejoins the road, and shortly thereafter, reaches Jerry Cabin at mile 8.6. Water is available from a good spring a short distance down a side trail near the shelter.

Continue along the A.T. for .25 mile, and reach the junction with the Fork Ridge Trail on your left. It is 2 miles down this trail to Big Creek Road and 2 miles farther to Carmen, North Carolina. The A.T. continues along the dirt road for another .75 mile to where the road turns to the right, heading 3 miles to Round Knob Spring and Round Knob Campground Road. The A.T. then continues along graded trail to the right of Big Firescald Knob.

At mile 11.1, pass a spring to the left of the trail and pass through a rhododendron grove. In another .75 mile, you will reach the rhododendron "gardens" at Bearwallow Gap. Here, the forest service Whiteoak Flats Trail heads left 2.5 miles to Hickey Fork Road. The A.T. continues through the rhododendron for .25 mile to the junction with a wide side trail that leads a short distance to Blackstack Cliffs, which offer great views of Tennessee. The A.T. forks left and continues through rhododendron.

In another .25 mile, a side trail heads left a short distance to White Rock Cliffs, a rock outcropping with good views, particularly of the Black Mountains and Mount Mitchell (elevation 6,684 feet). A short descent along switchbacks offers good views to the south and east. Pass a spring to the left of the trail in .1 mile, and continue along the A.T. below the developed Jones Meadow.

Nearly a mile later, reach an old lumber road, which shortly joins with Camp Creek Bald Fire Road. Follow the old lumber road to the left, and within the next .1 mile, turn right uphill. There is a spring to the right of the trail a short distance later. Continue to the left, climbing the eastern ridge of Camp Creek Bald, and circle just below the summit through a thick growth of rhododendron. Reach another trail junction at mile 14. This trail heads left down Seng Ridge to Pounding Mill Trail, Whiteoak Flats Trail, and Shelton Laurel Road. To the right, the trail leads .25 mile to Camp Creek Bald firetower (elevation 4,844 feet), which offers great views of the Smokies.

The A.T. continues ahead, descending slightly. Reach Little Laurel Shelter to your left at mile 15.3. Water is available from a boxed spring down the blue-blazed trail to your right. The trail to the spring is also the start of the Dixon Trail, which heads 1.5 miles to the Camp Creek Bald Fire

Road. The A.T. continues to descend, reaching a fork in the trail in another 2 miles.

Take the left fork (the former route of the A.T. is straight ahead) and in just over .25 mile, cross Old Hayesville Road in a stand of white pine. Begin to climb, switchbacking to the left around a hill. In another .25 mile, pass a blocked trail to your right, and descend to your left. Hike nearly .5 mile to return to the crest in a sag, and cross an old dirt road. Take the right fork of the trail, climb uphill, and in .1 mile, turn left onto the trail coming up the ridge and continue to climb.

At mile 19.6, turn right, away from the route of the former A.T., continue along ridge, and reach Allen Gap at Tennessee 70 in .6 mile.

Trailhead Directions

The A.T. crossing at Devil Fork Gap is on the Tennessee/North Carolina border. From Erwin, Tennessee, reach Devil Fork Gap by taking US 23 south for 12 miles to Rocky Fork and then Tennessee 352 for 4.2 miles to Devil Fork Gap.

To reach the trail crossing at Allen Gap, take Tennessee 70 for 25 miles south of Greeneville, Tennessee, or by taking US 25W/70 for 6 miles east of Hot Springs, North Carolina, and then North Carolina 208 north 9 miles to Allen Gap.

MAX PATCH/HOT SPRINGS

MODERATE
20.2 mile traverse

This hike offers some tremendous views from the top of Max Patch and takes you over Walnut and Bluff Mountains on the hike into Hot Springs, North Carolina. Max Patch is the southernmost open, grassy bald on the A.T., and the panoramic view takes in the Black Mountains to the east, including Mount Mitchell, and many of the peaks in the Great Smokies to the west. Walnut and Bluff Mountains do not offer any views, but the hike follows a beautiful wooded section of trail and crosses several small streams as it passes through the Roaring Fork Valley. Three shelters along this hike create several options for overnighting, but to divide the hike into two nearly equal days, you will need to use a tent. This hike gains less than 1,000 feet in elevation in the first 7 miles.

The Hike

From Max Patch Road, hike north on the A.T. and cross a creek before beginning the climb up the south slope of Max Patch. At mile .4, cross the gravel road and continue climbing Max Patch on steps cut into the side of the bald. Reach the summit (elevation 4,629 feet) in another .4 mile. Continue following the white-blazed post leading across the bald, and begin descending. In .4 mile, enter the woods.

At mile 2.2, cross Roaring Fork, and in .25 mile, reach an old railroad grade which the A.T. follows for .25 mile. The trail crosses several small footbridges during the next 3 miles as you cross the northwest side of Roaring Fork Valley. At mile 5.7, reach a short side trail that leads to Roaring Fork Shelter. Water is available from a piped spring nearby. The privy offers a nice view of Roaring Fork Valley.

From the shelter, hike .5 mile to Lemon Gap, where the A.T. reaches, but does not cross, North Carolina 1182 (and Tennessee 107). In another .5 mile, begin climbing steadily up Walnut Mountain, and pass near the wooded summit (elevation 4,280 feet) at mile 7.3. In .25 mile, reach Walnut Mountain Shelter. Water is available from a somewhat unreliable spring near the shelter.

Continue north and descend, passing through fields on the way to Kale Gap in .75 mile. The trail follows an old road bed for the next .25 mile and then passes around the side of Tennessee Bluff Mountain. The trail passes through Catpen Gap in .75 mile and climbs to the wooded summit of Bluff Mountain (elevation 4,686 feet) at mile 9.9. During the remainder of the hike to Hot Springs, the A.T. loses well over 3,000 feet in elevation.

From Bluff Mountain, the trail descends steadily. Pass through the forest service boundary fence in .75 mile, cross a forest service road in another .25 mile, and cross several small roads in the next 2.6 miles as the A.T. descends to Garenflo Gap (elevation 2,500 feet) at mile 13.6. The trail passes to the left of a forest service road in the gap. Continue north on the A.T., pass under powerlines, turn right, and descend. Take a left .5 mile beyond Garenflo Gap and continue following the A.T. when you reach the junction with an old section of the A.T. that leads to right. The old A.T. rejoins the new path in .6 mile. Hike 1 mile, reach Little Bottom Gap, and climb a short steep section of trail. In another 1.3 miles, at mile 17, reach Gragg Gap. Deer Park Mountain Shelter is down a short side trail. Water is available from the small spring located between the A.T. and the shelter.

From Gragg Gap, climb Deer Park Mountain along the ridge. Reach a highpoint in about 1.5 miles and descend steadily into Hot Springs, North Carolina. During this descent, enjoy several good views of the town, particularly in the winter. At mile 19.9, reach the parking lot near the Jesuit Hostel for hikers, the end of this hike.

Trailhead Directions

To get to Max Patch, the southern end of the hike, turn onto North Carolina 1175 from North Carolina 209, approximately 20 miles north of Interstate 40 near Lake Junaluska and 7 miles south of Hot Springs, North Carolina. Follow North Carolina 1175 for 5.3 miles and then turn onto Max Patch Road (North Carolina 1182). The parking area at the foot of the bald is 25 miles down Max Patch Road.

The northern trailhead is a forest service parking lot in Hot Springs, North Carolina. Hot Springs is 26 miles east of Newport, Tennessee and 17 miles northwest of Marshall, North Carolina, at the intersection of US 25/ 70 and North Carolina 209. Inquire at the French Broad Ranger District Office on US 25/70 in Hot Springs (or at other businesses in town) for directions to the small parking lot, which is on the A.T. beside the Jesuit Hostel.

MOUNT CAMMERER LOOP
Great Smoky Mountains National Park

STRENUOUS
18 mile loop

The highlight of this hike is the commanding panoramic view from the stone firetower on the summit of Mount Cammerer. The mountain is the easternmost big peak in the park. Once known as White Rock, this peak was renamed for the former National Park Service Director, Arno Cammerer. Along this hike, you may witness some of the decline in the spruce-fir forest, caused in part by the balsam wooly adelgid. Acid rain is also believed to be a contributing factor in the demise of the trees because it makes mature firs easier prey for the adelgid.

This hike is set up with Cosby Knob Shelter as your overnight stop. Get a backcountry permit in advance from Great Smoky Mountains National Park, Gatlinburg, Tennessee 37738, or call (615) 436-5615 for more information. The permits are free, but there is a fine for not obtaining one. In spite of this, you may want to bring a tent: illegal campers often fill up shelters before the hikers with permits arrive. We have had this happen more than once, and have had to sleep outside the shelter in our tent.

This strenuous hike should not be underestimated. The climbs and descents are quite difficult. There is a more than 3,000 feet difference in elevation between Davenport Gap and the firetower on Cammerer.

The Hike
From the trailhead at the Big Creek Ranger station, follow the Chestnut Branch Trail as it ascends gradually alongside Chestnut Branch for the first mile. The trail then turns right and climbs steadily to its junction with the A.T. at mile 2 of the hike. Turn left and follow the white-blazed A.T. as it climbs Cammerer Ridge. At mile 2.9, pass the junction with the Lower Mount Cammerer Trail.

The A.T. climbs, often sharply, up the ridge. At mile 5.3, reach a side trail to the right that leads .6 mile to the summit of Mount Cammerer (elevation 5,025 feet). Turn right and follow the side trail up the ridge. After enjoying the tremendous view from the stone firetower, return to the A.T.and continue hiking north as the trail climbs for another .25 mile. (All hike mileages include the 1.2 roundtrip to the firetower) In 1.3 miles, (mile 8), cross the top of Rocky Face Mountain and descend .6 mile to Low Gap.

Begin climbing Cosby Knob, and in .75 mile, reach Cosby Knob Shelter just to the left of the A.T. Water is available from a nearby spring. After spending the night at the shelter, hike south on the A.T. for .75 mile to Low Gap. Turn right on Low Gap Trail, and descend steeply off the ridge as you follow Low Gap Branch down to Walnut Bottoms. In 2.5 miles, reach the junction with the Big Creek Trail. Turn left and follow that trail on a gravel road as it winds alongside Big Creek for 5 miles. At the Big Creek Primitive Campground, turn left and walk .5 mile down the road to the Big Creek Ranger Station, the end of this hike.

Trailhead Directions
From Interstate 40, take exit 451 (Waterville, Tennessee) and follow North Carolina 284 south. The Big Creek Ranger Station is just past the village of Mount Sterling on North Carolina 284.

MOUNT COLLINS/CLINGMANS DOME
Great Smoky Mountains National Park

MODERATE
21.6 miles roundtrip

This overnight hike will take you over the highest point on the A.T.—Clingmans Dome (elevation 6,643 feet). On clear days, there are outstanding views of the peaks of the Great Smokies from the observation tower. Formerly Smoky Dome, the peak is named after Thomas L. Clingman, a Civil War General and U.S. Senator. Clingman was known for his heated debate with Elisha Mitchell. The two argued over which peak in the state was the highest—Grandfather Mountain or Balsam Mountain. The debate took place through editorials in rival Asheville, North Carolina, newspapers. Mitchell died in a fall while trying to prove his claim that Balsam Mountain was the tallest. History proved Mitchell right, however, and the highest peak east of the Mississippi bears his name.

Another interesting site is found in Indian Gap, where an old roadbed crosses the trail. It was built during the Civil War to get saltpeter mined from Alum Bluff Cave over the mountain to supply Confederate troops with gunpowder.

It is a roundtrip hike from Newfound Gap to Double Springs Shelter. You will need to get a backcountry permit in advance from Great Smoky Mountains National Park, Gatlinburg, Tennesse 37738, or call (615) 436-5615 for more information. The permits are free, but there is a fine for not obtaining one. In spite of this, you may want to bring a tent: illegal campers often fill up shelters before the hikers with permits arrive. We have had this happen more than once, and have had to sleep outside the shelter in our tent.

Along this hike, you may witness some of the decline in the spruce-fir forest caused in part by the balsam Wooly adelgid. Acid rain is also believed to be a contributing factor in the trees demise as it makes mature firs easier prey for the adelgid.

The Hike
From the trailhead at Newfound Gap, hike south on the A.T. Pass through a gap in the guardrail, and enter the woods. In .9 mile, pass the junction with the former A.T. on the left, and begin climbing along the southeast

slope of Mount Mingus. In .25 mile, reach a highpoint on the side of Mount Mingus, and continue for .5 mile to Indian Gap. In the gap, you will also see the road to Clingmans Dome, which the trail parallels but usually cannot be seen.

From Indian Gap, the A.T. climbs the ridge on the North Carolina/Tennessee state line, and reaches Little Indian Gap in .5 mile. In 1.9 miles, pass the junction with the Fork Ridge Trail on the left. In another .4 mile (mile 4.5), pass the junction with the Sugarland Mountain Trail on the right. The Mount Collins Shelter is .5 mile down this trail. Water is available from a nearby spring.

Hike .5 mile beyond the Sugarland Mountain Trail, pass over the wooded summit of Mount Collins (elevation 6,188 feet), and begin a gentle descent on its southwest slope. In .6 mile, reach Collins Gap, then climb 1.1 miles to the tree-covered summit of Mount Love (elevation 6,446 feet). From Mount Love, descend to a sag on the eastern slope of Clingmans Dome, and climb steeply.

At mile 6.7, reach the trail's highpoint on Clingmans Dome. A short side trail leads to the observation tower on the summit, which offers spectacular views on clear days. Unfortunately, the summit is often covered in clouds.

After returning to the A.T., continue hiking south and descend for .4 mile to a trail junction with Clingmans bypass trail. Continue following the A.T. and climb for .1 mile to the summit of Mount Buckley (elevation 6,582 feet). From Buckley, the trail descends sharply and then more gradually. Pass the junction with the Goshen Prong Trail at mile 10.2, and arrive at Double Springs Shelter at mile 10.8.

The shelter gets its name from springs located on both the North Carolina and the Tennessee side of the ridge. Since bears are often seen in this area, the chain link fence across the front of the shelter keeps the people in and the bears out. Carelessly leaving the door open can reverse this usual arrangement. This is not a good idea.

The return hike is north on the A.T. Hiking north from the shelter, reach the highpoint on Clingmans Dome in 2.9 miles, Mount Collins in another 2.9 miles, and Newfound Gap is 5 miles beyond Collins.

Trailhead Directions

Newfound Gap is on US 441 at the North Carolina/Tennessee state line, 16 miles south of Gatlinburg, Tennessee, and 20 miles north of Cherokee, North Carolina. There is ample parking in the gap.

Russell Field/Spence Field/ Rocky Top Loop
Great Smoky Mountains National Park

STRENUOUS
14.7 miles roundtrip

This hike features a loop through Russell and Spence Fields, a grassy ridge dotted with mature trees,to the bald summit of Rocky Top. Although it uses very little of the A.T. (5 miles), it is a spectacular overnight hike.

The hike begins at Cades Cove on the Tennessee side of the Smoky Mountains. You can pick up a map of the area at the ranger station. The loop follows the Anthony Creek Trail to the Russell Field Trail. At Russell Field, you pick up the A.T. to Spence Field and Rocky Top. Return by way of the A.T. to Spence Field, where you will pick up the Bote Mountain Trail, then follow it back to the Anthony Creek Trail.

Because you will stay at either Russell Field or Spence Field, you will need to get a backcountry permit in advance from Great Smoky Mountains National Park, Gatlinburg, Tennessee 37738, or call (615) 436-5615 for more information. The permits are free, but there is a fine for not obtaining one. In spite of this, you may want to bring a tent: illegal campers often fill up shelters before the hikers with permits arrive. We have had this happen more than once, and have had to sleep outside the shelter in our tent.

Along this hike, you may witness some of the decline in the spruce-fir forest caused in part by the balsam wooly adelgid. Acid rain is also believed to be a contributing factor in the trees demise as it makes mature firs easier prey for the adelgid.

The Hike
Starting from Cades Cove, follow the Anthony Creek Trail. You will follow this trail for 1.3 miles, mostly along a graded, gravel bed through a hardwood forest. The trail follows and criss-crosses Anthony Creek, which makes for a pleasant walk.

At mile 1.3, turn right onto the Russell Field Trail, which at first follows the right prong of Anthony Creek through a hemlock and rhododendron forest. The growth is so thick and moss-covered here that it is very nearly tropical in appearance. From the right prong of Anthony Creek, the trail follows Leadbetter Ridge for 1 mile, passes through a virgin hardwood forest in .5 mile, and crosses a grassy ridge in another .5 mile. Reach Russell Field and shelter at mile 4.8, 3.5 miles after turning onto Russell Field Trail. Water is available a short distance down the Russell Field Trail (toward Cades Cove).

From the shelter, turn left (north) onto the A.T. and hike just over .25 mile to McCampbell Gap (elevation 4,328 feet). Just over a mile later, reach the edge of the meadow at Little Bald, and enjoy excellent views to the south. Turn left, hike a short distance, and leave the meadow. Then turn right and enter the woods.

Follow the crest of the ridge through open woods, descend slightly, and reach Spence Field at mile 6.4. Spence Field is often considered the western end of Thunderhead, the magnificent bald visible ahead. From the edge of this grassy field, it is just over a mile (2.6 miles total from Russell Field) to Spence Field Shelter.

At mile 7.4, reach the junction with the Eagle Creek Trail. It is a short distance down this trail to the shelter. The tributary of Eagle Creek is the Spence Cabin Branch of Gunna Creek. Water is available from a spring on the trail past the shelter.

Continue along the A.T. for 1.2 miles to the summit of Rocky Top. You will descend slightly for nearly .5 mile to a grassy sag, where the Jenkins Ridge Trail heads right 6 miles to the Lakeshore Trail at Pickens Gap. From the sag, begin to climb up the grassy slope to Rocky Top. From the summit of Rocky Top (elevation 5,441 feet) there are great views of Fontana Lake. The summit of Thunderhead (elevation 5,527 feet) is another .6 mile from Rocky Top. It is covered in rhododendron and is particulary beautiful in mid to late June. The sidetrip would add an extra 1.2 miles to the hike (a total of 15.9 miles).

Return to Spence Field by hiking south on the A.T. The Bote Mountain Trail enters the A.T. from the right. Take the graded Bote Mountain Trail for 1.7 miles. The first .5 mile is through a beech and birch forest, and the next .5 mile is through hemlock. The last .75 mile, before you rejoin the Anthony Creek Trail, is through a laurel grove. Rejoining the Anthony Creek Trail, you will pass through hardwood forest for 3.2 miles on the moderate to strenuous descent to Cades Cove, the end of the hike.

Trailhead Directions

The trailhead for the Anthony Creek Trail is located at the Cades Cove Ranger Station. Take US 321 from US 441 south of Gatlinburg and Pigeon

Forge. From US 321, take Tennessee 73 to Laurel Creek Road and follow the signs to the Great Smoky Mountains and Cades Cove.

Northern Nantahala Traverse

STRENUOUS
21.4 mile traverse

This hike takes you over Wayah and Wesser Balds, where spectacular views are afforded from old firetower platforms. From these two lookouts, you can see many major peaks of the Great Smokies, other peaks south into the Nantahalas of North Carolina, and some of the mountains of Georgia. There is also a tremendous view from "Jumpup" on the long desecnt into the Nantahala Gorge.

The hike can be cut short by 4 miles by driving the forest service road to the top of Wayah Bald at the start of the hike. You will forego the long slow climb up from Wayah Gap, but may also miss a profusion of flame azaleas, rhododendron and mountain laurel in mid to late June and other seasonal wildflowers.

This hike is listed as strenuous because of the knee jarring descent from Wesser Bald down to the Nantahala River. This traverse is difficult to set up because of the distance (by road) between the trailheads, but it is worth it.

The Hike
From the trailhead at Wayah Crest (elevation 4,180 feet), cross Wayah Road and hike north on the A.T., beginning the long climb up from the gap. During the first mile, USFS 69 will often be visible to the left of the trail. At mile 1.3, pass the junction with the blue-blazed Wilson Lick Trail, which leads .1 mile to the left to an historic ranger station. Continue climbing for .5 mile, and at the top of a short steep climb, cross USFS 69. The piped in Rattlesnake Spring is located just to the right of the trail on USFS 69.

Climb the steps up from the road and continue a graded ascent. Reach the junction with the yellow-blazed Bartram Trail in another .5 mile. There is a campsite on the right and Wine Spring is just ahead on the left side of the trail. The Bartram Trail and the A.T. share the same footpath for the next 2.1 miles. Beyond the spring, the trail follows an old road bed for .25 mile before turning left off the road.

Continue hiking on a sidehill trail, and cross another old road in 1:4 miles. In .25 mile, the trail joins a paved path leading from a gravel parking area to the top of Wayah Bald. As the A.T. turns onto the pavement, there is a USFS pit toilet on the left of the trail. At mile 4.2, reach the stone observation tower on the summit of Wayah Bald (elevation 5,342 feet). Follow the A.T. north off the summit for .25 mile to where the Bartram Trail turns right and the A.T. continues ahead.

Continue north on the A.T. and reach Licklog Gap in 2 miles. Climb out of the gap to a highpoint on the ridge, and descend to Burningtown Gap in the next 2.3 miles. The dirt road in the gap is North Carolina 1397. The trail climbs out of the gap and reaches Cold Spring Shelter in 1.2 miles (mile 9.9). Water is available from the spring immediately in front of the shelter. This makes a good spot to overnight in order to break up the hike. Another good spot with potential campsites lies 2.2 miles beyond at a spring on the trail.

Hike north from the shelter and climb on the western slope of Copper Ridge Bald. As the trail continues following the ridgeline, it passes below the summits of Tellico, Black, and Rocky Balds. At mile 13.5, reach Tellico Gap. The gravel road is North Carolina 1365. Climb 1.4 miles from the gap to the highpoint on Wesser Bald (elevation 4,627 feet). A short side trail leads to the summit, where there is an old firetower. The forest service, with help from the Nantahala Hiking Club, added a platform to the tower frame in 1993, and the tower now offers a tremendous view.

From Wesser Bald, descend .7 mile and pass the blue-blazed Wesser Creek Trail. In another .1 mile reach the Wesser Bald Shelter, built in 1994 (Wesser Creek is the shelter's water source). The A.T. follows a rough up-and-down route for the next 1.6 miles over to Jumpup, a rocky outlook with an awesome view down to the Nantahala Gorge. From Jumpup, at mile 17.3, hike a tough 3.3 miles downhill to the A. Rufus Morgan Shelter. The shelter took a direct hit from a tree during a winter storm in 1993, but the roof was rebuilt by a local scout troop later that year. At mile 21.4, reach US 19 just across the highway from the Nantahala River. The Nantahala Outdoor Center is just to the left of the trail along the highway.

Trailhead Directions
The southern trailhead at Wayah Crest is on North Carolina 1310 (locally known as Wayah Road), 12 miles east of Franklin, North Carolina. The northern trailhead on US 19 in Wesser, North Carolina, is 15 miles west of Bryson City and 38 miles north of Murphy.

WAYAH BALD/SILER BALD

MODERATE
19.5 mile traverse

This hike traverses two historic balds, both of which have been covered again in trees. From the top of Wayah Bald, there is, however, a tremendous view. Peaks from the Great Smokies south into Georgia can be viewed from the stone firetower on the summit of Wayah.

The second bald, Siler Bald, though historically a bald, has also become covered once again with trees. Several years ago, the forest service cleared part of the summit and now maintains the meadow on Siler as a bald.

The Hike
From the trailhead in Winding Stair Gap, cross the highway from the parking area, and hike north on the A.T. Climb up the slope by the road, and turn left to enter the woods. At mile .4, and again at mile 1, cross small streams as the trail climbs to Panther Gap at mile 2.1. From that gap, descend for .5 mile and then begin climbing on the southeast slope of Siler Bald.

At mile 3.8, pass the junction with the blue-blazed Siler Bald Shelter Loop Trail, which turns off to the right .5 mile to the shelter and another .6 mile to rejoin the A.T. at mile 4.3. At the northern junction with the Loop Trail, a second trail leads .25 mile to the left to the cleared summit of Siler Bald (elevation 5,216 feet). The bald boasts fine views of the surrounding Nantahala Mountains. Wine Spring Bald (with the radio towers) and Wayah Bald with its stone tower can be seen to the northwest and north.

From the side trails to the summit and shelter, hike 1.7 miles down to Wayah Gap. The Wayah Crest Picnic Area is just to the left of the trail, right before you get to North Carolina 1310 in the gap. Cross the highway (locally known as Wayah Road), and hike north on the A.T. Begin the long climb up from the gap. During the first mile of the hike, USFS 69 will often be visible to the left of the trail. At mile 1.3, pass the junction with the blue-blazed Wilson Lick Trail, which leads .1 mile to the left to a historic ranger station. Continue climbing for .5 mile, and at the top of a short steep climb, cross USFS 69. The piped in Rattlesnake Spring is located just to the right of the trail on USFS 69.

Climb the steps up from the road and continue a graded ascent. Reach the junction with the yellow-blazed Bartram Trail in another .5 mile. There is a campsite on the right, and Wine Spring is just ahead on the left side of the trail. The Bartram Trail and the A.T. share the same footpath for the next 2.1 miles. Beyond the spring, the trail follows an old road bed for .25 mile before turning left off the road.

Continue hiking on a sidehill trail, and cross another old road in 1.4 miles. In .25 mile, the trail joins a paved path leading from a gravel parking area to the top of Wayah Bald. As the A.T. turns onto the pavement, there is a USFS pit toilet on the left of the trail. At mile 10.2, reach the stone observation tower on the summit of Wayah Bald (elevation 5,342 feet). Follow the A.T. north off the summit for .25 mile to where the Bartram Trail turns right and the white-blazed A.T. continues ahead.

Continue north on the A.T. and reach Licklog Gap in 2 miles. Climb out of the gap to a highpoint on the ridge, and descend to Burningtown Gap in the next 2.3 miles. The dirt road in the gap is North Carolina 1397. The trail climbs out of the gap and reaches Cold Spring Shelter in 1.2 miles (mile 15.9). Water is available from the spring immediately in front of the shelter. In 2.2 miles, reach another spring on the trail with possible campsites nearby.

Hike north from the shelter and climb on the western slope of Copper Ridge Bald. As the trail continues following the ridgeline, it passes below the summits of Tellico, Black, and Rocky Balds. At mile 19.5, reach Tellico Gap, the northern end of the hike.

Trailhead Directions
The southern trailhead at Winding Stair Gap is on US 64, 10 miles east of Franklin, North Carolina. The northern trailhead is on gravel North Carolina 1365 in Tellico Gap. Take paved North Carolina 1310 from US 19 in Beechertown, North Carolina. Drive a little over 5 miles from US 19, and follow North Carolina 1365 when it turns to the left. Then drive 4 miles alongside Otter Creek to Tellico Gap.

STANDING INDIAN LOOP

STRENUOUS
25.4 miles loop

On this loop, you will be hiking through the Nantahala and Blue Ridge Mountains. A short side trail leads to Standing Indian (elevation 5,498 feet), which is the A.T.'s highest point south of the Smoky Mountains. From the summit, you can see the mountain ranges that the A.T. follows south to Springer Mountain (the southern terminus of the A.T.).

Albert Mountain is another highlight of this hike. Boasting one of the few remaining firetowers in the south, Albert affords spectacular views of the Blue Ridge and the Little Tennessee River Valley.

The Hike
This hike begins at Deep Gap (elevation 4,341 feet). Follow the A.T. south and immediately begin your ascent of Standing Indian Mountain. Note the blue-blazed Kimsey Creek Trail to your left. You will later take this 3.7-mile trail from Standing Indian Campground to complete your hike. From Deep Gap, it is only .75 mile to Standing Indian Shelter. This shelter was to be removed in 1995 and replaced by a new shelter located nearby on a sidetrail.

The A.T. continues ahead, ascending along an old road. In another 1.5 miles or so, you will pass an unmarked trail on your left that leads to a spring. A short distance farther, you will reach the junction with the blue-blazed Lower Ridge Trail, which heads .1 mile to the summit of Standing Indian (to your right). To the left, the side trail heads 4.2 miles to Standing Indian Campground.

At mile 5.3, arrive at Beech Gap, where there are campsites and an intermittent spring to the right of the trail. The blue-blazed Beech Gap Trail heads 2.8 miles to USFS 67, 4 miles south of Standing Indian Campground. Continue along the trail and cross a number of streams in the next mile. Hike another 1.8 miles to Coleman Gap, located in a thick growth of rhododendron.

In another mile, reach the junction with the blue-blazed Timber Ridge Trail to your left. This trail heads 2.3 miles to USFS 67, 4.4 miles south of Standing Indian Campground. Hike nearly .5 mile and reach Carter Gap at mile 8.5. Campsites and a shelter are a short distance to the left on a blue-blazed trail. Water is available from a spring is located just beyond the shelter.

At mile 9.9, the A.T. heads left onto Little Ridgepole Mountain. This is where the A.T. leaves the Blue Ridge for the Nantahala Mountains. In just over .25 mile, reach the junction with an unmarked trail to your right that heads a short distance to good views. Hike another 2 miles to Betty Creek Gap (more campsites). A blue-blazed trail to your left heads .25 mile to a stream and USFS 67, 6.3 miles south of Standing Indian Campground.

The A.T. crosses the clearing and passes through a thick rhododendron growth. Nearly a mile later, the trail reaches Mooney Gap and crosses USFS 83. To the right, this road heads to the Coweeta Hydrologic Laboratory and U.S. 441. To the left, it joins USFS 67. From Deep Gap to Mooney Gap, the A.T. has been traveling through the Southern Nantahala Wilderness Area. At Mooney Gap, the trail leaves the wilderness area, and in .1 mile, the trail crosses a culvert that diverts water from the spring above the trail.

Turn left, climb log steps, and leave the old road for a footpath. In another .25 mile, pass a cliff on Big Butt Mountain, and enjoy views of the Coweeta Valley. Hike just under .5 mile to Bearpen Gap where the A.T. passes near USFS 67.

At mile 14.4, reach the junction with two blue-blazed trails to your left. The Bear Pen Trail heads left across USFS 67 and descends 2.5 miles to join USFS 67 in the valley. The Albert Mountain Bypass Trail heads right, following the road around the mountain. The A.T. continues up Albert Mountain, a rocky .25-mile climb.

The summit of Albert (elevation 5,250 feet) has a firetower that offers great views. The trail then descends Albert for .25 mile and reaches the junction of the bypass trail to the left. A good spring is located several hundred yards down the bypass trail. Continue along the A.T. for another .4 mile to Big Spring Gap and the convergence of a number of trails. The blue-blazed trail to the left heads a short distance to Big Spring Shelter (mile 15.3). Water is available just beyond the shelter on the same trail.

The blue-blazed trail to the right is the Little Pinnacle Trail, which descends to Coweeta. The other trail to the right heads .25 mile to an outlook on Pinnacle Mountain. The A.T. continues to the left, crossing a stream in a boggy area in 2 miles.

Less than .5 mile after crossing the stream, reach Glassmine Gap, where the blue-blazed Long Branch Trail heads 2.3 miles to USFS 67 near Standing Indian Campground. One mile later, pass an intermittent spring to the left of the trail. During the next mile, you will pass several potential campsites and intermittent water sources.

At mile 20.6, reach the blue-blazed trail that heads left to Rock Gap Shelter. Water is available from two springs just beyond and behind the shelter. In another .1 mile, pass the parking area at Rock Gap. Turn left on paved USFS 67 and hike one mile to Standing Indian Campground, where you will pick up the Kimsey Creek Trail. At Rock Gap, USFS 67 heads right .5 mile to Wallace Gap. The blue-blazed trail on the right leads .75 mile to the huge John Wasilik Memorial Poplar.

Pick up the Kimsey Creek Trail at Standing Indian Campground, and follow Kimsey Creek 3.7 miles back to Deep Gap. The trail begins at the Backcountry Information Center and crosses the river on the campground road before turning right and following the edge of the campground. In just over .25 mile, the Kimsey Creek Trail turns left and leaves the trails that follow the river. About .5 mile later, the trail enters a clearing and turns right along a gated road that follows the creek.

At mile 23.8, cross a log bridge over another creek, and at mile 25.4, reach Deep Gap by way of the former picnic and camping area.

Trailhead Directions
Reach Deep Gap by taking USFS 71 from US 64 (south of Franklin, North Carolina) near the Clay-Macon county line. The road is to the left if you are coming from Franklin. Drive 6 miles on USFS71 to Deep Gap.

GEORGIA

GEORGIA

Georgia is the last state on the trail (or the first for most thru-hikers). Its more than 75 miles of trail are extremely popular year round. The trail traverses the Chattahoochee National Forest and is noted for its rugged wilderness areas and high elevations. Popular hiking spots include the Swag of the Blue Ridge, Tray Mountain, Rocky Mountain, Blue Mountain, Wolf Laurel Top, Blood Mountain, and Big Cedar Mountain.

Neels Gap, at the base of Blood Mountain, offers the Walasi-Yi Trail Crossings Store. It is the only building through which the A.T. passes. Springer Mountain is the southern terminus of the A.T. In 1993, the trail to the summit was re-routed and a new bronze plaque, marking the mountain as the southern terminus of the A.T., was added.

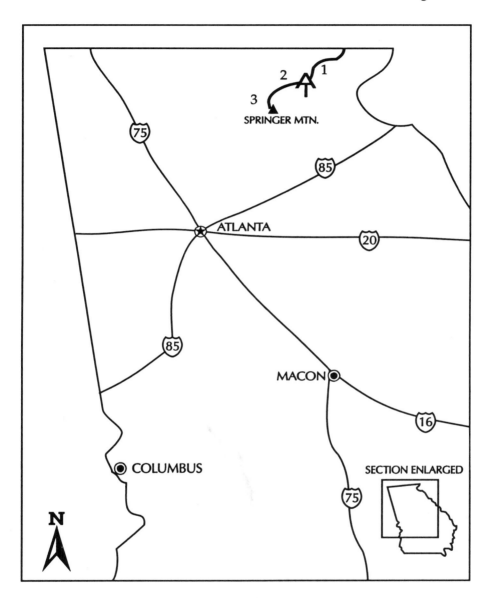

1. Tray Mountain Wilderness
2. Wolf Laurel Top/Blood Mountain
3. Woody Gap/Springer Mountain

TRAY MOUNTAIN WILDERNESS

MODERATE
16.1 mile traverse

This short overnight hike crosses some of the biggest mountains on the Georgia section of the A.T. and has several long gap-to-mountain ascents. During the 6.4-mile section from Addis Gap to Tray Gap, you will hike through the heart of the Tray Mountain Wilderness Area. You will also cross the rocky summit of Tray Mountain, which offers tremendous views of the surrounding mountains from the foothills in the south to the Nantahala Mountains in North Carolina. Though there are a few tough climbs and descents, this hike is listed as moderate, in part, because it is only 16 miles long.

The Hike
From Dicks Creek Gap, hike south on the A.T., following the road briefly, and turn left to enter the woods. Climb up out of the gap, cross several creeks, and reach Moreland Gap at mile 1.2. Climb 1 mile to the top of Powell Mountain (elevation 3,850 feet). Descend .25 mile to McClure Gap, climb then descend along the ridge, and reach Deep Gap 1.1 miles later. A .25-mile blue-blazed trail leads to Deep Gap Shelter. Water is available from the spring you pass on the way to the shelter.

Climb up from Deep Gap, reaching a highpoint on Kelly Knob (the trail does not cross the summit) at mile 4.2. Descend 1.1 miles to Addis Gap. Some old guidebooks mention an Addis Gap Shelter, which has been removed. From Addis Gap, climb .6 mile to a highpoint on the ridge and descend .25 mile to Sassafras Gap at mile 6.1.

Cross over the east side of Round Top, and traverse the broad gap known as the Swag of the Blue Ridge (elevation 3,400 feet), about a mile beyond Sassafras Gap. Climb up from the Swag and pass around the western slope of Young Lick Knob. Descend to Steeltrap Gap at mile 8.9. *The Appalachian Trail Guide to North Carolina-Georgia* states that water is available to the left of the trail in this gap.

Ascend and then descend on the ridge during the 1.5 miles to Wolfpen Gap. Begin climbing on the eastern slope of Tray Mountain. In 1.2 miles, at mile 10.6, reach the junction with a blue-blazed side trail that leads .25 mile to the right to Tray Mountain Shelter. Water is available from a piped spring on a blue-blazed trail a short distance behind the shelter. Although it does not break the hike up into two equal sections, we suggest you camp here. It is a nice place to camp whether you stay in the shelter or not, and there is easy access to water.

After passing the shelter side trail, continue to climb, sometimes steeply, for .25 mile to the rocky summit of Tray Mountain (elevation 4,430 feet). Enjoy a spectacular view from the peak. Descend on switchbacks to Tray Gap at mile 11.7, cross the dirt USFS 79 in the gap, and enter the woods beside the small parking area. Descend, crossing USFS 79 again in 1 mile, and reach Indian Grave Gap and a dirt forest service road in another .75 mile. A blue-blazed bypass trail leads to the right (down the road) and rejoins the A.T. in 2.5 miles on the other side of Rocky Mountain.

After crossing the dirt road, climb the eastern slope of Rocky Mountain, reaching the summit (elevation 4,017 feet) at mile 14.8. Descend steadily from Rocky Mountain, and in .25 mile, pass the junction with the blue-blazed bypass trail that leads back to Indian Grave Gap. In another .25 mile, cross a tributary of the Hiawasee River, and .6 mile later, reach the southern end of the hike in Unicoi Gap.

Trailhead Directions
Dicks Creek Gap is on US 76, 11 miles east of Hiawasee, Georgia. The southern trailhead at Unicoi Gap is on Georgia 75, 9 miles north of Helen, Georgia.

WOLF LAUREL TOP/ BLOOD MOUNTAIN

MODERATE
16.2 mile traverse

Good views and the highest peak on the A.T. in Georgia are the highlights of this relatively short overnight hike. On this section, the A.T. passes good viewpoints on Cowrock and Wolf Laurel Top Mountains, and climbs up to Blood Mountain to offer another spectacular view. There is also a fine view from Big Cedar Mountain.

The nearly 11 miles from Neels Gap to Woody Gap attract more visitors than any other section of the A.T. in Georgia. The biggest attraction, Blood Mountain, was named after a battle between the Creek and Cherokee Indians that caused the mountain to run red with blood.

At Neels Gap you will pass under the arch at the Walasi-Yi Center, which is the only coveredsection on the entire A.T. The center's name is Indian for Frogtown and Neels Gap was once known as Frogtown Gap. The center has a good selection of books, backpacking equipment, food, and more. This is a tough hike that is listed as moderate because it is only 16 miles long.

The Hike

From the trailhead in Tesnatee Gap, hike south on the A.T. and climb steadily for .75 mile to the top of Cowrock Mountain (elevation 3,842 feet). Enjoy a fine view from the rocks just before the suumit and another fine view from the campsite to the left of the trail on the summit. Descend to a sag and then climb Wolf Laurel Top, reaching the summit (elevation 3,766 feet) at mile 2.1, where there is a good viewpoint on the rocks to the left of the trail. Descend and follow the ridge, passing below the summits of Rock Spring Top and Turkeypen Mountain, and reaching Swaim Gap at mile 3.4.

Climb Levelland Mountain on switchbacks, reaching the summit (elevation 3,942 feet) .6 mile from Swaim Gap. Descend from Levelland, and in 1.5 miles, pass under the arch at the Walasi-Yi Center in Neels Gap, which is the only covered section on the entire A.T. If you would like to camp on Blood Mountain, you will want to carry your water up from here because there is no water on the summit.

In Neels Gap (elevation 3,125 feet), cross US 19/129 and enter the woods. After crossing the road, look on the right side of the trail at the base of the steps for the brass plaque set in the rock that is identical to the one at the southern terminus of the trail on Springer Mountain. In .9 mile, pass the blue-blazed trail on the right that leads .25 mile to a parking area for day hikers. Shortly thereafter, the trail begins to climb Blood Mountain in earnest. The steady 1.4-mile climb is generally well-graded on switchbacks. There are a couple of excellent views from the trail near the top of the climb as well as from the rocks over the shelter on the summit (elevation 4,461 feet). The two-room stone cabin was built by the CCC in the 1930s. At mile 7.9, the summit makes a good place to spend the night, leaving 8.3 miles for the second day.

Descend steeply from Blood Mountain on switchbacks and reach Slaughter Gap in another 1.1 miles. In Slaughter Gap, the A.T. reaches the junction with two other blue-blazed trails. Continue following the A.T. and pass a spring about .25 mile beyond the gap. In the next .25 mile, cross two small creeks and reach Bird Gap at mile 9.9. Pass a blue-blazed trail on the left that leads around Blood Mountain. Climb out of the gap on the side of Turkey Stamp Mountain and then descend to Horsebone Gap. Climb up from that gap on the side of Gaddis Mountain, and descend to Jarrard Gap at mile 10.9.

In Jarrad Gap, pass a blue-blazed trail on the right that leads down to Lake Winfield Scott, and climb .5 mile to a highpoint on Burnett Field Mountain (elevation 3,478 feet). In another 1.2 miles, pass the Dockery Lake Trail and begin climbing Granny Top Mountain, reaching the summit at mile 14.

Descend Granny Top, and in .25 mile, begin the 1-mile climb up Big Cedar Mountain (elevation 3,737 feet). There are fine views from the rocks near the top of the mountain. Big Cedar is referred to as Preaching Rock on the Chattahoochee National Forest Map. Descend sharply for .25 mile from Big Cedar to Lunsford Gap. From that gap, climb slightly and then descend to Woody Gap at mile 16.2, the end of the hike.

Trailhead Directions
From Helen, Georgia, drive north on Georgia 75 to Georgia 356. From Georgia 356, drive to Georgia 348 and turn right. Drive about 12 miles from the town of Helen to the trailhead in Tesnatee Gap.

Woody Gap is on US 60 at a point 5.6 miles north of Stone Pile Gap, which is about 9 miles north of Dahlonega on US 19. There is a picnic area at the trailhead.

Woody Gap/Springer Mountain

MODERATE
20.9 mile traverse

The first 12 miles of this traverse follow long ridges as the A.T. winds its way toward the southern terminus of the A.T.—Springer Mountain. Along the way, the trail skirts the 3,742-foot Black Mountain near Woody Gap, and from Hightower Gap, it is just 8 miles to the summit of Springer.

At Three Forks, three mountain streams join to form Noontootla Creek. The trail then follows Stover Creek through one of the highlights of this hike—a stand of virgin hemlocks known as the Cathedral Hemlocks. Hiking north from Springer, you won't see trees like this again until the Great Smoky Mountains.

The Hike

From Woody Gap (elevation 3,050 feet), cross through a picnic area and begin your ascent along Black Mountain. You will climb then descend to Tritt Gap (elevation 3,050 feet) in the next mile. From Tritt Gap, hike just under .5 mile to the crest of Ramrock Mountain (elevation 3,200 feet) and enjoy nice views to the south. Descend along switchbacks for .1 mile to Jacks Gap (elevation 3,000 feet), and begin to climb again before descending to Liss Gap (elevation 2,952 feet) at mile 2.1.

At mile 2.6, cross an old road, begin to climb, reach the top of the ridge at mile 3, and then descend to Gooch Gap. Just before you reach the gap, you will pass a blue-blazed side trail to your left that heads a short distance to a spring. At mile 3.6, reach USFS 42 at Gooch Gap (elevation 2,784 feet). USFS 42 heads right 2.7 miles to Suches, Georgia, and left 6.1 miles to Cooper Gap and (eventually) the base of Springer Mountain.

Shortly beyond USFS 42, reach the junction with another blue-blazed side trail, which forms a .25-mile loop back to the A.T. as it passes Gooch Gap Shelter. Water is available from a spring near the shelter sign at the southern approach to the loop. Continue along the A.T. for .25 mile to the southern end of the loop where the blue-blazed trail rejoins the A.T.

After passing the side trail, hike nearly another .75 mile to a gap (elevation 2,950 feet). Climb to the ridgetop and reach the high point of Horseshoe Ridge at mile 5. Descend to the right, following a stream.

In nearly .5 mile, cross the stream, turn left at the bottom of the hill, and continue along the A.T. with former pastures to your right. Hike .75 mile to Blackwell Creek and cross on a footbridge. There are good campsites to your right. Continue along the A.T., ascend through rhododendron, and cross another stream in .5 mile.

In .25 mile, cross Justus Creek on a footbridge (more campsites along the creek), and in another .1 mile, reach an old logging road. A left on this road will take you to Suches-Cooper Gap Road (USFS 42). Begin to climb Justus Mountain, reaching Phyllis Spur (elevation 3,081 feet) in .75 mile; descend into a sag (elevation 2,900 feet) .25 mile later, and reach the summit of Justus (elevation 3,224 feet) at mile 7.8. From the summit, head left along the ridge before descending along switchbacks.

In just over .5 mile, reach the intersection of three roads at Cooper Gap (elevation 2,828 feet). The road heading downhill to the left is Cooper Gap Road (USFS 80), which heads 14 miles to Dahlonega. To your left and ahead is USFS 42, which heads left back to Gooch Gap and Suches, and ahead to Springer Mountain. To your right is USFS 15, which heads to the small settlement Gaddistown. Cross USFS 42 and begin an ascent up Sassafras Mountain.

Reach the summit (elevation 3,336 feet) at mile 9. As you descend off the ridgetop, keep an eye out for U.S. Army Rangers who perform maneuvers in this area (often well into the night), which include automatic weapon fire. It is 1 mile from the summit of Sassafras to Horse Gap (elevation 2,673 feet). You should be able to see USFS 42 to your right. Climb the ridge again, hike along the ridgecrest, and descend to Hightower Gap at mile 11.7.

Reach the intersection of USFS 42 in Hightower Gap (elevation 2,854 feet) at mile 11.9. To your right, USFS 42 heads back to Cooper Gap and Suches. Ahead, USFS 42 heads on to Winding Stair Gap and Springer Mountain. Between these two roads is USFS 69, which heads 2 miles to Rock Creek Lake. Continue along the A.T. and climb .5 mile passing the .1 mile side trail to Hawk Mountain Shelter. Built in 1993, the post and beam shelter has a loft and can accomodate a number of hikers. Water is available from the stream downhill, and in front of the shelter.

The A.T. continues along the north side of Hawk Mountain. The trail over the summit was abandoned in 1979. Reach the ridge crest and the intersection of the former A.T. in just over .5 mile. Begin to descend, and at mile 14.2, arrive at a logging road. Hickory Flats Cemetery Road heads left to USFS 58 near Three Forks. To reach the cemetery, hike a short distance down this road. At the left turn in the gravel road, take a right along a dirt road. There are picnic tables and a pavilion at the cemetery.

Continue along the A.T., cross the road, descend for just over .25 mile, and turn left onto an old logging road. In another .4 mile, reach the intersection of the Benton MacKaye Trail (white diamond blazes) and Duncan Ridge Trail (blue blazes) to your right. The three trails (A.T. included) share the same footpath for the next mile.

In .1 mile, reach a blue-blazed side trail that heads right to Long Creek Falls, a pretty waterfall. As the A.T. parallels Long Creek, you will pass many possible campsites. At mile 15.9, reach USFS 58 at Three Forks. USFS 58 heads left 2.6 miles to Winding Stair Gap and USFS 42. The Duncan Ridge Trail ends here, but the Benton MacKaye continues to follow the A.T.'s path for a short distance before turning left up Rich Mountain. Cross the road, and soon thereafter, Chester Creek.

Hike .5 mile past Three Forks, and cross Stover Creek. Turn left, and follow an old logging road that parallels the creek. Here, the trail passes through Cathedral Hemlocks, a virgin stand of timber. One mile later, turn left off the road and soon cross a bridge over a stream before climbing log steps. In .1 mile, reach another logging road. Stover Creek Shelter is to the right. The A.T. turns left and follows the road a short distance before ascending log steps to the right. At the top of the steps, reach another road, turn left, and follow it for .25 mile before ascending more steps to your right.

As you climb the north slope of Rich Mountain, cross a stream at mile 17.9 and reach the ridgetop (and the intersection of the Benton MacKaye Trail) in just over .25 mile. Head right, continue to climb along Rich Mountain, and cross another old road in just over .5 mile. The Benton MacKaye Trail leaves the A.T. here, but rejoins it on Springer Mountain. The old road heads left to a blue-blazed side trail that leads downhill to water.

At mile 19.1, reach the junction of USFS 42 just below Springer Mountain. Ascend along a recently relocated section of trail up Springer Mountain. At mile 19.8, reach the junction with the Benton MacKaye Trail where it leaves the A.T. for the first time after sharing its southern terminus with Springer. A short distance later, reach the blue-blazed side trail that leads to Springer Mountain Shelter. The mountain boasts a shelter, built in 1992, that accomodates more hikers than the earlier shelter and includes a sleeping loft. Water is available from a nearby spring.

The summit of Springer (elevation 3,782 feet) is reached at mile 20. To the left of the trail is a bronze marker set into the rock marking this as the southern terminus of the Appalachian National Scenic Trail. The plaque, placed here in 1993, features a map of the trail's route from Maine to Georgia. After passing this marker, the trail turns to the right, where the southernmost blaze is painted on a rock outcropping with wonderful views of the Blue Ridge. A bronze plaque in this rock near the blaze features a backpacker and the words "Appalachian Trail. Georgia to Maine. A footpath for those who seek fellowship with the wilderness. The Georgia Appalachian Trail Club." This marker was made in 1933 and placed here in 1959 by the Georgia cluib, when the southern terminus was moved from Mount Ogelthorpe to Springer Mountain because of encroaching development.

A blue-blazed trail heads 8.3 miles to Amicalola Falls State Park. Return to the base of Springer (.9 mile) to complete this overnight hike.

Trailhead Directions
Woody Gap is on US 60 at a point 5.6 miles north of Stone Pile Gap, which is about 9 miles north of Dahlonega on US 19. There is a picnic area at the trailhead.

The parking area at Springer Mountain can be reached by taking US 60 north from Woody Gap. Turn left on USFS 42, which is paved for the first several miles, and continue to the trail crossing. You will cross the A.T. in Gooch, Cooper, and Hightower Gaps before reaching the trailhead near Springer. It is a long drive down USFS 42, but this road is often open when other forest service roads in the area are not.

Appendix

Trail Maintenance Clubs

The Appalachian Trail owes its existence to the hiking clubs, which are charged with its maintenance. These clubs are responsible not only for the maintenance of the footpath but also for relocating the trail, managing its surrounding lands, helping with land acquisition negotiations, compiling and updating guidebook and map information, working with trail communities on both problems and special events, and recruiting and training new maintainers.

The clubs also sponsor backpacking and hiking trips as well as workshops. These are a great way to meet others interested in hiking.

The following list contains the names and trail assignments of clubs along the Appalachian Trail. Addresses appear for those with permanent offices or post office boxes. In other cases, please contact ATC headquarters for the address of the current club president or other appropriate officer (P.O. Box 807, Harpers Ferry, West Virginia 25425).

Maine Appalachian Trail Club, P.O. Box 283, Augusta, ME 04330.
MATC covers 264 miles from Katahdin to ME 26 (Grafton Notch, ME).

Appalachian Mountain Club, 5 Joy Street, Boston, MA 02108.
AMC covers 119 miles from Grafton Notch, ME to Kinsman Notch, NH.

Dartmouth Outing Club, P.O. Box 9, Hanover, NH 03755.
DOC covers 75 miles from Kinsman Notch, NH to VT 12.

Green Mountain Club, Rural Route 1, Box 650, Waterbury Center, VT 05677.
GMC covers 116 miles from VT 12 to the Massachusetts border. They also cover the entire Long Trail.

AMC—Berkshire Chapter, 5 Joy Street, Boston, MA 02108.
The Berkshire Chapter covers 87 miles from the Vermont border to Sages Ravine, MA.

AMC—Connecticut Chapter, 5 Joy Street, Boston, MA 02108.
The Connecticut Chapter covers 50 miles from Sages Ravine, MA to the New York border.

The New York-New Jersey Trail Conference, 232 Madison Avenue, Room 908, New York, NY 10016.
NY-NJTC covers 163 miles from the Connecticut border to Delaware Water Gap, PA.

Keystone Trails Association, P.O. Box 251, Cogan Station, PA 17728.
KTA is the blanket association for the following 10 independent trail clubs, all of which can be contacted at the above address.

Springfield Trail Club: 7 miles from Delaware Water Gap, PA to Fox Gap, PA.

Batona Hiking Club: 8 miles from Fox Gap, PA to Wind Gap, PA.

AMC—Delaware Valley Chapter: 16 miles from Wind Gap, PA to Little Gap, PA.

Philadelphia Trail Club: 10 miles from Little Gap, PA to Lehigh Furnace Gap, PA.

Blue Mountain Eagle Climbing Club: Split into two sections—66 miles from Lehigh Furnace Gap, PA to Bake Oven Knob, PA and from Tri-County Corner, PA to Rausch Creek, PA.

Allentown Hiking Club: 12 miles from Bake Oven Knob, PA to Tri-County Corner, PA.

Brandywine Valley Outing Club: 11 miles from Rausch Creek, PA to PA 325.

Susquehanna Appalachian Trail Club: 9 miles from PA 325 to PA 225.

York Hiking Club: 8 miles from PA 225 to the Susquehanna River.

Cumberland Valley Appalachian Trail Management Association: 18 miles from Darlington Trail to Center Point Knob.

Mountain Club of Maryland: 30 miles from the Susquehanna River to Darlington Trail and from Center Point Knob to Pine Grove Furnace State Park, PA.

Potomac Appalachian Trail Club, 118 Park Street S.E., Vienna, VA 22180-4609. Arrangements can be made for renting PATC cabins by calling Cabin Reservations at PATC headquarters at (202) 638-5306 between 7 p.m. and 10 p.m. on weeknights.
The PATC covers 238 miles from Pine Grove Furnace State Park, PA, to Rockfish Gap, VA.

Old Dominion Appalachian Trail Club, P.O. Box 25283, Richmond, VA 23260-5283.
ODATC covers 17 miles from Rockfish Gap, VA to Reeds Gap, VA.

Tidewater Appalachian Trail Club, P.O. Box 8246, Norfolk, VA 23503.
  Tidewater covers 10 miles from Reeds Gap, VA to Tye River, VA.

Natural Bridge Appalachian Trail Club, P.O. Box 3012, Lynchburg, VA 24503.
  NBATC covers 88 miles from the Tye River, VA to Black Horse Gap, VA.

Roanoke Appalachian Trail Club. Contact ATC for current address.
  RATC covers 114 miles from Black Horse Gap, VA to Stony Creek Valley, VA.

Kanawha Trail Club. Contact ATC for current address.
  Kanawha covers 21 miles from Stony Creek Valley, VA to New River, VA.

Virginia Tech Outing Club. Contact ATC for current address.
  Virginia Tech covers 25 miles from VA 608 to Garden Mountain, VA.

Piedmont Appalachian Trail Hikers, P.O. Box 4423, Greensboro, NC 27404.
  PATH covers 43 miles from Garden Mountain, VA to VA 16.

Mount Rogers Appalachian Trail Club. Contact ATC for current address.
  Mount Rogers covers 64 miles from VA 16 to Damascus, VA.

Tennessee Eastman Hiking Club, P.O. Box 511, Kingsport, TN 37662.
  TEHC covers 126 miles from Damascus, VA, to Spivey Gap, NC.

Carolina Mountain Club. Contact ATC for current address.
  CMC covers 90 miles from Spivey Gap, NC, to Davenport Gap, TN/NC.

The Smoky Mountains Hiking Club. Contact ATC for current address.
  Smoky Mountains covers 97 miles from Davenport Gap, TN/NC, to the Nantahala River, NC.

Nantahala Hiking Club, 31 Carl Slagle Road, Franklin, NC 28734.
  NHC covers 60 miles from the Nantahala River to Bly Gap on the Georgia border.

Georgia Appalachian Trail Club, P.O. Box 654, Atlanta, GA 30301.
  GATC covers 78 miles from the North Carolina border to Springer Mountain.